"That Time Cannot Be Forgotten"

"That Time Cannot Be Forgotten"

A Correspondence on the Holocaust

Dr. Emil Georg Sold & Paul Friedhoff

TRANSLATED FROM THE GERMAN AND EDITED BY
Ivan Fehrenbach

AFTERWORD BY
John K. Roth

INDIANA
University Press
Bloomington • Indianapolis

This book is a publication of

Indiana University Press
601 North Morton Street
Bloomington, Indiana 47404-3797 USA

http://iupress.indiana.edu

Telephone orders   800-842-6796
Fax orders   812-855-7931
Orders by email   iuporder@indiana.edu

The paper used in this publication meets the minimum
requirements of American National Standard for Information
Sciences—Permanence of Paper for Printed Library
Materials, ANSI Z39.48-1984.

Manufactured in the United States of America

Library of Congress Cataloging-in-Publication Data

Sold, Emil Georg.
"That time cannot be forgotten" : a correspondence on the Holocaust / by
Dr. Emil Georg Sold and Paul Friedhoff ; translated from the German and
edited by Ivan Fehrenbach ; afterword by John K. Roth.
p.   cm.
Includes bibliographical references and index.
ISBN 0-253-34092-6
1. Jews—Germany—History—1933–1945.   2. Holocaust, Jewish (1939–
1945)—Germany.   3. Holocaust, Jewish (1939–1945)—Influence.
4. Sold, Emil Georg—Correspondence.   5. Friedhoff, Paul, 1907–
—Correspondence.   I. Friedhoff, Paul, 1907–
II. Fehrenbach, Ivan, date   III. Title.
DS135.G3 S65 2002
940.53'18—dc21
2001007493

1   2   3   4   5   07   06   05   04   03   02

CONTENTS

Editor's Introduction

"There are so many questions without answers," writes Paul Friedhoff in a letter to Dr. Emil Georg Sold. But one of those questions—how could the Holocaust have happened?—bears a personal significance for both of these men. Therefore, in an exchange made all the more powerful because of who they are and where they come from, Friedhoff and Sold struggle together in an attempt to answer the unanswerable.

Both were born in the Rhineland-Palatinate region of Germany, and though Friedhoff was older than Sold by thirteen years, they witnessed many of the same political and social changes that occurred during the first half of the century. Their perspectives, however, could not have been more different—Sold was Catholic and served in the Wehrmacht during World War II, while Friedhoff, as a Jew, escaped from Germany and Hitler and fled to the United States.

At the age of twenty-seven in 1934, Friedhoff sensed the course that Germany would take with Hitler, and he convinced his family to leave the small town where his mother had been born, where they had a home, friends and relatives, and where they had spent their lives. Subsequently, he helped over three hundred Jews escape from Germany, and as a result he has been likened to Oskar Schindler.

Sold has spent much of his later years revisiting the Hitler period in his mind, trying to promote understanding and relations between peoples and religions. In an attempt to atone for a national history that gnaws at him personally, he has lectured, erected memorials, and written books. He wrote, for example, a book on the Jews of Schifferstadt (a town in the Rhineland-Palatinate), and it was that book that led to the initial contact of the two men: Friedhoff received the book from a bank in Schifferstadt, and when he responded with comments on the text, the bank forwarded his letter to Sold.

Thus, a half-century after circumstances had placed them in different worlds, Friedhoff and Sold suddenly found themselves in a correspondence that covered the many issues surrounding that earlier time, and in particular, the many issues surrounding the Holocaust—racism, hatred, religion, philosophy, government, and education. Their discussions often lead to conflict and only sometimes end in resolution, for theirs is not a genteel rehashing of generally accepted views on human rights. Rather, Sold and Friedhoff tackle difficult issues and do not blunt their arguments for fear of offending the other. In several sections, for instance, they discuss whether ordinary Germans knew of the concentration camps—Friedhoff vehemently insists that they did; Sold says that they, or at least he, did not.

Their candor also exposes the true complexity of their subject. Sold admits that he had never talked to a Jew until 1978, and yet, he discovers years later that his daughter has married someone of Jewish descent. Friedhoff acknowledges that even he had once been a proud German—recalling how, during the First World War, his father hung the national flag out the window whenever the Germans captured a Russian city—and yet Friedhoff has not considered himself a German from the day he dropped his bags on American soil.

Despite the obstacles that result because they have never seen each other, the two become very good friends, and the correspondence becomes an integral part of both their lives. Even if they cannot agree, they learn to respect the other's position, and, especially because of the volatile nature of their topics, that mutual respect alone provides a stunning example for others in all kinds of conflicts. It also provides hope that perhaps other disagreements could be resolved without people and countries resorting to violence or war.

If Friedhoff and Sold cannot answer the unanswerable—how could the Holocaust have happened?—what they do know is that it cannot be forgotten. In remembering and attempting to understand, they hope to save the next generations from enduring what their generation had, and has to endure. And in that way, their letters are not so much about the past as they are about the future.

Editorial Note

Dr. Emil Georg Sold was born in 1920 in Schifferstadt, Germany, in the same town where his wife, Elli, was born four years later. Before he finished his study of medicine, Sold served in World War II as a medical officer in an armored division; he was taken prisoner by the Americans near the end of the war. After completing his degree in Heidelberg and working in Ludwigshafen, he chose to become a general practitioner in his hometown. In 1984, he began transferring his practice to his son-in-law. Since then, he has been able to devote almost all of his time to his other interests—studying history and religion, attending (and presenting) lectures, organizing meetings and services, and writing and reading books.

Paul Friedhoff was born in Rülzheim, Germany in 1907. At the age of twenty, he moved to Amsterdam, where he worked sorting, evaluating, and pricing tobacco, skills that soon led him to a position in Indonesia. Four years later, however, finances and other concerns drove him back to Germany; news about Germany's political state had troubled him, and he was worried about his family. After Hitler was sworn in as chancellor in 1933, Friedhoff convinced his family to emigrate to Philadelphia, where they had relatives. There Friedhoff met his future wife, Greta. For twenty years, while Paul worked in the export-import and furniture manufacturing businesses, the couple lived in Puerto Rico. In 1975 they moved to Florida, and, in 1997, they relocated to Virginia to be closer to their daughter and her family. Friedhoff died August 29, 2001, while these letters were being prepared for publication.

Some material, such as personal information and discussion unrelated to their main topics, has been removed. The original German correspondence is in the National Holocaust Museum in Washington, D.C.

Emil Georg Sold, 1944

Emil Georg Sold, 1995

Paul Friedhoff, 1931

Paul Friedhoff, 1993

"That Time Cannot Be Forgotten"

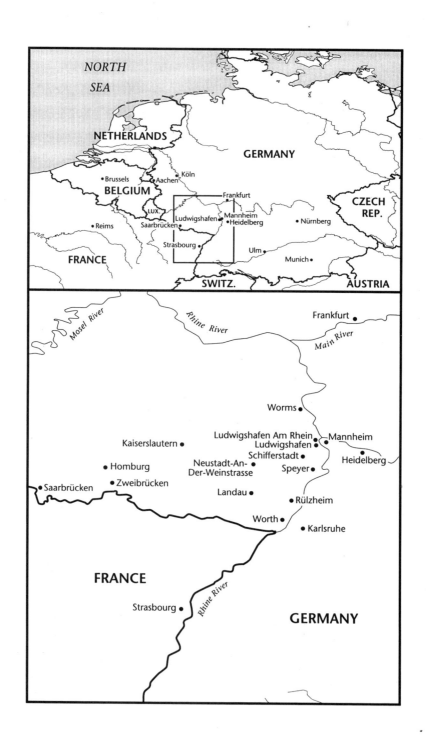

THE CORRESPONDENCE

Paul Friedhoff
Clearwater, FL

Stadtsparkasse Schifferstadt
Germany
SEPTEMBER 16, 1994

Dear Sir or Madam,

Your book *Die Schifferstadter Juden* has arrived safely, and I thank you very
much for your effort. [The full title is *Die Schifferstadter Juden: ein Lesebuch*
(The Schifferstadt Jews: A Reader), co-authored by Bernhard Kukatzki
(Schifferstadt: Stadtsparkasse Schifferstadt, 1988).]

I am only surprised that Michael Rosenstiel, a Jewish teacher from about
1920 to 1930, was not mentioned. He was the brother of my Aunt Bertha
Feibelmann, born Rosenstiel, who lived in Rülzheim. She was the widow of
Heinrich Feibelmann, also a schoolteacher, who died in 1911 at the age of
forty-four.

Every once in a while Michael came to Rülzheim to visit his sister. I can
remember him well. I didn't know his wife, and I think that they had two
daughters. I don't know what became of the family. Perhaps they suffered
the same lot as so many other Jews.

Sincerely,
Paul Friedhoff

————— 🌀 —————

Emil Georg Sold

SEPTEMBER 24, 1994

Esteemed Mr. Friedhoff,

[*Sehr geehrter* would probably be translated as "Dear" instead of "Esteemed,"
but since it is more formal than *Lieber* and a reference to that distinction is
made in the correspondence, I have left it as "Esteemed" to highlight the
formality.]

The Stadtsparkasse Schifferstadt left it up to me to answer your letter of September 16, 1994, since I am the author of the book you named, *Die Schifferstadter Juden.* Because I have a general knowledge of the fates of Jews in our area, I can answer your questions without any difficulty:

The Jewish teacher Michael Rosenstiel was not referred to in our book because he didn't work in Schifferstadt, but in the neighboring town of Mutterstadt about six kilometers away. The same holds true for the Feibelmann family. You can find further details about the fates of both families in the photocopies I am enclosing with this letter. They come from a book about that town, *Mutterstadt.*

As you will gather from the Mutterstadt text, on June 16, 1933, ninety-one Jewish citizens were still living there. Among them were two people named Rosenstiel, possibly the family that included Michael. Michael Rosenstiel was a teacher at the Jewish school for twenty-eight years (1897–1925).

Of these ninety-one citizens, seven people who died during the Third Reich are buried in Mutterstadt. I cannot comment on the 18 + 5 + 4 people who moved to North or South America before 1940 (evidently they succeeded in emigrating). Ten to twelve people "moved to other towns within Germany's prewar boundaries" or "to other countries within Europe." I don't know their names. You could find more information about them at the Mutterstadt town hall. Yet it is very possible that these people also fell victim to the persecution by the Nazis, for toward the end of the Third Reich the tentacles of the Holocaust extended across all of Europe.

On October 22, 1940, thirty-five people from Mutterstadt (along with all the other Jews from the Rhineland/Upper Palatinate) were put in the French internment camp Gurs or Rivesaltes in the Pyrenees of South France. They only had one chance to survive, namely, if they had already filled out a visa application before their deportation. Those who had been accepted by the country they applied to were able to leave the internment camp for America. But that was the case for only a very few. As for the others, one must unfortunately assume that they did not survive the deportation.

There were very bad conditions in the camps of southern France. From 1940 to 1942 every fourth camp inmate died. After the summer of 1942, the transports ran to the extermination camps in the east, mainly to Auschwitz. Only the very old and weak were left in the French camps, and this was because their natural deaths were just a matter of time. Even so, a few survived and were able to be saved.

We know the identity of the people transported to Auschwitz because exact lists were kept on each transport. The French authorities were in charge of handling these transports. The lists included names, birthdates, and places of origin, and are still accessible today. Thus it is possible to find out what happened to the Rosenstiels by searching these transport lists for their personnel data.

These lists are located in the papers at the Centre de Documentation Juive in Paris, assembled by Serge Klarsfeld. But they are also in the camp documentation at Auschwitz. Also, all of these lists have been transcribed in the documentation at the memorial Yad Vashem in Jerusalem. The easiest process for you would probably be to inquire in Jerusalem, since all of the documents are stored there electronically. For that reason they are much more accessible than the typewritten lists that the French have.

Mr. Friedhoff, I hope that I have been of service with this information. In the meantime, I am going to see if I can obtain any additional information about the Rosenstiel and Feibelmann families from another source, the Institut für Pfälzische Geschichte und Volkskunde in Kaiserslautern. If I do, I will get in touch with you again.

Sincerely,

Emil Sold

———❀———

OCTOBER 3, 1994

Esteemed Dr. Sold,

I thank you very, very much for your nice and detailed letter of September 24, 1994. Yes, I made a mistake. Michael Rosenstiel lived in Mutterstadt and taught there. At my age—eighty-seven—it can happen that you mix up two towns.

First I would like to pay you a compliment. You have written the first part of the Schifferstadt book with a great deal of understanding and compassion. It certainly could not have been easy to look at the atrocities of the Schifferstadt population at that time and to remember the few Jews who were there. It is impossible to put Hitler on a par with Germany's great poets (Goethe, Schiller, Heine), great composers (Beethoven, Bach, Brahms, Schubert), and the great thinkers and scientists (Einstein, Habe, Schopenhauer, and others). It is difficult to find an answer for what happened. I can only imagine that the principalities in the Middle Ages, and later on the kaisers, oppressed the people in such a way that they did not develop their own ideas. They just became sheep who followed the leader of the herd. Germany—in contrast with France—has never had a proper revolution to free itself of its shackles. So the Germans also followed Hitler; he put them under a spell with his outstanding rhetoric. It shouldn't be an excuse, but perhaps it's an explanation of the German character at the time of the Nazis.

Due to these lords and kaisers, Germany became a country of war. Remember 1870 and 1914, and then the Second World War. We can only hope that the new generations have different leaders, and that they learn to take different paths. That should begin with different teachers, unlike those I remember from the high schools in Landau and Speyer.

I hope that I have not offended you by expressing my feelings. I would like to hear your views about such a dark point in the history of Germany. There is a lot of material here for a stimulating correspondence.

Sincerely,

Paul Friedhoff

———❦———

OCTOBER 9, 1994

Esteemed Mr. Friedhoff,

Many thanks for your letter of October 3, 1994. It had already arrived here by October 7. No, I am not at all offended that the memory of all that happened must be a lifelong occupation for you, and I understand that there must be a scar remaining that probably can never heal. It is similar for the many of us who as a people belong to the perpetrators, and who did not have to suffer like you and others. We, too, are unable to escape the terrible atrocities of our people, and must face the responsibility in front of the world and in front of history. But this responsibility means that we must actively work to prevent anything similar in our history from repeating itself. And we must also be prepared to make reparations, in the widest sense, as much as is possible. I am trying to do that with what I am doing now. My first task was to inform myself about everything that had happened. And then I wanted to pass on that information by going to the public with it. Then I wanted to revive and strengthen the humanitarian way of thinking, which is just as natural to our people as it is to all others.

You write, "There is a lot material for a stimulating correspondence." Perhaps it would be easiest if I present you with a few lecture plans that I have used in the past years, which have to do with this topic. Naturally, they also deal with the motives for the persecution of the Jews, which indeed found its terrible climax in the Holocaust, but which was not at all an invention of the Nazis. The texts are in my computer only as theses, without any rhetorical embellishments. Since they were prepared for various situations in various atmospheres, they are somewhat unorganized and repetitious. Yet in varied ways they will show you my present view of the situation.

Unfortunately, I cannot undo what happened (even though that is what

I would want the most). I have only two possibilities: a humanitarian one, to help ease the suffering as best I can, and then the other possibility, to search for the causes and consider how one can deal with them. I would be very happy if you were able to help me with additional thoughts about these causes. If we want to progress, we must not only think, but maybe even learn to change our views. After looking at the facts, I have done that more than once during the time in which I have been occupied with this topic. When I returned home from prison, I, too, still believed that it was impossible that what obviously had happened in other towns could have happened to the Jews from Schifferstadt. And yet they, too, suffered exactly as did the Jews elsewhere.

I hope that it will be possible for you to decipher the small writing of my computer printout. Since it is written on one of the old (Commodore) machines, I cannot change it very easily anymore. I was born in 1920 and already have difficulties with my eyes. But perhaps you will still succeed in deciphering what I have written. All that you read is the result of a passionate preoccupation with the topic. It has lasted for years now, and I have dedicated as much time as possible to it. And this must all be discussed, for we must know exactly what happened.

For example, there is a point that time and again causes quite a stir, and which is often discussed with faulty logic. A man came from America to Germany and explained his thesis in public lectures. He was concerned with the so-called Auschwitz lies: that the statements concerning Auschwitz are simply not true (!); and that everything is a complete and malicious invention of pressure groups(!).

For his thesis he offered numerous pieces of evidence. That was naturally grist for the mill for those around us who, for understandable reasons, simply do not want what happened to have been true. But the foundation for these so-called "Auschwitz lies" was based on an easily resolved mistake: Auschwitz was an old (Austrian) barracks from the time of the First World War, and they were, as I was able to see for myself when I was there, really much too small for the crimes associated with the name. Just for spatial reasons, all of that could not have happened there. In reality, however, the huge extermination camp that is always shown in the pictures was first built in 1941/42, with a connection to the railroad tracks. In fact, the camp is about two to three kilometers away from the Auschwitz barracks, in a town called Birkenau. If people would just get used to distinguishing the two camps in their speech, or for example say Auschwitz-Birkenau when they speak of the extermination camp, then all of the debates about the so-called "Auschwitz lies" would disappear with a poof in the air. We have to investigate precisely if we really want to know what happened.

Mr. Friedhoff, I hope that with my "materials" I have shown you how I see things now. Check it all over closely and take your time. I would be very pleased if we could get into a conversation about one point or another. It is like studying the Torah: one shouldn't read it merely for oneself. There should always be a *chaver* [friend] or a friend nearby for discussion, for truth reveals itself in dialogue and not in unchecked, solitary study.

I am very much looking forward to your next letter!

Sincerely,
Emil Sold

———— ❀ ————

OCTOBER 21, 1994

Dear Dr. Sold,

Why don't we drop the "esteemed" so that we can be a little more personal now? We might even say "Dear Emil," and make the acquaintance or friendship stronger that way. When my mother-in-law died at the age of ninety-three, her friend was still the "esteemed so and so." Terms like these are just the peculiarities of different cultures. Here when we are introduced to someone we immediately address each other by the first names.

But first of all, many thanks for your very informative letter. I did not have any problem reading the small writing, even though I am eighty-seven. Thus my memories go a little further back than yours, and my German is a bit rusty and out of date. That, too, must be overcome. In any case, you have made an exceptional search to find the reason for anti-semitism. Yet, it is not only the definitive answer for the hatred of the Jews that must be discovered, but also the reason for hatred between all religions.

The existence of a God is not proven. The existence of a supernatural being is only an assumption, and in most cases the concept was used by men as a means to power. When we look back, we find that all religions began as a cult, and that they spread because a single person was very talented at speaking to groups. Yet hatred between different religions developed and still exists even today. Every religion claims to be the right, and the only, path to "heaven."

Most people need these crutches in order to cope with the problems of every day. But it would be fine if the people limping around would only use the stick for themselves, and didn't want to share the stick with others. Religion should be a personal affair, and people shouldn't try to convince others of their own religion. That's the "teaching" that I extracted from your speech. You say yourself that the murdering took place in the name of God. I will add that the sword has killed the most people when used in the name of God, and that it continues to do so.

Religion is a must for mankind. It is only too bad that the leaders behind the different religions don't believe in working for the good of their supporters. They strive only to spread their interpretation of God and to find more believers. Reformations and simplifications of the ceremonies have little to do with actually going to heaven.

Those are general views. Now to the particulars of your talk: by your description you were a prisoner of war, and for that reason didn't know what went on in Germany. I cannot share your claim that the Germans didn't know anything about the killing of the Jews and other nationalities. The people in the towns in the regions of the extermination camps certainly knew what was happening. The facts passed from mouth to mouth, and everyone knew them. Even we here in America were completely informed. The Germans didn't tell you when you came back from the war, perhaps for your protection and perhaps also out of shame.

I can give you a pretty good analogy. I lived in Homburg Saar and lodged in a two-story house. Above me lived the owner, Mr. K., who was a blacksmith. It was in the years 1933–1934. Mr. K., as a Catholic, was not a friend of Hitler. At the time the Saar was still under French control. Hitler came to Zweibrücken and Mr. K. wanted to go hear him just to see why he was so worshiped in Germany. He came back ecstatic: this man would save Germany. After the war my wife and I visited Mr. K. We sat around the table, had coffee and cake, and I reminded him of his visit to Zweibrücken. He didn't know anything about it. He had never heard Hitler speak, and he had never been his friend. In general, that was the attitude in Germany. There were no Nazis there. Naturally there were exceptions, but very few. An editor of *Der Stern* told the story of how, as a nine-year-old boy, he had laughed on Kristallnacht when the Nazis threw a piano out of a house. Not everyone had "done" such acts, but many like him had enjoyed seeing them done. He writes movingly about the feelings and thoughts he has today when he thinks back. It is estimated that Hitler murdered twelve million people, half of whom where Jews.

You write that one should not overlook the Jewish successes in certain areas, which the awardings of the Nobel Prize have shown so clearly. I have investigated this and have come to the conclusion that the Jews seem always to excel in extraordinary numbers. I don't have the answer for this. The Jews have always been called the "people of the book," and this has to do with the books of religion. As you yourself write, neither the Germans nor the Jews are a pure race. I acknowledge that, though it still does not answer why the Jews are so successful. Perhaps you have an explanation for it.

That should be enough for today. I would also be interested in knowing what field you used to be in, or still work in now. Why do you have the title of doctor? I founded a furniture factory in Puerto Rico and retired in 1975.

We have been living for nineteen years now in Florida, the so-called old people's paradise.

Yours very truly,

Dear Mr. Friedhoff,

Thank you very much for your letter of October 21. It contained a lot of starting points for a great number of topics, each of which would require its own long letter. Thus I will start first with answers to the easier questions you brought up.

With the help of your letter we have both already (for the most part) managed the problem of addressing each other. We should have a little patience, since in the course of this exchange we both must make some sort of departure from our habits. It is easier to approach each other in writing. Yet at the same time, the way we greet each other is not the crucial factor. The important aspect is what we have to say in the long run. We both, you more than I (I'm seventy-four), have some very momentous life journeys behind us, and we also have both had a series of life experiences that have determined our opinions. But I will begin with myself:

You ask about my occupation. Well, I am a doctor, and I have just now finished forty-two years of work in my own country practice. Ten years ago the practice was handed over to my son-in-law. I make daily house visits to someone or another, and two times a week I do surgery, but I only do it to assist my son-in-law in my former practice. Now I have a bit more time and can devote myself to topics that I could not even think about earlier.

For example, I am taking courses for senior citizens at the University of Mannheim (in Archaeology, Art History, the History of Religion), in an attempt to fill my gaps in these subjects. Among these courses is also a seminar in Landau that I have attended for a few years now. In it Christians and Jews read the Bible together, a highly interesting thing. . . .

We are of the opinion that the relationships on our planet will get better only insofar as people learn to talk with each other, first of all by listening to the other one in silence, then by thinking, and then by asking additional questions—in order to be better informed at the end. We—that is, Catholics, Protestants, and Jews—are a truly ecumenical group that also makes public appearances. We have visited synagogues in Mannheim and have had services together, at which the rabbi stood—in his robe in the Catholic church—with the other clergy at the altar. And everyone prayed with the rest of the parish, each in his own way to the same God.

We must finally learn to understand and cultivate our common ground. During this process we must not try to convert the others (contrary to earlier habits, when people preached to fight against others). Up until now it has worked so well that in the last two years we have even invited Muslim professors or Imams to our talks—and those were always very productive days. When we assemble at the Schifferstadt *Judengedenkstein* [memorial stone for the Jews] (for example, in memory of *Kristallnacht* on the ninth of November), the Muslim Imam is always there as well. He, too, delivers a prayer for peace in his own language.

Also in your letter you touch on the extraordinary successes of the Jews in the spiritual and scientific areas. We discussed this topic in my house last year, when Professor Z. P., a rector emeritus of the University of Beersheva in Israel, was a guest of mine here. I explained my perspective: for two thousand years the Jews in Europe have been trying to survive under the most difficult of conditions. In this fight for existence, only the most competent and capable have been able to survive. None of them could "sleep through" his lifetime, and each had to be awake constantly. That finally led to a genetic selection that favored the most capable.

To my surprise Z. P. did not accept that theory. He gave the opinion that such a natural selection, with a concentration of the best talents from the Jewish side, had not taken place. Investigations would indicate that the Jews have the same "mean value" as other populations. The capacity of the "talented" is based much more on the need for each person to make some sort of special effort. Thus, for example, the country of Israel, in which today everyone qualified can find an expert professional position, cannot show a single Nobel Prize winner for itself. [This is not true. A few notable Israeli recipients are Yosef Shmuel Agnon (Literature), Menachem Begin (Peace), and Yitzhak Rabin (Peace).] And in America at the moment, the not-so-privileged Puerto Ricans are completely outdoing the Jews in this field. Both he and I would have agreed that the particular personal pressures to do well play a decisive role. However, he argued, the acquired capacities of each individual were not passed on to the next generation.

There is still another important thing that we must take into consideration here. For two and a half thousand years the Jews have been a "people of the book" and a "people of writing." The Jews have the earliest existing religious code, which discusses learning to read and write. And there is not any other (religious) code in which the believer is always expected to study the writings with a *chaver* or someone else. Then they are supposed to have a discussion during which everyone is able to defend and maintain a different opinion without being excluded or persecuted. The upbringing in the Jewish *shul* [synagogue: Yiddish from the German for school] never promoted the development of stringent religious dogmas with the compulsion for people to accept them (and in the case of nonobservance of these dogmas, to be persecuted or even executed).

You yourself wrote: the existence of a God is not proven. And yet that does not affect your Jewishness at all, and no one would get the idea that because of this sentence you should be persecuted or excommunicated from the Jewish community. But consider Christianity, where scientists in the Middle Ages were still executed (for example, Giordano Bruno) because they defended their conclusion that the earth revolved around the sun!

Jewish schoolchildren debate from the beginning and learn to argue with everything they have. It keeps them mentally awake and develops their imagination. And they are advantaged compared to the person who, under different pressures, has only had particular doctrines and dogmas to choose from, and who is used to accepting a preformed philosophy of life (and of whom some "leader personality" later makes easy prey for his spiritual manipulations). As you yourself must have experienced, that situation has taken place over and over again with the Germans!

Mr. Friedhoff, there are certainly many more ways to look at this last question that neither one of us has touched upon yet, as with all of the other problems. The longer we inform ourselves about the specific points, the more comprehensive our views will become. In your letter you touched on a whole string of additional questions that I cannot go into today because of the potential length of such a letter. But I hope you have some different points of view on these things, just as one would not expect anything less from a *chaver*, or a true discussion friend from the *shul*.

I am already looking forward to your next letter and I remain, Yours truly,

Emil Sold

DECEMBER 26, 1994

Dear Dr. Sold,

The New Year will have made its appearance by the time this letter arrives. Even though it is somewhat late, I wish you and your family a happy and healthy New Year. . . .

Your last letter discussed in particular the extraordinary successes of the Jews. You mentioned the survival of the fittest and the religious study of the Ancients, which made the Jews the "people of the book." There is a third possibility, however, which you did not mention: the inner drive to pull oneself from the quagmire. We see this today in the people who came from the Far East and took up residence here in America. Very often their children are the best in the class. They have the inner drive to do better in some way because they are looked at with mistrust. Often they are seen merely as immigrants with a different skin color.

"The yellow peril," words minted by Kaiser Wilhelm II, was certainly not an empty threat. Here it can be assumed that the future belongs to the Far East, and it seems that things will turn that way at the end of the next century. When we reflect on the past and see what happened to the earlier ruling countries—for example Greece and the Roman Empire—we should not be surprised that the descendants of the ruling people would become mentally lazy, and that they would hand over the scepter to different nations. The same is the case in the socialist countries where the government makes sure that every citizen has food on the table. Why work when it isn't necessary? But I have come to a topic that I didn't wish to touch upon.

Today I must show you that we cannot escape fate. Our local newspaper and the *Los Angeles Times* reported that a family named Topf, who had a factory in East Germany, was demanding back its factory and its mansions. When my wife saw the name Topf, old memories rushed back. It was the year 1927, and her mother had knee pains. The doctor sent her to Marienbad for treatment. My wife's parents went with their two daughters—my wife Greta, at that time seven years old and called "Gretel"—and her sister Lili, nineteen years old. In the park of the health resort Lili met a nice young man, Ludwig Topf. During the three weeks there, the two young people were inseparable, but Gretel always had to be with them so that nothing could happen. Ludwig was in Marienbad with a nurse because he had been in an auto accident and the climate and the water were supposed to heal him. Lili kept up a long correspondence with Ludwig, until she met Hugo, whom she married. She met Ludwig a second time when her husband had to go to Berlin on business. Lili informed Ludwig that the train would be stopping in Erfurt for a little while. Ludwig met Lili and her husband at the train station, and that was the last that she heard of him.

The newspaper article explained that the Topf company manufactured the ovens for the concentration camps. Ludwig killed himself shortly after the war. In the Holocaust Museum today the oven doors from different concentration camps still show the name "Topf."

I wrote an article about that and sent it to *Der Stern,* which promptly sent it back with the friendly explanation that they would have nothing to do with the Topf family. That in itself is understandable, but I only wanted to show them that often time alone is incapable of healing old wounds.

I am sorry to be so negative today. I received a letter from the Mayor of

Rülzheim, where I was born, and I could only answer that I thanked him for his attempt to forget the way things were. But one remains homeless anyway, for no one that I knew is there anymore. Or is it maybe the season that depresses people?

I am very much looking forward to your next letter. Yours truly, and from Greta as well,

———— ❧ ————

JANUARY 2, 1995

Dear Mr. Friedhoff,

The New Year had not yet arrived when your letter of December 26, 1994 reached us. It came exactly on New Year's Eve. Many thanks for your good wishes for the New Year, which I return to you and your family.

In your letter is a reference to a Topf family who is demanding back its business and its mansions from the former DDR. That is an explosive topic, and I must discuss it before all the others.

At reunification, a treaty was negotiated "in a rush" between the two German states. It was supposed to sort out a number of legal items and partly it proved to be effective, but afterwards it also proved to be full of inconsistencies. At that time it had been decided that the rule for all of the postwar expropriations was "return before compensation," but in every case there was at least compensation. Thus, whoever was dispossessed of something was supposed to get his property back. If for some special reason that was not possible, the former owner received financial compensation. Therefore, it could very well happen that people like the Topf family got its former property returned in the DDR, since in civil law the question of whether it should have been returned is very clear. But the morality remains completely out of the picture. That is another issue that you touched on in your letter—their company supplied crematorium ovens. Today these people would certainly say that they were supplying them to city and state crematoriums, and therefore also to concentration camps. Thus, suddenly, they are completely without guilt. In fact, they were really forced to do it, they would say—a protective statement used everywhere that you yourself have certainly come to know well enough. But so that you can know more than many other people, I will share the following with you:

As I read about your family's memories of Ludwig Topf, the name Topf actually electrified me. I had run into this name somewhere before, and could not get any rest until I had dug up the sources where I had seen it. According to these sources, the company's involvement in the KZ [concentration camp] was considerably more extensive than it must have appeared.

In some way, this company was involved with the mass exterminations, and if you read and study what patents it had already officially registered at the patent office, it can only make you shudder.

So that you, too, will really know everything, I am photocopying what I have at home on the topic of *Ludwig Topf and Sons*. Most likely, like me, you will need some time before you are able to digest everything that is written there.

The material comes from a book by Ralph Giordano, with whom I have talked now and then. It bears the title *Wenn Hitler den Krieg gewonnen hätte.* [If Hitler Had Won the War. The full title is *Wenn Hitler den Krieg gewonnen hätte: die Pläne der Nazis nach dem Endsieg* (Hamburg: Rasch & Röhring, 1989).] . . . It has to do with the Nazis' plans after the *Endsieg* [final victory]. It is well researched and full of unimaginable pieces of information. It makes you freeze occasionally when you read it, and you just lose your breath with many of the details. If you want to read the book anyway and are unable to obtain it at home, I could try to find it here to send to you. But it is not everyone's thing to read about these kinds of details.

Mr. Friedhoff, many years ago I studied in school, and—as one says— "got my M.D." For us, something like that stays with somebody for his whole life. But first, the young generation forgot how to address doctors with their title. And today, even for us, that formality is not as important anymore. In addition, we are not talking to each other about medical things, but speaking with each other as people who really have had very different lives. Without choosing to do so, we each belong to a group that has every reason finally to speak frankly about the past with the other group, but also to talk about a better future. In the future, please forget about the "doctor" title, which for our conversations is really of no importance.

I think that you now have some ideas that must be read several times, not only once. The other topics that I have ignored, since they are not as pressing as the one touched on today, still haven't escaped us.

Please send my regards, this time directly, to your good wife Greta. I didn't know about her until your last letter. Has she had to overcome a fate similar to yours?

To a bearable year for 1995!

FEBRUARY 2, 1995

Dear Mr. Sold,

I am somewhat late with my answer to your letter of January 2. I was in the hospital for several days because I had to have my pacemaker repaired.

The small operation—it lasted only twenty-four hours—had unexpected results. My right leg was nearly paralyzed, and it is only just now close to normal again. The one should not have had anything to do with the other. Who knew!

Many thanks for your letter and your views about the Topf family. I wrote an article about this matter that was published yesterday in our newspaper. Please let me know if you can read English, and I will send you the article with my next letter.

You still have not written about how much of the German population knew of the concentration camps. I would very much like to hear your views on this. Also on that point, I still need to tell you that in the year 1944, two important documents appeared that left no doubt as to what was happening there. One of them was written by a former Polish prisoner. His name was Jerzy Tabeau, and he succeeded in escaping from a camp with several other prisoners. His report was circulated by the Polish government-in-exile in London. The other shocking report was written by two Slovakian Jews. Specific details of the mass gassings were passed on to all the remaining governments. Some men succeeded in escaping from Auschwitz, and their reports on camp conditions traveled mouth to mouth and must have been heard in Germany as well.

I still have not had the opportunity to go to a bookstore to see whether the book *Wenn Hitler den Krieg gewonnen hätte* is translated and can be found here. I will let you know the next time I write.

Today I have to stop my letter a little sooner, since the doctor has prescribed complete rest for me for some time. Our continued regards from family to family,

———— ✿ ————

FEBRUARY 14, 1995

Dear Mr. Friedhoff,

Many thanks for your letter of February 2, 1995. I see that despite the difficulties with your right leg, you have made it through the recent operation quite well—and I offer you my congratulations since that is all I can do.

I will turn to today's topics right away:

Naturally I would be very happy to get your article about the Topf family. I did not actually learn any English in school, but what I learned in the American prisons and otherwise "without trying" will probably be sufficient, with the help of a dictionary, for me to be able to translate a text from a newspaper. So, if it is possible, please send me your article.

In the meantime I will try to find Ralph Giordano's book here, *Wenn*

Hitler den Krieg gewonnen hätte. If it is not out of print I will gladly send it to you. The readings leave you speechless and partly horrified, but also partly in disbelief. The megalomaniacal ideas that these people had on their minds are amazing. You'll see for yourself. They had serious thoughts about how the U.S.A. could be conquered and then governed!

And now to the question about the knowledge of the concentration camps:

Naturally, everyone knew about the existence of these camps, from the beginning on. As early as 1933 all of the "comrades" who were unpopular with the party were put there for "re-education." The knowledge of the entrance doors came from there as well: *Arbeit macht frei!* [Work makes you free]. My father-in-law, who until 1933 was the mayor and head of a business in Schifferstadt, was taken into "preventative detention" as well. At the time they said that the purpose was to prevent him from being harmed by the outraged population. Since he was not willing to accept their offer and join the party in order to become mayor again, he was placed in prison until he was ready to give up a certain portion of his pension. For two years after his release, he did not receive his pension at all, and then it was cut to half of what it was supposed to be. Communists, Social democrats, those who refused to work, and other unpopular people went to Dachau for "re-education." But everyone survived Dachau and returned after varying times of imprisonment, except for one man. He had distinguished himself as a Palatine separatist leader after the First World War, and was probably murdered in Dachau. None of them ever said anything about what they had experienced and suffered during their stay in the camp.

After the Reichskristallnacht, the men from the Jewish families in Schifferstadt were sent to Dachau for the first time. They stayed there until they signed a document saying that they "no longer felt capable of sensibly managing their own property" (after about six weeks). The management of this property went to the "Society for the management of Jewish property." The result was practically the same thing as expropriation. These files still exist today, and a few years ago I was able to see them. All of the Schifferstadt Jews were released from the KZ again. Everyone, with one exception—he and his wife did not succeed in obtaining an entry visa for America—was able to emigrate in 1939 before the war (to England, the United States, Argentina). I contacted all of them after the war. One of them had some strange bad luck. He emigrated to England with his family, and at the outbreak of the war, he had his family move on to the U.S.A. He, however, was interned until the end of war in Scotland in an English camp, just because he had been a German officer in the First World War and had earned a lot of war decorations!

There were many crimes committed against humanity in these prewar concentration camps. Many prisoners died because of the prison conditions. Up until the end of the war, a few thousand people were executed in Dachau after formally run "trials," for the most part by shooting. Near the end of the war, a gas chamber was installed at Dachau as well, but it could not be put into operation.

The existence of these prewar concentration camps, and the suspicions about what happened within them, were common knowledge. Many "comrades" were admitted there for "re-education" because of verdicts from the courts. But many came back and were silent. All of the people knew about the "jokes" of the Munich clown Weiss Ferdl [a well-known humorist and folksinger of the time, famous for his indirect political and social commentary] as well, who one time on the stage is supposed to have said, "And if the fence in Dachau is still really high, I am coming in anyway."

The KZ served—in addition to the legitimately sanctioned "legal" methods of public persecution—to pressure the Jews to emigrate. I also talked about that in my book *Die Schifferstadter Juden,* as you can see on pages 49–50. In my attempts to make reparations for the little girl Hannele (see pages 129ff), it struck me again that they even used certain methods that were not generally known, and that are apparently forgotten today (the Hakhsharah camps tolerated by the SS, pages 50–51). [The Hakhsharah program consisted of, among other things, agricultural training and the study of Hebrew in preparation for the building of a national Jewish homeland. Until the November pogroms in 1938, the SS actually permitted these camps in order to pressure the Jews to emigrate.] Because of the labor law, today the participants in the Jewish Hakhsharah emigration camps are paid a certain pension for their recognized and thus "official time of employment."

A completely different thing was the construction of the extermination camps in Poland after the beginning of the war. You find that on pages 51–52, and what happened there should probably overshadow everything that human minds had ever thought up before on how to murder. Theresienstadt in Czechoslovakia was probably only a token camp for the international Red Cross. They led commissions from Switzerland and Sweden there in order to mislead the foreign countries. Thus they could have documented evidence so that all possible rumors could be completely denied ("the führer gives the Jews a city!")

As you yourself know, the Allies did not find out about the extermination camps in Poland until late in the war. Everything there ran as secret commando missions. No one could enter the entire *Generalgouvernement* [Polish territory under German rule] without a special permit. The people who were involved were strictly committed to complete silence. The local population certainly knew about transports of Jews to labor duties in the eastern regions. Yet they never heard anything about Auschwitz, etc. The names of these camps, their purposes, and the conditions inside them became common knowledge to the Allies only after the war.

Several years ago, two people from Schifferstadt came to me. They had been in the Wehrmacht and were deployed as anti-aircraft men around the camp at Auschwitz. At the time, they had been about sixteen years old. They had thought that the smoking chimneys were just like the many normal factory smokestacks scattered about the region. They thought that this was where the labor union, Farben, had constructed a production plant for important war materials, and that the prisoners had to manufacture highly dangerous products. They never actually saw the extermination camp nor the prisoners, and there was only one time the SS commander Höss showed up. That was at a Christmas party, and it struck them that he hardly spoke a word.

After the war, we always heard and read about Auschwitz, even though the camp at Auschwitz consisted of relatively small Austrian soldiers' barracks from the First World War, and I think that that is why the slogan "Auschwitz lies" has gained more popularity. Today for the first time in fifty years, the world press correctly referred to the camp constructed in the area of Auschwitz as the Birkenau extermination camp. Even people who don't have any personal knowledge of the situation talk about these topics. Auschwitz has become a "symbol" to represent many other "camps." But this year's ceremonies disappointed me because they focused only on this one "symbol"—no one even thought about the hundreds of thousands of Jews who were systematically murdered on the spot, silently and discreetly, by so-called special units behind the advancing fronts. As we know today, the majority of the so-called "Eastern Jews" were never even put into the camps! There are no records of them. Their murders behind the front proceeded completely anonymously, and as for their number, we have nothing but estimations.

The extermination camps in the East had a completely different purpose. The western European Jews were brought there systematically in registered transports that ran throughout Europe. This was done so that they could be murdered discreetly and unnoticed, out of the sight of the European community (some of them after a short time of work duty). These transports were managed very carefully—could it be any other way with us? I was able to fully reconstruct the path that the Schifferstadt Jews took from the camps of Gurs and Rivesaltes in southern France to the gas chamber at Auschwitz-Birkenau. I even got the particulars, including the departure times of the trains, the names of the transport drivers, and the names, birthdates, and nationalities of the victims. Everything was carefully documented.

One thing that the two anti-aircraft men noticed at Auschwitz: Auschwitz also had an industrial combine that was very important to the war effort, and only a single small railway led there, running for long stretches across flat country. But there was never an air attack at the combine. The Allies could have stopped what was happening there with a single blow—it would have been easy. Their bomber squadrons even flew over the area to get to Berlin. But the anti-aircraft emplacements never got any action there.

You asked what I thought of the claim, "We didn't know anything about it!"

I have said as follows in all of my lectures:

1. Since 1933 everyone had clearly witnessed the persecution of the Jews.

2. Everyone knew about their forced emigration.

3. Everyone knew of the Reichskristallnacht and its consequences, as well as the ensuing, temporary removal of the male Jews to concentration camps.

4. Everyone noticed the deportation and disappearance of their Jewish neighbors to "Work camps" from 1940 on.

5. The *Endlösung* [final solution, the extermination of all the Jews] after the Wannsee conference in January of 1942 was a "secret of the Reich." It happened in the hidden camps of the East. Extermination camps like Auschwitz-Birkenau and their gigantic "shuttle services" were organized after the end of 1941. Everyone involved knew about that, as well as those who happened to hear of it by accident. But news of these things didn't reach the majority of the people until after the war.

I know that worldwide public opinion does not agree with my fifth point. It is much easier for the journalists to act with headlines when all is said and done, and too unpleasant for them to differentiate precisely. But what I say is true. The object of the Wannsee conference (and also the fact that it even took place) wasn't first discovered until long after the war!

That doesn't prevent me from studying other historical sources and being open to all new discoveries. Above all, it doesn't prevent me from being ashamed down to the deepest part of my heart for all the atrocities of those years. And it doesn't keep me from recognizing my responsibility for the future as one of these people, even though I was not able to choose which group I belonged to.

But I want to add that it is still very damaging to attribute this "historical and collective guilt" to every single German without distinction, in the same breath identifying him for the rest of his life with the murderers. After a while, a large portion of the people has become defensive and defiant, and they no longer want to know about anything. They simply shut their ears when the topic arises, instead of being willing to learn more about it.

Who is guilty?

1. There are the actively guilty, the initiators, the commanders, the insiders, the masterminds behind the scenes, the thugs, the executioners, the slave drivers. They sentenced people to death, sent them to concentration camps; they arranged or carried out the tortures, killings, and mass murders. Those who could be found were put on trial in Nuremberg and other towns. These trials are still continuing today, decades later.

2. There are the passively guilty. They knew about it and allowed it to happen. Where it had been possible to help, they didn't. They continue to live, often without the knowledge of their guilt ("I only did my duty"), and sometimes with even a more or less good conscience!

3. But there is also the army of people who are not guilty. They had nothing to do with it, either because it just happened that way or because they made a conscious choice. In particular cases they even helped the less fortunate.

It is simply a mistake to assume that for twelve years, eighty million people had nothing on their minds except murdering Jews. Several thousand Germans were themselves victims of the brutal justice system. The majority of the Germans lived in the perfect police state—in constant fear of being discovered and persecuted. And for many, the only concern was to make sure that they themselves survived the chaos.

4. Most likely, however, all Germans share a common responsibility. Together as a people they have the duty to make reparations for the atrocities that, in the history books, they committed collectively. To do that, every single person must make his own contribution.

I have finally decided, for myself, to accept all the (so very justifiable) resentment against the Germans. We cannot demand "rights and justice" when someone is standing across from us who had to endure such horrible injustices, and who will never be able to get over his deep, psychological wounds. I was standing in the archive at Yad Vashem next to the explanation of the fates of the Jews from Schifferstadt. I was across from an older man and I asked him whether he spoke German. He answered me in German, *"Nein, ich spreche nicht deutsch"* [incorrect German]. We then spoke to each other in French, and he was an extremely nice man. He belonged to the comrades who tried to erase all of their German roots after everything that happened here.

I am ready to do everything at my disposal to help heal the disaster that is still affecting the generations on both sides. In order to do that, we must not talk around the painful and unpleasant things, but must name them clearly. And we must be willing to listen to the person we are talking to, and to consider and respect his arguments, even when, at the moment, they do not conform to our own.

Mr. Friedhoff, today the place where the Schifferstadt synagogue used to stand has been rebuilt as an office block. After the release of the male Schifferstadt Jews from the concentration camp at Dachau in December 1938, they found it necessary to sell the destroyed synagogue's building site in a notarial bill of sale to the city administration. How were they supposed to defend themselves? Later the city resold it to a private individual. After the war, that was seen as a perfectly legal exchange of property.

I own an apartment building two houses down. Since it was not possible to put it in the former synagogue square, I have a Jewish memorial in my front yard on the street. It corresponds to the front of our former synagogue. It's about as high as a man, with special text written on it. In past years on appropriate days, Catholics and Protestants have assembled there together with the rabbi Dr. Meir Ydit, and finally with the Imam from the local Muslims as well. They come together to memorialize, and to pray for peace among men. The text on the stone is intentionally peaceful. On the pediment I have set the places in the Torah: Gen. 4.9: "Cain, where is your brother Abel?" And then Dan 3.17, "If it is meant to be, our God, whom we worship, can free us from the burning fiery furnace, and he will deliver us from your hand, oh King."

Despite all the denominational boundaries, we have finally begun to talk with one another. We are learning how to listen to the other person and to think about what he says. That makes it possible to see the other as a person, just like ourselves, and to realize that there is no rational reason to fear or fight him. There are two main reasons for hate and war: religious (and political) fanaticism, and the disastrous striving for someone else's possessions. As long as these two things exist, there can't be any peace. It is the task of the future to overcome both of them.

Yet neither one of us will see this goal attained. These harmful mechanisms are too deeply rooted in people, and changing ideas or views always takes generations. But that must not prevent us from working toward this goal, despite all the difficulties.

I am ready to discuss in detail how I see the KZ topic at the moment. Object to anything I say if you know more about it than I do. There isn't any reason to hold back any questions, even the probing ones.

To answer a question that you haven't yet asked: when I was younger I was not a member of any party organization. According to the verdict from the Allies' Heidelberg tribunal after the war, the aim of which was "liberation from Nazism and militarism through the law," I was classified as "not affected." But I didn't regard that as any credit to me. At that time I still didn't have much of the knowledge that I have at my disposal today. My lack of interest in politics was based primarily on religious reasons, and also because I saw my parents under a great deal of pressure due to their "political unreliability." I still don't belong to any political organization today—my membership is limited to work at the German Red Cross and to the Life Saving Service. Privately I am trying to improve and revive the long-lost, humane way of thinking in public life, as much as I am in the position to do so.

Well, that should be enough difficult topics for today. My best regards to you and your wife, especially with the hope of many more healthy years. If you happen to end up on our old continent sometime, I would really be happy if we could meet each other. Until then, I will await your next letter.

Giordano's book is out in a new edition here. To make things easier I am simply going to enclose it for you. Don't be startled by some of the details he has discovered. We, too, feel liberated from this madness!

MARCH 4, 1995

Dear Mr. Sold,

My answer to your last letter is somewhat late. I was in the hospital again, and they couldn't figure out whether I had gout or phlebitis. I am now being treated for both until they are sure which it is.

Many thanks for your last letter with the enclosure of Ralph Giordano's book and the Federal President's speech. I am nearly finished with the book and would like to note a few points: On page 11, Ralph speaks (to abbreviate) about the "collective consensus between the leadership and an overwhelming majority of the people." On page 34, he talks about the Wilhemian Imperialism, but I will come back to that later. On page 118, Ralph says "Our entire society collaborated on Auschwitz." The upper part of page 119 speaks about Speer's ignorance of any genocide—even Speer knew nothing of it. On page 124, Ralph mints the word *Geständnisunfähigkeit* [the inability to confess]. Only Eichmann had bloody hands.

Ralph goes into Germany's past only rather cursorily (pages 190 and 191). The pressure to the East was already well known under both Wilhelms. Wilhelm II also spoke about the Yellow Peril. Neither Ralph nor you speak of the German Reich, and how it served as the foundation for the Wilhelms and then in the end for Hitler. When we look back, we find that Germany was once a country of princes (I am including kaisers, kings, princes, etc. in the shortened form of just "princes"). The country consisted of farmers, a small middle class, and the blue-blooded nobles and their army. They sat in their castles, watching over everything and plundering the country streets.

Germany has never had a Robespierre and a Danton. It has never had a revolution in order to get its rights and cut off the princes' heads. The people were the sheep who followed the leader of the herd. And they followed Hitler in the same way, as a legacy from the Middle Ages and the time of the Wilhelms. Bismarck united the principalities and gave the population a small piece of meat, as someone gives the dogs a scrap in order to pacify them. The princes gave up their positions themselves, after they received the land and title from kaiser or king, and more or less made servants (slaves) out of the farmers.

I remember my history teachers from the high schools in Speyer and Landau. I was the best in the class because I knew the dates of all the princes and wars. Everything else was completely irrelevant. The teachers were always to the right, were nationalistic, and tried to teach the students their dogmas. The attitude of today's German youth will again depend on their teachers. I am eager for you to tell me the outlook on this situation. Who converts the teachers?

I am cutting my letter short today, since I have to keep my right foot propped up and cannot do that while I am writing at the computer. I am enclosing my article about Ludwig Topf for you, and would also like to hear your opinion on it. I hope that my health condition gives me time to tell you more in my next letter,

Yours truly,

MARCH 19, 1995

Dear Mr. Friedhoff,

Many thanks for your letter of March 4, 1995. I gather that your health problem wasn't entirely solved yet. I assume, however, that differentiating between gout and phlebitis wasn't a continuing problem, and that since writing you have gotten better. At our age it's no surprise that something like that is always getting in the way.

I was able to translate your newspaper article on Ludwig Topf without any great difficulties. He made me think about the innumerable examples from that time period where so many normal human relationships were sacrificed overnight because of ideological and societal pressures. And only a few "comrades" continued to keep up relationships that had been started before. He also reminded me of the story that I told in the book *Die Schifferstadter Juden* (page 61, the two pictures to the left), where the mixed-race lovers Walter Schmitt and Else Oppenheimer were separated after a very short amount of time. And then Schmitt found himself as the first Nazi mayor of Schifferstadt!

You mention Ralph Giordano in your letter, and his discussion of people's *Geständnisunfähigkeit* [the inability to confess]. That is actually a very strange phenomenon. There are obviously circumstances in which the phrase is valid—memory says, "I did that." But then conscience says, "I could not have done that." Finally memory gives in . . . Strangely enough, this behavior is practiced by all of mankind. We see that in the daily trials, during which no one is willing to admit his own transgressions. It was that way at the trial for the burning of our synagogue in 1938. Those who at the time had boasted about their "heroic deed" (two of them even had to go to the hospital for a short time because they didn't know how to handle the lighter for their fuel) not only didn't remember their action, but also were able to "prove" that they were only at the place of the fire because they felt obligated to help (which in reality no one did at all!). It is also strange that the so-called political and religious criminals immediately swore off their own beliefs when they were supposed to be imprisoned for their actions. Obviously there are things and beliefs that we are only prepared to defend if they don't cause us any unpleasantness.

Germany, as a "land of princes." I agree with you entirely. But we must examine what that means historically.

All human societies go through certain stages. Since primeval times, the whole world, as in nature, has been governed first and foremost by "might makes right." The strong make others their subjects and control them. In the end the neighbors are not only the servants of the strong person, but his soldiers as well. And if it is necessary, they are even prepared to go to their deaths for him and his aims. The "strong" become the chiefs, the bosses, the presidents, the employers, and the lawmakers; the "weak" become their followers. The weak can even learn to find their personal happiness in a servant position that is dependent on the strong. But none of this goes smoothly or without continual battles for power. These battles can take place with brutal force, cleverness, or with the tricks of experienced people.

The state governed by philosophers already failed with the ancient Greeks, who two and a half thousand years ago "invented" democracy. From a certain stage of development on (and above all after painful experiences), human beings began to think and search for agreeable, easy solutions. As a historical country of immigrants, North America won over its new citizens because in fleeing their bondage and going to America, they liberated themselves from their former way of life. And also because these new citizens came together from very different cultural sectors, they built up an especially strong potential for freedom-loving people. But are the true conditions in this democratic country, the way they rule in domestic and foreign affairs, really fundamentally different from the mechanisms that have controlled evolution everywhere else in the world?

We in Germany are indebted to the Allies for sweeping away our ruling class in 1945, along with its ideological superstructure. The developments in the direction of democracy made that possible. We see, however, that people today still have difficulties fighting against (if they have already attained a certain status of freedom at all) the innate human desire for power. Otherwise, how could the wars after 1945 have been possible? They were against all human reason! Mankind still hasn't progressed much farther, despite the insights of certain people. Nearly three thousand years ago, philosophers had already realized that "My freedom ends where it infringes on the freedom of my neighbor." "True freedom means that freedom exists everywhere, for my neighbor as well." That also counts for states.

For the most part, revolutionaries have only exchanged the heads of the leaders for different heads, and the new ones were subject to the same mechanisms and behavior as their predecessors. Nevertheless, it seems that more and more people today recognize these mechanisms and think about how the individual and the people in the world can resolve the common power dilemma. But that will be a whole process that will demand the spiritual and moral development of many generations of people, if you want to look at it optimistically. Yet that is only if mankind doesn't catapult itself out of history beforehand, due to its stupidity.

You ask about the situation in our schools and the views of the teachers.

Here it is possible to detect a decisive break with earlier tendencies. Liberalization is Trump! Everyone has disassociated himself from the slogans of "Freedom, Honor, and Fatherland." The older generations of teachers have died off; our youth has broken away from the old Prussian "ideals" (at the very latest, in the student revolution of 1968). Moreover, the influence of the school has long been diminished due to the appeal of the media, which attacks the youth day and night.

Today everyone who can dodge his military service does. Our English and French friends have even reproached the Germans with the claim of "cowardice" in recent years. Our people have forgotten the militarism of earlier times. The shock of 1945, the total destruction of not only our cities but our country, and also its complete ideological breakdown inspired the youth to act and reform. It was called the "Belief in Germany," and generations later, the healing power of that shock will still be working wonders.

But there is another point that we should think about:

Right now the third postwar generation is growing up. This generation can hardly understand that for good or ill they have taken over the poisonous past of their grandfathers, and that constantly and indiscriminately it is being laid upon their heads. They consider this to be unjust. One young man said to me, "Today there are obviously two groups of people in this world who are always guilty, for whom there is misery on the earth. These groups are (according to the convictions of the Christian and Islamic peoples) the Jews, and since the last war, the Germans." I replied that as a member of the "generation of perpetrators," I can understand the world very well when it points its fingers at the Germans. And it will certainly require several generations of good human behavior (or even a sizeable amount of human atrocities in other parts of the world?) before the Holocaust can slowly move from the world's field of vision. Today many young people simply close their ears when "this old and tiresome topic" is mentioned. Naturally the Holocaust is vividly depicted and taught in a variety of places, including the schools. Several months ago in a local high school I helped to lay out a presentation about the fate of Jewish young people in the concentration camps. I gave a lecture on the topic there as well. We simply must make sure that it is not forgotten. But here, as well, something has changed: the first postwar generation turned against their parents because they, the younger generation, did not want to deal with these things at all. In fact, they defended themselves violently against the charges, and this led to problems in many families. The second postwar generation, however, can no longer regard their parents as the "actual perpetrators" and thus as "the guilty." Now the youth often feels attacked itself, and are unjustly held responsible without distinction for every single thing that the topic includes. And they react accordingly.

Naturally the new teachers cannot escape this process either. We have the phrase, "What doesn't taste good is only swallowed unhappily." It is the same way everywhere in the world. But in this situation the facts are too strong to escape. The teachers grew up differently than the generation "that had something to hide." The process of changing the ideas of an entire people takes generations. I hope that our youth has the chance and the time that they need for this process.

After all, if mankind wants to continue to exist, not only here but throughout the world, we must all recognize the necessity for everyone to change his views. When we look at the world and its problems today, it is sometimes tempting to give up.

Mr. Friedhoff, I think that I have provided you with some good things for discussion today, which we can both think about together. Unfortunately I don't know of a situation anywhere in the world with which we could undoubtedly identify ourselves. The individual persons and all the different peoples continually produce new problems, though they aren't nearly as skillful at producing the solutions. Yet at the same time I defend myself against the fundamental pessimism that suggests itself when one looks at the ways of the world. Wasn't reason supposed to win through at some point, enabling an existence on this planet fit for human beings?

With my best wishes for your health and my regards to your dear wife,

Dear Mr. Sold,

For Easter, though a little bit late, I send my best wishes to you and your family, and hope you have a wonderful holiday. This evening we are having our Seder in memory of the Jews' exodus from Egypt. As you can see, even the events from very ancient times are not forgotten. How could one simply shove such events to the side, when there were witnesses? Both sides would very happily change things so that they never would have happened, but unfortunately that can't be. I'm inserting some reports that I received about Germany. They prove that hatred of the Jews still surfaces in different regions. One wonders why and is unable to find any answer for it. It is terribly sad that people cannot live peacefully with one another.

My health problem has now been diagnosed definitively as gout, and the pain has been reduced by Predison. When I see the doctor again next week, he is going to take another specimen.

I must come back to the "land of princes" for just a moment. You say that all societies have to pass through certain stages. That is very true. But one wonders why Germany took a path different from the other powers. The liberation in Germany didn't come from its own people, but was imposed, more or less, by other powers in the two world wars. The few kings or queens that still exist today have become puppets in order to preserve the reputation of their countries.

In St. Petersburg (Florida)—the so-called sister city of the Russian St. Petersburg—there is an exhibition right now that shows the life of the royal house of Romanov. It is in glaring contrast to the poverty of the population. The jewels on a horse's legs would have been enough to build schools and hospitals. Even today. Why the Russian government doesn't sell these and other art pieces instead of begging for money from other countries is not understandable.

I completely agree with your view when you say that after many failures, going as far back as the ancient Greeks, people think about how to find agreeable and peaceful solutions. Do you think that we will ever experience the final result of that? The search for power by individuals and by countries is too large to make it possible for people to live next to one another peacefully. You call it "greed" and "lust for power," and I agree.

In your views about the present generation you are simultaneously a pessimist and an optimist. I can understand that, and I can see that you feel as if you were a forced participant in the Hitler period. It would be nice to show the leaders of today's government a new path, to show them how people can get along peacefully with each other. Egotism makes people bad listeners. I always say that our politicians forget their promises and change their views as soon as they see Washington after the election.

At one point you wrote me that you were a prisoner of war of the Americans. What year was that and where were you held? Were you in America at that time? I worked some time with German prisoners of war, since I could communicate with them. It would be an enormous coincidence if we had met each other then.

All the best for today, to you and your wife, and from my wife as well,

Yours,

———❀———

MAY 1, 1995

Dear Mr. Friedhoff,
Many thanks for your letter of April 14, and thanks for the good wishes on Easter. I hope that your health problem has found a satisfactory solution; we are not as defenseless in this area as we were before.

I agree with you on all of your points; therefore, we don't need to discuss any of them. I have some news for you today:

To our surprise, we had visitors from America: Otto Landman and his family, whom you obviously know well. Unfortunately, we were hardly able to do anything for our guests since their time was limited. Thus we had to restrict ourselves to the questions that couldn't be ignored. I hope that Landman finds his way back here, and then we will have the opportunity for further conversations. I would also like to take him to visit certain towns that all Jews should see. Once I got the chance to see the nine-hundred-year-old Speyer Mikve [ritual bath, an important part of the traditional Jewish community] with the Fritz Löb family (Buenos Aires). He was a child from Schifferstadt (emigrated in 1938!) and had stood behind it, and had never even heard before that it existed. Our Palatinate countryside was an important center of the Jewry in the Middle Ages, with important *shuls* in Speyer, Worms, and Mainz. In fact, the Yiddish language developed here in the Middle Ages, which brings me to a short tale:

When we visited Poland several years ago, our path also led us to Crakow and the old synagogues there. We were supposed to be shown around by an old woman who felt bad because she wasn't able to speak German. She could only explain the synagogue to us in Russian or Polish. I suggested that she try Yiddish, and the next thing you knew the two of us were having a lively discussion. I was helped by our Palatinate dialect because Yiddish is based on that dialect as it was spoken in our countryside a few hundred years ago. It was enriched by many Hebraic terms, as well as by a good deal of Russian and Polish after the eastward migration of the Jews in the fourteenth century. The other visitors (also Palatinate) were very impressed that we could communicate in Yiddish. There is always a lot of interest in Yiddish song recitals here, for with a little assistance we can get a general understanding of the text.

Now a little bit about my imprisonment: In mid-April 1945 I was surrounded in Ruhrkessel with the rest of my armored division (116. P.D.). We were at the end. Our army commander (General Model) surrendered at 19:04 after saying goodbye with the day's orders, and then he shot himself. His adjutant did the same thing. Two days later I handed over my medical corps (eight men) to the Americans, along with the accompanying material from my motorized first aid station. To our astonishment, we were permitted to continue driving our vehicles. Military policemen eventually guided us to a valley in the region—and then we were automatically taken prisoner in a POW camp (at Brilon). To our great surprise, we found almost all the members of our division whom we had "lost" in the few weeks before. So the individual companies were reconstructed under their former leadership and reunited. This made us all think that we would now be deployed by the Americans as a unit against the Russians. They wouldn't have needed to persuade us; American rations and weapons would have been enough. We stayed in the quarry at Brilon for a short time. Then we were loaded up on American trucks without our materials, and after a long trip we ended up in an enormous camp at Remagen. Tens of thousands of soldiers were spread across the field between the Rhine and the western train line, as far as the eye could see. And new transports with prisoners continued to arrive for days. The officers were separated from the enlisted men, and existing units were broken up. There wasn't any barbed wire, but in its place Jeeps circled the camp day and night. Anyone who ran toward the edges was shot indiscriminately; and after a few days barbed wire was set up. Chaos ruled. There was hardly any food at all, but everyone understood that the army was overtaxed by the over two hundred thousand prisoners brought to Remagen from Ruhrkessel alone.

Unfortunately an incessant rain lasted for ten days, and there was no protection against it. The prisoners tried digging themselves holes in the earth, or hiding from the rain with pieces of clothing. But the holes filled quickly with water and then caved in, and many drowned when the earth collapsed around them at night. Diarrhea broke out, and the makeshift latrines overflowed. Every morning, trucks came into the camp and were loaded up with dead bodies. Many prisoners died in these disorganized first days; it was said a several thousand. But after about two weeks, the situation changed. The camp leadership had obviously switched hands, and a captain "Cane" appeared who completely changed our lives. The rationing was better organized. We received material to build a system that provided us with water (there were a few "water towers" that tankers filled with water from the Rhine. The water was then disinfected with [a bit too much] chlorine, but it was certainly better than no water at all). At the same time, streets were built throughout the camp, and so-called "cages" were constructed to hold a hundred men each. In your cage you were "at home." Tents were erected for the wounded and the sick, and the construction of field latrines was also begun. The bad times were over.

A special camp was constructed for the extra medical personnel (I was sent here as well). We were put up in tents, and cared for in strict accordance with the International Red Cross POW guidelines. We received the same rations as the American soldiers (though the cigarettes were removed from the packs beforehand), so we were able to pass some food over the fence to other prisoners. There was a timetable arranged for each day. In the afternoons we had lectures (on medicine and history) by professors in the camp. Those weeks were filled with discussions about God and the world. We also tried to figure out the intentions of the Americans (the Morgenthau Plan was leaked to us, though I don't know how). Captain "Cane" had become a very well-known person around the camp, and often was at these lectures as well. He even obtained some musical instruments from outside so that some people could form a band. In the evening, the band played at the fence of the camp, and the guards from outside gathered nearby to listen. The band stayed together for a few years after our release: the conductor was Fritz Weber; later they were the combo in an American club in Bad Ems.

To our astonishment, the release from the camp began at the end of May. The Americans tried to filter out the important Party leaders hiding among the other prisoners. Everyone had learned to appreciate Captain "Cane," since he had been so interested in improving the camp conditions. Before we were released, he gave a speech, and for the first time he spoke in German! We all lost our breath: he told us that he wasn't an American, but a German-Jewish doctor from Kaiserslautern, and that he had escaped to America in 1936 just ahead of the persecution. His real name was Dr. Kahn. He certainly had no personal reasons to commit himself so entirely to the well-being of the German prisoners, yet he respected his human duty to the prisoners. I will never forget that afternoon. I wonder if at that time he knew about the events in the German extermination camps.

The release to our hometowns was very well organized, and at the beginning of June, I was put on a truck with thirteen other comrades from Schifferstadt. It was a beautiful and sunny June day. We had survived the war and were free. Everyone had his discharge papers from the American prison, and the mood was ecstatic. But we drove right past Schifferstadt without stopping! We went down the main street in Speyer, and colossal posters hung on the walls of the houses with the first pictures from the concentration camps. We read in huge letters: YOU ARE TO BLAME! Next to the post office, our truck was surrounded by the machine guns of French soldiers. We weren't allowed to get out; instead we were taken to an old work camp in Speyer. No one talked about the Geneva convention there. The news of our arrival spread to the local population, who supplied us with food through the barbed wire for several days. Then we were taken to Landau and were imprisoned in the high school. The majority of us were transported to France; one man was imprisoned there for over two years, but I had managed to make special arrangements in the camp at Landau. So as the camp grew empty at the end of June 1945, I was given French discharge papers and released to go home to Schifferstadt.

At that time, Schifferstadt was occupied by the French; the crew of a (French) Sherman tank had taken over my parents' house. They were willing to talk to me and give me a hand, but I couldn't stay there. In many ways, the men who had returned home were made the scapegoats, and we had to endure a lot of punishment. So I fled to a wine-growing estate in Diedesfeld and became a farmhand. I met two Russian men there and one of their wives. They had been POWs in Germany and had refused to repatriate to the Soviet Union. They got caught in Diedesfeld when they fled to the west, away from their fellow countrymen. And they did so because they knew what would happen to them if they went back. I became friends with them and we had wonderful conversations day and night. One was a physicist, the other a chemist (his father a surgeon in Leningrad), and the wife was studying medicine. When Diedesfeld was handed over to the French by the Americans, a commission of Russian officers, with the help of the French, searched for former Russian POWs. When this happened, I took them on a risky trip into the zone occupied by the English, where they would be safe. They have been there ever since. Others in their situation were extradited, and a horrible fate awaited them: those who survived their journeys home were sent to work camps, where they often suffered a worse fate than German POWs. In a few weeks we will be celebrating our fiftieth year of a loyal and fruitful friendship. It will be the same day that I approached them in the field, and told them that the Americans had dropped an atomic bomb on Hiroshima.

In December 1945, Heidelberg University was able to reopen its study programs, contrary to the fears caused by Morgenthau and thanks to American initiative. And everything was under the control of an administrator from an American university!

He was a very intelligent and sensible man. There is a brief story about him: at the end of the Nuremberg trials several Nazi leaders were hanged, including some generals. The next day, at an old war memorial at the university, there lay a garland with a commemorative ribbon: "to our murdered army commanders Keitel and Jodl." We expected some considerable sanctions, possibly even the closing of the university. But what did the university administrator do? He said absolutely nothing. A few days later he invited the students to the biggest movie theater in the city, and showed a film about the Nuremberg trials. Those trials were the first attempt to dispense justice in an area that had not been covered by international law, but the world could not possibly ignore what had happened without suffering severe consequences. Following that film, we saw the movies that Hitler had made—of the show trials in front of the Reich's supreme court. His supreme court judge Freisler decided against the men from July 20, 1944, and this led to the "extermination" of hundreds of people who had nothing at all to do with the assassination attempt. Before the trial, Hitler had already given instructions that he wanted "to see the assassins hang like dogs. . . ." This university administrator's "practical instruction" on two different types of justice certainly affected those students who had not yet healed since the end of the war. And after that there was peace, as well as a clear change from the previous rule of "nonfraternization."

This, then, is a short summary of my time as a prisoner of war, in response to your question.

Mr. Friedhoff, it seems natural that during the fifty-year commemoration when the media will constantly reflect and talk about the events at the end of the war, there will be every reason to talk in detail about that time period. The rebellious attempts of many right-wing, nationalistic groups have almost completely collapsed under the pressure of several enlightened publications. They travel around our country in search of trouble, but for the moment these professional right-wing revolutionaries have grown strangely quiet. For the first time, the youth has at its disposal substantial documentation that reveals the results of such harebrained and inhuman policies. Before, the young people knew only the slogans and their accompanying actions, and they used them in attempts to shock and frighten their parents. But they had never really informed themselves about the realities of that time. It is strange to me that printed material and promotional literature are delivered from abroad in support of our good ideas, and I find the use of the swastika at demonstrations in foreign capitals, even in Moscow, absolutely grotesque. It seems as though an international collaboration is taking place among the extreme right terrorist groups, and I cannot imagine what these people are trying to achieve. I have read that these types of problems have surfaced recently in America as well. The police of a democracy are defenseless against the attacks of well-aimed terrorism; they can do nothing but run around investigating after the event, and if one day they were to retaliate, that would be the end of a constitutional state and the beginning of total chaos. And—as the ancient Greek philosophers knew—only a strong man, a new dictator, could lead a people from that.

The ancient philosophers show the evolutionary possibilities for a human society: the absolute control of the strong then leads to a dictatorship (to tyranny). When the dictator's end comes, he is removed and succeeded by a small collective (oligarchy), which is less effective in imposing "order" and "leadership." Then many lesser leaders come to power, with additional damage to private and state authority. It finally reaches the point where the people control themselves—in the democracy.

As long as the individuals follow the rules of democracy, this "operation" can progress even further, and the result will be a more and more humane form of government. The greatest possible freedom prevails, that of everyone—the ideal society. But: in this society, egoistic groups can very easily appear and abuse their freedom in order to serve their own interests. With the individual's exaggerated search for freedom, the "anarchy of democrats" can develop very easily. What results is a growing struggle between different interest groups. In particular, whenever the economic and/or social situation is bad, deadly arguments begin to rise, and in the end they lead to a new chaos. In the long term this is intolerable, and the people will call for the strong hand of deliverance, the hand that will end the chaos with force. And once again we will have reached the starting point of the evolution I just described: the beginning of a new dictatorship.

That is the reason I see the emergence of an "opposition outside of parliament" as highly dangerous, especially when this opposition has begun to arm itself and destroy the democratic order. Chaos has no power to heal itself. At the end of these trials, people will begin to trust in a new "strong man," who is able to restore order. The collective reason of a human society should not be overestimated—experience shows that humans only learn through bad experiences.

In Heidelberg in 1946, I learned from Gustav Radbruch that history doesn't run in a linear fashion, though philosophical frameworks try their best to make it seem that way. History has often made leaps or taken completely unexpected paths. With one blow, the world finds itself in a new situation, which leads to new reactions that are just as unexpected. For example, what would become of our world if a madman somewhere sparked an atomic bomb? or if somewhere another great flood arose? or if a meteor impact changed the equilibrium of the earth? To defend themselves from foreign threats, humans join together in new communities and groups. And then the evolution develops in directions that were never even considered before.

In 1945, who would have anticipated the speed at which a destroyed German Reich would become an integral part of the international alliance? It was against all logic!

Well, I've bombarded you today with several of my concerns and ideas. What else is there to do in a situation like this? We must observe, and we must think—and we must do everything in our power to steer against a visible development in the wrong direction. In the end, we really can't do any more than that.

And to you Mr. Friedhoff, more best wishes for your recovery, and best regards from old Europe, to your wife as well,

———❀———

MAY 8, 1995

Dear Mr. Friedhoff,

In my last letter of May 1, 1995, which perhaps you have not yet received, I wrote: ". . . and I find the use of the swastika in demonstrations in foreign capitals, even in Moscow, absolutely grotesque. It seems as though an international collaboration is taking place among the extreme right terrorist groups, and I cannot imagine what these people are trying to achieve. I have read that these types of problems have surfaced recently in America as well."

Since last writing, I contacted a friend of mine about this topic. Since he is Russian-born, he follows the developments there very closely. Well, I received a letter from him today, the day when the entire world is thinking about the end of the Second World War. I very much want you to see what he wrote, and so I am immediately sending you a photocopy. The beginning of the letter refers to several questions that I had asked Juri earlier in a different context. Among other things they had to do with the "Russian nihilists" of 1905. . . .

But now, to touch on another topic, a few words on the situation in our dear Rhineland:

Spring has broken out here in Germany. A few warm days have transformed the country into a sea of flowers. On the roads with chestnut trees down the Weinstrasse, the blossoms fell off some time ago. The walnut tree in front of my window has already sprouted a thick cover of leaves, and the fig tree has produced several big jumbles of fruit. Blue and white lilacs spot the yard, and their fragrance surrounds you. In the fields, the rhubarb has almost been harvested. A few weeks ago we picked the first asparagus in the garden. Entire columns of seasonal workers have marched to the fields to harvest the different types of radishes. Each time they come, they work here for six weeks, and then they are exchanged for others from Poland. It is all very well organized, and with the money that they earn here, they can live well for two years at home.

More than twelve hundred Turks live in Schifferstadt. They came here as tobacco workers, and brought along their close relatives. They have permanent residence here. Their children go to school with our children, and they receive their religious instruction from the trained Turkish staff. The town council has constructed a mosque for them, but it hasn't been attended by many for a long time. There are several types of Islamic denominations with slight differences among them. Many of the women walk around covered up, even some young girls, and there isn't the slightest problem with any of this (as of now). Our Turks are very active in wrestling (the wrestlers from Schifferstadt are well-known for their ability). They also have their own soccer club, which is integrated into the general club life. That is, their club participates in the qualifying games with the German teams. On the floor above my practice, I took in a Turkish family who has lived there for eight years now. We understand each other very well. Before Christmas, the daughters of these Turks came to my wife and baked German Christmas cookies with her. In the sixties, the Italians and the Spaniards came as foreign workers, and they assimilated into the German population a long time ago. Their children have married here. Very few of the Greeks who worked here in the sixties have remained; for the most part they returned to their hometowns. There were also many Yugoslavians in Germany, but since the military conflicts, many of them have returned to that poor country.

With the enormous waves of refugees from the Asian countries and from Africa, we have sheltered a mass of asylum-seekers from all over the world. Someone told these people that they could live here fairly well, even when they didn't have any connections. There are international organizations that arrange their transportation into the Federal Republic of Germany in exchange for many thousands of marks or dollars. Naturally, the German population has been under a strain because these poor people must be given a place to stay, and in one blow they increase the number of unemployed. Meanwhile, however, a law has made it possible to deport the asylum-seekers who have come only for economic reasons, and who are not threatened in their home country. Yet, more often than not, this procedure takes nearly two years. Our world has become truly international. Every morning a group of French-speaking Africans passes by our house on the way to work. They take the train from Metz (France) every day because they can get higher wages here than there. As you see, our country has made an interesting evolution after the war. The people from the Rhineland have become a mixed group.

Despite the difficulties brought on by a mixed society, we have every reason to be happy with the development of our country. In those difficult years after the war, who would have thought that today, fifty years later, the partial reduction of the allied occupation forces would not be felt as an additional "liberation?" And who would have guessed that because of this second "liberation," which in recent years had become necessary, tears would flow on both sides?

The process of our liberation has dragged on for a half a century. "Yanks go home" could be read on many walls in the first years, but today that would be seen as an absolute perversion. We "received" the Americans in 1945 with mixed feelings, and it wasn't only the Germans—the French, too, disapproved of the American occupation for many years. Yet both countries also had great emotional difficulties when the Americans suddenly got the idea to withdraw completely. We need to say it: we are greatly indebted to America. The development of our country today would not have been possible without America. You have protected our country and guaranteed peace in Europe for fifty years now. That has been the longest, most peaceful, and most pleasant period in our history for centuries!

Well, once again I have gotten to politics. But is that any wonder, when every day we confront new images from our past?

In closing I would like to add: I would very much like to have you and your wife stay with us for several days in the Rhineland. Would that be possible? The Rhineland is really wonderful country. There are no more traces of the last war's (terrible) consequences. There is peace everywhere. And the traces of Jewish history have by no means been wiped out, as the *Gauleiter* once desired [a *Gau* was the largest administrative region of the Nazi Party, and the *Gauleiter* was in charge of this region]. We would have some things to look at here (even in Rülzheim!). And together we could reflect upon God and the world. . . .

Yours truly, with my best regards to you and your wife, and, if it is possible, to the Landman family as well,

MAY 22, 1995

Dear Mr. Sold,

Today I owe you a response to two letters. I will try to refer to the different points that you made. But first I would like to tell you that my health has improved considerably. The gout is completely gone, even though walking is still causing a few difficulties. Meanwhile I had my eighty-eighth birthday, an anniversary that was last reached in my family by my great grandfather. One should be happy still to possess mental and physical abilities at this age.

I am happy that you met Ruth and Otto Landman. I'm sorry that the time was too short. They are especially wonderful people, enjoyable to be with and to talk with. I still haven't heard anything from them, and I don't know if they are back yet, but I'm going to call them this evening.

I was in high school for three years in Speyer. During the week I lived with the teacher Mr. Waldbott (22 Landauerstrasse). Mrs. Waldbott was distantly related to my mother. It was close to the end of the First World War, when the French occupied the Rhineland. I still remember that near the train station a bust of Jahn, the father of gymnastics, was lightly damaged by a bomb. And in my three years there I didn't visit the Mikve a single time. Young people my age had no interest in that. I just remember that food was extremely scarce. At the Waldbott's we often had potatoes and red beets for the main meal. They had two sons who emigrated to America, long before Hitler. Georg became a doctor, and Emil, the older of the two, had a cigar factory. I don't know when and for what reason they came to America. In any case, they were spared many unpleasant things. Georg brought a man named Karl Haas to America from Speyer. He is a classical musician (a pianist), and has made himself quite a reputation throughout the country. . . . Perhaps you have heard of him. I know that many years ago he visited Speyer and received a welcome from the mayor.

You mention the Yiddish language. It is very strange that I didn't know any Yiddish until I came to America. Men with long beards and black gowns often came to our town to sell religious articles, and they spoke a strange form of German. I thought that they were Polish, and that they were speaking German with a Polish accent. Now I know that their language came from Middle High German mixed together with Hebrew, as well as with Polish in Poland, Russian in Russia, etc. Many Jews in America who came from Eastern Europe, or whose parents did, can still speak Yiddish today, and they are very proud of it.

Your story about your imprisonment during the war sounded better than the accounts of Americans in German prisons, but I assume that the problems of the Americans had a lot to do with the shortage of food in Germany. Your description of Captain Cane (Dr. Kahn) was very touching. My wife wants to write an article about it. The French didn't behave themselves as well as he did, but that in itself was understandable. Even the university administrator only showed his good side. Is the present generation conscious of the way America helped Germany back to its feet?

You are right. Hitler continues to live on in different countries with the symbol of the swastika. What happened here in Oklahoma City is certainly the result of different forms of hate. It is just amazing that thinking people could come up with these kinds of ideas. Is it a lack of intelligence, or is it revenge for an unsuccessful life? Does every country have such vindictive people and if so, why? Where have people failed when such monsters are raised? There are so many questions without answers.

Your friend in Russia described the same type of situation that exists in many other countries. He said what happened, but he didn't talk at all about the reason for racial hatred in Russia, nor how it can be combated. Again, that is a question without an answer. It is certainly a possibility that Russia will come to have another dictator. Where were there ever benevolent dictators? Perhaps the authoritarian kaiser was indeed the right solution compared to the flawed democracy we know today. But could we count on the reason of a single person? The politicians who lead the democracy are only after getting power into their own hands. We can't leave ourselves entirely to their judgment either. What is your answer to it all?

You actually answered that question generally in your last letter. But one question leads to another. You say that humans only become intelligent through bad experiences. I will happily admit to that. But do we have to stand on the side then, and watch the skinheads destroy the world? I don't think that you would accept that idea. The democratic countries should unite just as the hate groups who work together internationally, and democracy should make it impossible for the skinheads to exist any longer. Do we have to wait until it is too late?

I have to come back to an old topic again. We don't entirely agree on how much the German population knew about the mass murders. You hold the opinion that they first discovered the truth after the war. I claim that they knew what was happening and didn't want to admit it. In an earlier letter I told you that we in America knew about it, and thus the Germans must have known it as well.

Several days ago an article appeared in our newspaper, written by Annette Wronka. She was born in Germany twenty years after the end of the war, and she asked her mother what she had known. Her friend, Liesel Kroehnen, had been twenty-eight years old when Hitler came to power. She said in the article that she listened to BBC and learned about the gas ovens. Annette says that no one in her own family had killed a Jew, but also that none of them had saved a Jew either. She says that she continually senses "the taste of guilt." I hope that you will read this article and that you will be able to understand it. It is written from the heart; Annette cannot forget what happened, and she cannot forgive them. Perhaps she goes too far with her accusations, but her opinion is understandable.

Many thanks for your invitation. You are younger and perhaps have the intention to come visit the United States at some point, and you are warmly invited to be our guest here. We think that "if the dear God remains healthy," we will want to visit Europe again next year. We would then meet you and Elli either in Schifferstadt or perhaps in the Alsace.

For today, best regards to you and Elli, and from my wife as well,

JUNE 20, 1995

Dear Mr. Friedhoff,

After catching up with the "business" mail that had piled up during my vacation, I have finally gotten to answering your long letter of May 22. So:

I read with joy that since you last wrote you have recovered very well, and that you turned eighty-eight years old. Congratulations on your "ripe old" age and many good wishes for the future. I don't know many other people of your age who can still be as active as you. Nowadays people withdraw from public life very early, even at age sixty, and try to enjoy the fruits of their life without doing anything. More and more often a bureaucratic mentality takes over, which is often detrimental to the individual. The socialist state indeed cares for everyone for his entire life, but as a result no one exerts himself and one loses mobility and activity. Many of my older friends have more or less passed away intellectually speaking, and they find it nice that way.

Georg Waldbott, as you wrote, brought the musician Karl Haas from Speyer to America. Does this Karl Haas have a brother (or relative) named Joseph Haas? Joseph Haas was also a musician in the thirties. He was highly decorated as a church musician, even by the pope. He wrote many masses and oratorios, as well as two operas. Among other things, he wrote the Speyer cathedral mass in 1930. But he also wrote a very slow and stately hymn that we high school students performed on May 1, 1934, German Labor Day. The text: "for a day let the working cease / let all the wheels stand still / today a holiday shines on us / put down the hammer and the quill / head and hand / city and land / string a ribbon tightly around everything / work for the fatherland / work for the fatherland / work for the German fatherland!" You see, there was a ribbon strung tightly around everything. . . .

Yiddish: when I was young, the Jews in Schifferstadt didn't speak Yiddish, but a Schifferstadt dialect. The Jews who had emigrated from here to the East after the pogroms of the fourteenth century took on the Middle Rhineland dialect of the time, and they went into the ghettos and enriched their new surroundings. But the Jews also left behind some parts of their language for us in the Rhineland, and these traces have remained in our speech for centuries. In 1992 an acquaintance of mine (Dr. Post) investigated examples of this mixture that still exist in our language, and he put them all together in a booklet. If it would be of any interest to you, I would happily send it to you.

Is the present generation in Germany still conscious of America's help after the war? Naturally my generation well remembers the Marshall plan, care packages, airlifts to Berlin, etc., even if today we aren't thinking about those things all the time. The longer term economic help was achieved by linking the two countries' economies closely together, and that has lifted our economy out of its deep valley. But then the cold war brought us Soviet propaganda, which was able to gain a foothold within the left-wing parties (*Yanks go home!*). Today many of the postwar economic problems have been solved. Happily it is said that everything has returned to normal, and that the youth don't really think about it anymore. They have completely assumed the American lifestyle. . . .

"Mom, what did you know?" It is a question that has followed my generation for a half a century now, and which has always stood between us and our children (even when this question wasn't asked by them). Four years ago in Saarbrücken at a weekend conference, I was standing across from two Abitur [the exam students must pass to leave school and qualify for entrance to the university] classes that had chosen history as their elective class, and they were all well-informed. They were simply unable to imagine, and could not even grasp everything that had happened here in the Nazi Reich. Even the two of us, you and I, could only partly agree with each other.

But one could naturally discuss, argue, and pick arguments apart. We could set one theory against another. But would that change anything that happened? An emotional disputation over the question, "Did everyone know, or were they only partially informed?" would obviously start a never-ending spiral. This question cannot be answered by emotions, but only through a careful examination of the facts. But it is also a question that sometimes can no longer be tackled objectively and sensibly. Because it is so laden with sorrow, a cool approach is hardly possible.

Perhaps I could make a suggestion that I learned in school from Dr. Max Meir Ydit. He survived Auschwitz and, until his death two years ago, was a country rabbi in the Rhineland-Palatinate. For many years he led a Christian/Jewish discussion circle in Landau, and I studied with him for four years until his death. We read the Torah together and talked about many other topics as well. I learned a lot from him. It never bothered us to hold different opinions and views on the same text! In Germany people are always prone to know-it-all attitudes and to the assertions of absolute truths (and they were, as history shows, often willing on both sides to kill for their dogmas—a Christian disease for many centuries now!). In the *shul,* however, they don't love these types of murderous antitheses. You simply accept the different opinion of your partner, and silently reflect on his arguments. Therefore, upon further thought, the *"chaver's"* questioning becomes necessary, and without the partner's assistance the Torah, for example, should not even be read at all.

Therefore, for our exchange I would like to make a suggestion: could we perhaps simply push our questions to the side every once in a while, until we gain better knowledge of the subject?

Or even, to talk like a rabbi: could you accept, for the moment, that there were some people in Germany who did not find out during the war about the extermination camps in the *Generalgouvernement?* I previously conceded that there were thousands upon thousands who were part of it all, and who must have known about it. But according to their rules, these people had to keep completely quiet during the war—and to protect themselves after the war, they certainly didn't speak about it freely. . . .

Annette Wronka's questions obviously came straight from her heart, and it is hardly possible to answer them with a cool head. She upset me very much, and I can understand why Annette received no answers to satisfy her. How could someone be satisfied with any answer when talking about this topic? You can shift and change the question however you want: yet even if the "guilt" for these crimes is not automatically assigned to all the Germans as a single people, in the future, the guilt will probably rest on all of us as a collective defect in our population. I, too, am helpless and stunned when I am questioned about Auschwitz, or even when I think about it. It simply chokes one up with emotion. It is a problem that my generation has to bear, and in every way it must make us recognize our responsibilities in the future.

Mr. Friedhoff, you wrote of your intention to come here perhaps next year "if the dear God remains healthy." We would be very happy to see you, either in Schifferstadt or in the Alsace. But you should set some time aside, so that we can talk with one another in peace. There really isn't anything better than a discussion face to face!

To end today, my best regards and best wishes to you and your wife,

———✸———

JULY 18, 1995

Dear Mr. Sold,

. . . Karl Haas: as far as I know, Karl only had a brother named George. Since he is Jewish, I cannot very well imagine that he has been decorated by the pope or has written masses or oratorios. The name Haas (my brother-in-law was a Haas from Rülzheim) must have been Jewish originally, but now it is widespread among non-Jews in America too.

Yiddish: for as long as I lived in Germany (twenty-seven years), I never heard the word "Yiddish." My religion teacher was apparently more interested in explaining the holidays and the events of recent history. . . . Until I came here I didn't learn that it was a Middle High German, which the emigrants had retained and mixed with Polish (or Russian) and Hebraic words, thus creating a new language that in later years would be acknowledged as literary. Yiddish is dying here because the younger generation neglects the language of its parents and grandparents. That is also the case with languages like German and French and others. . . .

"Mom, what did you know?" I don't think that we will ever agree on this topic, and it would probably be better to drop it. It is certainly a fact that a part of the population did not know about the mass murders. But only a part, and the others were silent about it. The generation that took part in it all is dying off, and the youth will never understand how those kinds of atrocities were ever possible. But the facts must be explained to them in any case, so that they don't repeat themselves in some other way. An author who writes for children dealt with it by saying that the people with blue eyes hated the people with green eyes and vice versa. In his imagination, a sly crook came into the picture who could make blue eyes green and the green ones blue. He sold the idea to both sides so that each could be the same as the others, yet with his manipulations he preserved the hostility. The author wanted to say that you can always find differences between people that can cause trouble. And he was also saying that mere color blindness will not save mankind. . . .

All our best wishes and regards to you and your wife, from both of us, Greta and Paul,

———— ✿ ————

AUGUST 5, 1995

Dear Mr. Friedhoff,

The Haas family: several generations ago, people in Europe took on an inheritable family name (the "last name") on top of their personal names (the "first name"). At first it was the Christians who did this, but then during the course of their gradual emancipation, the Jews did the same thing. These official names could be invented on your own, chosen freely, or randomly assigned by the town clerk. Frequently, the names were picked because the person had gained a "nickname" due to certain personal characteristics. So by no means does the name "Haas" belong to any particular denomination.

However, there was yet another way (all over Europe) to get a new family name, and it can complicate any research on names. Often a Jew who was baptized received the family name of his Christian godfather. So for generations in Europe there have been many Christian families whose earlier Jewishness cannot be recognized in their names, and has been long forgotten in their own families. These families are occasionally called "unknown Jews." And there are so many of them!

There is an index of the entire European nobility, the so-called *Gotha.* There is also an index of the old Jewish families who became nobility, the *Semi-Gotha.* And if you search in it for "unknown Jews," you often make some astonishing discoveries. . . . And to my surprise I also found the Jewish name "Baumann" in the *Semi-Gotha,* the maiden name of my mother! . . .

Yiddish: when I was in a Jerusalem hotel I met a little girl ("Hannele"), who, in 1940 at the age of five, had been taken with her parents from Schifferstadt to the KZ in Gurs, where they were separated. The parents were murdered at Auschwitz in 1942, and Hannele was saved from the camp by a secret organization (O.S.E.). She then came to Israel without any relatives. Several years ago, I searched for this girl from Schifferstadt, and I found her in Ramat Gan in Tel Aviv. Hannele couldn't speak German anymore, nor French, nor English. We had to get ourselves an interpreter who was born in Israel to parents from Munich and therefore spoke German. Neither woman could speak Yiddish. I made an attempt to speak to them: *"Hobt Ir de Mameloschn ganz vargessn?"* [Have you completely forgotten *Mameloschn?* (Yiddish, the mother-tongue)]. And right there both of them were electrified, for they had understood my question immediately.

". . . I don't think that we will ever agree on this topic, and it would probably be better to drop it . . ." That is true insofar as we can't achieve anything by merely repeating our different opinions back and forth to one another. And yet to be able to cultivate a good friendship, despite several differences in opinion, is a good sign of liberal mindedness and a cosmopolitan attitude. But beyond that, we must also remain open to new facts, even when they force us to make some corrections to our previous thoughts. That is what happened to me a few weeks ago, when I discovered something new:

While reading about the fifty-year memorial, I learned that there was still a country in Europe besides Denmark that had successfully prevented the transportation of its Jews to Poland: in 1943 the Jews of Bulgaria were supposed to be deported to Auschwitz. The (orthodox) ministry there already knew what was happening in Poland, and it announced the truth to the people from the pulpit. The people were also told that if this deportation were attempted in Bulgaria, the Bulgarian orthodox ministry would place itself in complete regalia at the front of the prison procession. And come what may, they would go along to Poland as well. How did the SS react to this action? They feared any possible unrest behind the German front, and so the Bulgarian Jews were excepted and left alone! So in that way this one group, at least, was saved from extermination.

At the same time (1943), the German clergy from both churches found out about the extermination of the Jews! And the same people who had fought successfully against the "extermination of lives unworthy to be lived [the handicapped and mentally insane]" just two years before, now were unable to find their way to the pulpit. They were silent—and there was no action whatsoever by the churches in Germany. Even the Vatican remained completely silent.

I knew about the behavior of the Danish population before. The king pinned on a Star of David as a sign of solidarity, and the population led their Jews over the border to Sweden, where they were safe because it was a neutral country, unoccupied by Germany. And the German occupying forces made no countermeasures here either!

The Bulgarian example of successful solidarity of the church and the people with their "own Jews" was new to me. It shows that a united opposition could indeed have been possible, if . . .

We just have to think about that—and I also wanted to say this to you as an addendum to our earlier discussion. . . .

Mr. Friedhoff, the sentence with which you closed your last letter really touched me. I return my best wishes in the same way: best regards to you and your wife as well, from both of us, Elli and Emil,

———— 🕮 ————

AUGUST 24, 1995

Dear Mr. Sold,

Your letter of August 5 was full of surprises; thank you very much for it. . . .

. . . I've tried to find the *Semi-Gotha* here, but the library only has it in Swedish. I asked for it anyway and am supposed to get it in the next few days. Perhaps I'll be able to deal with it since I speak Dutch. . . .

I had learned about the behavior of the population of Bulgaria. It proves again that countries like France agreed with Hitler's ideas, just like Germany and the majority of the Eastern countries and the Balkans. But with all of that, we come back to a topic that both of us would prefer not to discuss.

As far as the Church is concerned, I always find that the faithful are more interested in their own bliss than in that of their fellow human beings. People have tried in every possible way to attract others to their religion. History shows very clearly how often religions have been used as a political means—the Crusades and the Inquisition for example. Why should it have been any different during the time of Hitler?

Now I have something to tell you that perhaps will surprise you. The enclosed papers show you that I have been searching for my ancestors for many years now. At the beginning I found that there were no Jews to be found among all of the "Friedhoffs." My brother had the idea that perhaps a non-Jew married a Jewish woman, and that the man had been converted to Judaism. That wasn't the case, however. One day I was in Cologne, and as always I was leafing through the telephone book looking for my family name. I found an entire page of Friedhoffs, ripped it out, and later from home I wrote all of them the same letter. I explained to them that I was looking for my ancestors, and that I knew that everyone had a family tree because Hitler wanted to know whether there were any Jews in one's family three generations back. I received a lot of answers with negative results. A Gerd Friedhoff from Dortmund wrote me and said that he, too, was looking for his ancestors, and that we could do it together. Naturally I agreed. After several weeks he wrote me that he had found my family. My father came from Ergste, a suburb of Dortmund. The relevant archive was in Detmold.

During my next trip to Europe, we visited this archive and found plenty of information. Now I probably have over one hundred addresses of members of my family, of which I am sending you some copies. I am also sending you the order from Berlin saying that all Jews had to take a family name. Naturally I don't know why my great-grandfather chose the name Friedhoff. We have a photo of my grandfather in a uniform. He came back from the war with consumption and died as a young man. We found his grave in Ergste. Part of the public cemetery was reserved for the Jews, and my grandfather was the first Jew to be buried there. In Langerwehe near Aachen we found the double grave of my grandmother's parents. I wrote all of that down in a book eight years ago along with my family tree and illustrations in order to serve as my biography. Mr. Kukatzki {a contributor to the book and a scholar in the area} has the book and can lend it to you. Of course it is written in English.

I am also sending you a page that I copied from the archive, even though it has nothing to do with my family. It shows how dependably the German clerks did their job. A Jew was given the name Israel, and then the name was reversed after Hitler. [As a part of the race laws instituted by the Nazis, any male Jew who did not have a recognizably Jewish name was to add the name Israel.} It is almost funny.

I never asked my father how he got to Rülzheim and married my mother. Often by the time one thinks about these things, the sources of information are no longer alive. My father was a butcher, and at that time it was normal for a journeyman to wander through the country looking for a good position. Since my grandfather was a butcher as well, I assume that he either employed my father, or that my father "married into" the business. Among the Jews there was always a marriage broker, and so this "marrying into" is a distinct possibility. But the answer can't be found anymore. Again, best regards to you and your wife from both of us,

---

SEPTEMBER 17, 1995

Dear Mr. Friedhoff,

. . . So: *Semi-Gotha:* it is not in our regional library in Speyer, and my bookseller doesn't see any possibility of finding an edition either. It was last printed in 1912, and I've never actually had it in my hand. My knowledge of the *Semi-Gotha* comes only "secondhand," and that's how I knew those other things. . . .

. . . The Speyer regional library doesn't have the *Semi-Gotha,* but it has a similar book from the year 1913 which limits itself exclusively to the German relationships. That is called the *Semi-Kürschner.* . . .

However, this *Semi-Kürschner* reveals in the foreword and between the lines that it was not written with friendly intentions to the Jews. It is even "decorated" with a swastika on the book cover—in 1913, many years before the Nazi period. It only describes details from the period of 1813–1913. I got it in my hands last week when I was looking for the *Semi-Gotha,* and paged through it.

The name Sold isn't in the *Semi-Kürschner* (and, as I saw for myself, neither was the name "Friedhoff"). . . .

It completely surprised me when I discovered a Henrietta Szold in Jerusalem, but not because of the different spelling of her name. . . . For me it is a real comfort that a person with my name has become an important figure with social activities in Israel. A family from Tel Aviv with whom I am friends gave me an Israeli banknote two years ago with Henrietta's picture, and that really made me happy. So are the Solds "unknown Jews" as well? Years ago in Budapest I counted over a hundred people with the name Szold in the telephone book. Unfortunately, the book gave no details about their religious affiliations. Of course it can't be said whether I had any connection with them beyond the related name.

Now to the name Friedhoff:

. . . Your great-grandfather lived in Northern Germany, and the previous century's legislation concerning Jews lagged many years behind the present laws. That can also be seen in the municipal laws that you enclosed. Happily, your papers also provide us with information that your great-grandfather, Abraham Samuel, took the name Friedhoff only for himself and his own family, and not for his parents or his brothers. Thus we find out that next to your name, there exists another (or several?) parallel ancestral lines with different names (perhaps the descendants of Levy Samuel, quoted under number ten, with the present name Blumenfeld?).

Contrary to the situation of the Solds, there are some clear relationships for you: you can assume that the membership of your line of Friedhoffs is completely clear—and you cannot expect to be added to some "unknown Christians" one day. . . .

At our regional library in Speyer, one can get an "interlibrary loan." You put in your book request, and the library goes to different international institutions in search of the requested book. That is how I got the publication by Serge Klarsfeld years ago about French Jews, since it could not be found on the market. He talks about the Jews who were sent to Auschwitz from France, by order of the French authorities. And among the seventy-two thousand well-documented inmates at the French camps, I was able to "recover" the Schifferstadt Jews who had been deported to Gurs (see my book about the Jews, pages 103–116. It was just recently named "the best researched book about a Jewish community"). . . .

———❦———

OCTOBER 7, 1995

Dear Mr. Sold,

Many thanks for your nice letter of September 17, 1995. Since then we have celebrated our New Year and Yom Kippur—we ask God in advance to forgive those sins that we might commit during the next year. Whoever invented this practice had a very good understanding of human nature. I recently read a book that describes the foundations of all the major religions of our time. It reinforced my opinion that we humans invented God and not the other way around. If someone has a new idea and he is a good speaker, he will certainly find some followers. Then a new cult comes into being, which will very possibly lead to a new religion. And we individuals profess the religion into which we were born. The strange thing is that everyone believes in a God—even the same one—but we find different ways to worship Him. It is more or less the same thing with languages. People are motivated by the same things, but express themselves in different ways. Enough of that . . .

I ordered and received the book *Jüdische Lebensgeschichten aus der Pfalz* [Jewish Life Histories from the Rhineland] from the Evangelischen Presseverlag in Speyer. The history of my family is written in the book; Mr. Kukatzki more or less translated "my story" out of my book. I am honored that my parents were acknowledged in the book. How does your situation stand with Mr. Kukatzki? Have you asked him for my book? . . .

I still haven't received the *Semi-Gotha* in Swedish yet. The library says that it can take about six weeks. I will have to ask about it again. . . .

———❦———

OCTOBER 24, 1995

Dear Mr. Friedhoff,

. . . Now to our continually intriguing topic: the *Semi-Gotha.* As I write here, the three volumes that came out from 1912 to 1914 are lying next to me on the table. This is how it happened: in my attempt to get the *Semi-Gotha* on "interlibrary loan" by having the Rhineland regional library look for it in other libraries (I told you about this intention in my last letter), I noticed that *"Semi-Gotha"* was only the subheading or subtitle of the work, and that it would have to be ordered in the library under its correct title. Its correct title reads *Weimarer historisch-genealoges Taschenbuch des gesamten Adels jehudäischen Ursprunges* [Weimar Historical Genealogy of the Entire Nobility of Jewish Origin]. Only the third volume from 1914 is called *Semigo-*

thaisches Genealogisches Taschenbuch aristokratisch—jüdischer Heiraten [The Semi-Gotha Aristocratic Genealogy—Jewish Marriages]. And note this: I was able to obtain these books in the Speyer regional library immediately with these titles, and then I took them home and studied them in peace. I also found the *Semi-Kürschner* in the Speyer library. . . .

I don't have the book *Jüdische Lebensgeschichten aus der Pfalz,* but it will be no problem for me to get it. I am very excited about your story.

Best wishes to you and your wife, and in expectation of your next letter,

—————❦—————

DECEMBER 1, 1995

Dear Mr. Sold,

I am late in answering your letter of October 24—but many thanks for your letter and for the papers you enclosed. The reason for my tardiness is the following: my agent gave me the hope that he could perhaps find a publisher for one of my books. I am now in the process of making several changes, and this takes up a lot of time and concentration. The book is over three hundred pages long, and you certainly know what that means. And at my age it doesn't go so fast anymore. Therefore, you will have to have some patience with me until I can direct my thoughts to something else.

The political events keep on coming: it looks as if we—the U.S.A.—are going to support Yugoslavia. I hope it is not a repeat of Vietnam. I don't have a lot of faith in the Yugoslavians. I got to know them in my earlier business trips, and I know that the one side doesn't trust the other, and that they're full of hatred. They also made good guards for the concentration camps, which cannot be forgotten. I don't want to come back to this topic.

The holidays and the New Year are right around the corner. We hope that you and your family have a wonderful holiday and a happy and healthy New Year. You will find a card enclosed that I made on the computer.

Greetings and best wishes to you and Elli, from both of us,

—————❦—————

JANUARY 22, 1996

Dear Mr. Sold,

Just a few lines for today: I haven't received any answer from you to my letter of December 1, 1995. I haven't heard anything from you about the holidays or the New Year either. I hope that everything is all right with you.

Best regards from both of us, to Elli as well,

———❀———

JANUARY 25, 1996

Dear Mr. Friedhoff,

Many thanks for your letter of December 1, 1995. You wished us a healthy and happy New Year, and though a little late, we happily return those wishes to you and your wife.

You write that at the moment you are in the process of editing one of your books, which is a big priority and taking a lot of your time. I can well imagine that you are busy with it day and night (at least in your thoughts). Perhaps it is your book about Jewish life histories in the Rhineland. I have tried to buy a copy of that, but without luck. Finally someone told me that unfortunately the book was out of print at the moment, and that I would have to have to be patient while awaiting a new edition. . . .

Every day there are new reasons to get worked up about the way the world is going, and new reasons to take some time and look at various important issues. But we should learn to follow a kind of diet when reading the paper. That is, we cannot take all the events in the world and push them inside us and try to digest them without straining our nerves. Therefore, we must follow a "diet" while reading, just as we do at the table when we're eating. We have to make a selection from the issues, and then stay within the realm of possibility when considering solutions. And we must select according to the importance of the topics. Then we have to realize that our lifetimes are measured. For in the end we don't know, as you once put it and I liked so much—"whether the dear God will remain healthy next year as well."

President Weizmann visited us. He provided us Germans with many reasons to talk to one another, and we should really be thinking about the things he said. He also gave the Jews here a lot to think about and discuss with his extremely controversial demand that they should emigrate to Israel immediately. It can hardly be expected that in the coming decades the emotions that grew (and were taught!) over a period of centuries will simply disappear, and that love will suddenly break out on both sides. But it must be possible to achieve a level where people think, where we get to know and understand one another better, where we talk with one another and arrive at a reasonable point of cooperation—just as this has happened between current-day Germany and the state of Israel. And just like what has happened to people who have "ventured down the path to one another," and have proven that it is possible to do so.

We are anticipating a visit to Israel, which will probably occur in April. After our partner and friend of many years, Mrs. Reinemann, died in Tel

Aviv at the age of eighty-seven, we were able to talk her daughter Dania, who was born in Israel, into doing what her mother did (Mrs. Reinemann helped us for many years in looking after the Jewish girl Hannele, forsaken by the world and by God—she went to the KZ at the age of five; her parents were murdered in Auschwitz). So now with Dania, we are dealing with the generation of children who were born after the Third Reich, who as a whole have not developed any emotional ties to the country of their parents, and who approach us coolly, maintaining a watchful distance. Nevertheless, we have found great kindness and wonderful hospitality in Dania, and I hope we will be able to return it soon.

You, too, have hinted that a visit with us may be a possibility ("if the dear God remains healthy"). In May we are going to the resort for three weeks, again to Bad Hofgastein, and then during the last week of September we are obligated to attend a conference in Münster in Westphalia. The remaining time we will be at home and would very happily greet you here!

For today, our best regards, also to your wife,

———❦———

FEBRUARY 14, 1996

Dear Mr. Sold,

. . . Many thanks for your letter of January 25. Your wishes for a good New Year were happily received, and I thank you very much.

I am sorry that you weren't able to get the book *Jüdische Lebensgeschichten aus der Pfalz.* Mr. Kukatzki, who contributed to the book, could certainly help you or lend you his book.

You have surely heard about the Mormons, who have their own religion here in Utah. Recently it has come to light that these Mormons "posthumously" converted the Jews who died in the Holocaust to Mormonism. They not only took in three hundred and eighty thousand Jews, but also Hitler, Göring, Göbbels, and Dr. Mengele. It seems as though the devil is searching for souls. A man formerly from Mannheim, Ernest Michel, is trying to erase the names of the Jews from the Mormon books. But that is not easy: in total they have used this method to admit two hundred million deceased people to their religion. It sounds a bit like the Baptists here: they claim that you can only get to heaven through Jesus. When will human beings ever become human beings!

I agree with what you said about President Weizmann. But we should nevertheless consider whether there is another reason for his demand [for Jews] to leave Germany, or to say it better, to go to Israel. As with the Mormons, it seems that most other religions are politically active. As long as hate between religions continues to exist, there will be unrest not only between countries, but also between people. Religions have failed to preach peace and how to live among all men with a spirit of understanding. It is the religious leaders who enforce this negative behavior, and it will not disappear, because there will always be hunger for power. This very much resembles the political parties and their never-ending vicious circles (in Iran religion and politics have been combined).

This year things are going well for us: the presidential elections are of course occupying both parties and thus the entire country. As always, everyone is always right, and tries to pass that on to everyone else. With patience, we will see how it turns out.

With best wishes from our home to yours,

FEBRUARY 20, 1996

Dear Mr. Friedhoff,

Our last letters must have crossed each other over the Atlantic, so I wasn't able to refer to your letter in mine, and vice versa. I wanted to give you a little break in December, so that you could edit your book in peace. And I also didn't want to write you then because of Christmas and the Christian New Year; I didn't know if you took part in those celebrations at all. Our Israeli friends originally come from Munich. They celebrate a combined festival that they call *"Weih-Nukka,"* [*Weihnachten* = Christmas; Hanukkah] and which allows them to be at home in both traditions.

When you look around the world and ask yourself a few questions, it's impossible to be at a loss for discussion topics. But you must maintain an "intellectual diet" if you want to cope with the fast and furious events of every day. But also, no one has enough information to enable him to form sound ideas about every single problem that faces us. Yet this much seems to be certain: the attempt by the Western world to reorganize things after the Gulf War according to the wishes of George Bush has long since fallen on its face. And you don't get the impression that mankind has learned anything in the last years either. It seems that the traits passed on to us from our "biological primeval period" are again manifesting themselves all over the world, and there aren't many signs that could justify hoping for the improvement of the general human situation. I am also thinking about your pessimistic assessment of the situation in the Balkans, where the mutual destruction obviously hasn't been enough to pave the way for sensible talks. In the meantime, our country is crammed full with hundreds of thousands of "Balkan refugees." It's very easy to get into a conversation with them, and I get upset every time I hear how these people are plagued by personal tragedy, and it shatters me every time I find out that their sole aim is to go home and take revenge on the people who are doing the same thing to them. Every once in a while in Germany today, little Yugoslavian boys are prepared for the coming blood feud—when they grow older they are supposed to go and attack the homes of other families. It's completely dumbfounding! This kind of situation couldn't be settled by any "world peacekeeping force" or by bombers either. The clashes will continue, even if they take place with a knife in the still of the night. . . . Nevertheless, we hope that our fears do not come true, and that the American efforts will achieve the desired success.

Karl Jaspers, the Heidelberg philosopher who was persecuted by the Nazis (and whom I heard in person after the war), entreated us young students at the time, "We have to become like the Swiss if we don't want to become like the Balkans." What he had in mind (at the time) was the completely self-contained Swiss Confederation, in which many groups of people (even those who spoke different languages) shared a peaceful coexistence for centuries. The inextinguishable hostility among the peoples in the Balkans cannot be due to the high, rugged mountains that divide up the landscape. This hatred was suppressed for several decades by the machine guns of the authoritarian Tito state (and by the foreign threat of the Soviet Union!). Now the hatred has broken out again. The Serbs already promised us a new world war when the present conflict began. But will we be intelligent enough to avoid this possible development, and to keep out of it when it is necessary to do so?

Mr. Friedhoff, today is Shrove Tuesday (Mardi Gras), and I have a little free time while the others are romping around. So I thought that I would write you, and I wanted to hurry so that we didn't "cross over the Atlantic" a second time. But what a wonderful stroke of luck: just this moment I found your letter of February 14 in the mailbox, and I can answer it right now. . . .

The Mormons are also active in old Europe. Thirty years ago they visited me at my practice with their books (The Book of Mormon). My son-in-law Dr. Stabenow was in the United States last summer with his wife and four children (he went to school there for a year and still regularly visits the people who hosted him). He gave his local address during a tourist visit in Salt Lake City, and since then the family is "looked after" by two young people even though he never had asked for them. He can't get rid of them, but they are two very attractive Mormons and he does have some good conversations with them. The Mormons are friendly people, but I never would have guessed that their friendship goes so far as to accept posthumously into their community not only the victims of the Holocaust, but also their old mortal enemies, in order to live in close, blessed, companionship with them forever! (The Christian sect of Jehovah's Witness was taken to the KZ by the Nazis because of their beliefs as conscientious objectors). So in the end, do entire SS units receive absolution posthumously, and then find themselves in heaven, united with their leaders and all their victims?!

That reminds me of another progressive movement that should be taken seriously: two years ago representatives of all the current world religions met at a conference in America. There they realized that world peace would not be possible unless there was an effective elimination of religious and ideological conflicts as well as conversion attempts, and unless each group renounced all movements against the others. Such a world peace would only become possible through a slow changing of ideas that begins at the foundation, and by overcoming the fundamentalism that exists everywhere. One of the initiators of this conference was Hans Küng, a professor in Tübingen and a Catholic theologian and priest, who was suspended from Rome by the authorities because the Vatican disapproved of some of his activities. Küng is searching for common ground in all the existing religions. In his opinion, one possibility for this common ground (to serve as the "new world ethos") could be the rules of the covenant God had with Noah in the Torah (Genesis 9: 1–17). I have looked it up several times in order to inform myself. God's covenant with Noah was not only addressed to the people of Israel (which didn't exist at that time), but to all of mankind. And it contains no "laws" or "truths" that couldn't be accepted by all people, so perhaps these laws could serve as the common ground for a human society without aggression and hostility. Naturally all the different kinds of fundamentalists will find it extremely difficult simply to accept the opinions of other people, but if we don't learn how to do that, the course of human history will hardly change at all. I am living to see that tolerance can function; you know that we have met in small discussion groups (unfortunately still too small), and with those discussions we have learned to listen to one another and to talk to one another as friends—Christians, Jews, and Muslims! In the long term, there really isn't any other choice. And the strange thing is: I discovered that my former adversary, now suddenly my partner, has problems very similar to mine, and he is just as happy as I am about the newly found mutual understanding.

On the topic of Weizmann, I am enclosing an excerpt of his unusual speech in the Bundestag, as well as an article by Daniel Cohn-Bendit. Cohn-Bendit has transformed himself from his earlier role as one of the 1968 revolutionaries in France and Germany to a thoughtful and serious journalist. . . .

———✺———

MARCH 19, 1996

Dear Mr. Friedhoff,

Perhaps as I am writing you these lines, a letter from you is again on the way to me at the same time, and the two of them are waving to each other across the ocean! I haven't chosen any specific topic today from our stock of problems, but you can also write "just for the fun of it." So:

Here along the upper Rhine there are three cities that played an important role in German-Jewish history. They are Speyer (Sch), Worms, formerly written as Uormss (U), and Mainz (M). In the synagogue, they used the beginning letters of the cities for the common abbreviations. You could become a rabbi in these three cities, and using the abbreviations together they named them "SCHUM." In Worms, Rashi (Salomo ben Isaak, 1040–1105) also received his rabbinate instruction as a young man. You can still go there and sit and think in the same study room where Rashi sat as a yeshiva student nine hundred years ago. And from there he left his mark on Jewish spiritual history! Now, in the last few days I read some news in the newspaper that made me very happy:

The northern Israeli city of Safed came into Israeli hands in 1948 at the last moment, though still not too late, and then it was excellently restored. It is a charming town that I have visited twice, and it played a role in the old Jewish history as well. This city of Safed is at the moment negotiating with Speyer to establish a partnership between the two cities, a "town-twinning." If that is successful, it would be very happy news for me. I have already pointed out numerous times that I think the time has come for Jews and Christians to approach each other seriously and talk. The bottom line of their painful common history is that they finally need to develop better relationships with each other. They need to learn to talk with each other as friends, and to turn their sights to a better common future. After all, to start with, the Christians could be regarded as a Jewish sect that first began to dissociate itself radically from Judaism in the second century. This separation led to all the miserable events of the following centuries, up until the Holocaust at the end. But perhaps that connection between cities cannot yet move so fast, and we will have to be patient for another generation. Even if something will not be carried out in the foreseeable future, this is what has been passed around unofficially for some time now: the Golan Heights are supposed to be given back to Syria. A buffer zone will be established between the two parties, and the Israelis want a contingent of American and German troops to be stationed there as the buffer. That could be the result of secret dealings among the governments. We will see! . . .

———❦———

MARCH 30, 1996

Dear Mr. Sold,

Humans think and God directs. That's how it has been with me for the last week.

First of all I got a cataract in my right eye removed. My reading and writing were especially hindered because my left eye is particularly bad and has a scar from an earlier accident. And then at my last checkup my cardiologist was not happy with me and sent me to the hospital. . . .

The result was satisfactory. Next Wednesday the other eye will be taken care of. In the meantime, I am making an effort to write you a few lines, so that you know about my condition. I hope that you are not offended by the shortness of this letter. When my eyes are working again, I will make up for it. For now I wish you a happy Easter, and send greetings from our home to yours,

———❦———

APRIL 9, 1996

Dear Mr. Sold,

My eyes are working again, even though I haven't yet received the new lens for the left eye. That will take from two to three more weeks. The things that were yellowish yesterday have now changed back to white. The world looks completely different again. It is unbelievable when you think how exceptional the progress of medicine has been in this area. In the olden days—actually only twenty years ago—people went blind with cataracts.

I am reading your last letter again and am convinced that something was lost when you didn't become a rabbi. You are certainly better educated about Jewish history than I am. Our Jewish teachers in school, including Mr. Waldbott in Speyer, were happy when we were able to read Hebrew and could understand the meaning of the holidays. We never translated the texts or learned about their meaning. That's completely different from the Jews who came from Eastern Europe. Their general education was not nearly as important as the teaching of Jewish literature. In any case, they represented what people here call "the people of the book."

It is really inhuman what is happening in the Middle East and the Balkans. Individual lives are no longer worth anything. It seems as though the Germans were a good model during the Nazi period. Unfortunately that brings me back to the Holocaust again. Old wounds are starting to bleed again. I am sending you copies in the enclosure that refer to a book that will come out soon. The title is *Hitler's Willing Executioners: Ordinary*

Germans and the Holocaust [New York: Knopf: distributed by Random House, 1996]. Here the "ordinary Germans" are discussed, and not those in the SS or SA [the storm troopers, a paramilitary branch of the Nazi Party, initially more important than the SS]. A. M. Rosenthal, one of the most distinguished journalists here, says that only twice in his life did he feel obligated to write about what happened to him personally—otherwise he wouldn't be able to write about anything else. One time was when he was in Poland in 1958 as a correspondent for the *New York Times* and visited Auschwitz. The second time was when he read this book and was convinced that it was the ordinary Germans and not the SS who were responsible for the Holocaust. The author testifies that about one hundred thousand ordinary Germans were murderers. That does not include those who carried out the daily atrocities. The author (a professor at Harvard University: Daniel Jonah Goldhagen) claims that almost all of the fifty million Germans knew what was happening in the camps. The second article is from the writer himself, in which he provides examples for his claims. I don't assume that the book will be translated into German. If you would like to have it in English, I will happily send it to you as soon as it is released. When one sees what human beings are capable of, nothing should be surprising anymore.

I am sorry to have to reopen this chapter. The bureaucracy left behind evidence of many specific cases in the archives, and thereby gave the Germans a bad name. That is not only bad for the Germans; it is bad for mankind in general. There are many people who would not be able to understand that kind of behavior; among them, certainly, are you and me. It is unfortunate that we cannot change mankind—unfortunate yes, but also, I believe, human.

Well now I have to give my eyes some rest. Greetings and best wishes from both of us, to your wife as well,

———— ✿ ————

APRIL 16, 1996

Dear Mr. Friedhoff,

Many thanks for your letter of March 30, 1996. I see that since you last wrote you have put several health problems behind you. I hope that everything subsided nicely and that you can read and write well again. It is a considerable handicap on the typewriter, as I have just found out by testing it and trying to write with one eye covered. . . .

I am sure that at some point I have written you about "Hannele," the Jewish girl from Schifferstadt who was sent to the KZ in 1940 at the age of five. Two years later her parents were murdered in Auschwitz. Hannele herself (her name is now Chana I.) was saved and taken to Israel all on her own. She was ruined in body and soul, and now she just died during Pesach in Tel Aviv after a difficult illness at the age of sixty. I had organized a group in Schifferstadt for her (Catholics and Protestants), which privately provided her a supplementary income, so that at the very least she no longer had to suffer material deprivation. So that you can see it, I am sending you the obituary that we printed in the Schifferstadt daily paper.

During Easter week we had a visit from some Israeli friends. Hannele's brother Kurt (now Claude) also came from Paris to meet with us. At the age of eight in 1939, he was able to escape to Weissenberg in Alsace, and survived in France with a false identity (as an orphan of French parents killed in Algeria). Claude speaks French and Palatinate, both languages that I can communicate in very well. Hannele, however, had completely forgotten her German and spoke only Modern Hebrew. She could only communicate with me and her brother with the help of a translator (I visited her three times in Israel). She couldn't even have a letter correspondence with her brother. I received some letters from her in Modern Hebrew, which each time a young Israeli who had married someone from Schifferstadt translated for me. But for the most part, Hannele's friend wrote me in German, which she had learned from her Munich-born mother, and for many years this friend was our guest here every summer.

Your book: *Jüdische Lebensgeschichten aus der Pfalz* has come out since I last wrote you. Naturally first I read Kukatzki's article about the story of the Friedhoffs, which I found very interesting. . . . I will treat myself to the remaining articles during my coming vacation.

❦

April 17, 1996

Dear Mr. Friedhoff,

Early today I received your letter of April 9, 1996, and to my great joy I see that things are going better for you. Because of my inadequate knowledge of English, for the time being I have only been able to give the two photocopies a cursory reading. But I understand that after half a century, someone is speaking here who feels obligated to express his personal horror over what happened in Germany during the Third Reich. It is easy to relate to the wave of emotion aroused by the discovery of what happened. And I can empathize with the person whose wounds are reopened and bleeding again. I can assure you that every single time I am confronted with these things again it makes my stomach cringe, and then I wish that the ground would open beneath me and swallow me up. I still don't know the conclusions and hypotheses of these authors, nor what new sources or information they rely on. For that I'll have to take a bit more time, and at least make myself some exact translations of these reviews. At this time, for language reasons, I am hardly in the position to read these books critically myself.

About our exchange of ideas on these things—you suggested that we shouldn't speak about it anymore, but I do not believe that our views on this topic should be "irrevocably buried in a Genizah" [the storeroom of a synagogue used as a depository for biblical manuscripts that can no longer be used] as it were. It's not good to suppress these things forcefully; they always keep their potency in any case and then poison our interactions with one another. It is better to leave unresolved questions open for the time being, to speak about them when there is new information, and then think about them together.

By chance, the book you quoted by Daniel J. Goldhagen was discussed in our paper today, *Die Speyerer Tagespost* (by the way, it is predicted to be a hit here in Germany!). I am cutting out the article for you, and am enclosing it without comment.

I am also sending you an excerpt from the *Schifferstadter Tagblatt* from April 11, 1996 with the obituary that I mentioned above, of Chana I. She was the last KZ victim of the Jewish community in Schifferstadt, after a sickness that lasted half a century. On behalf of "Hitler's Willing Executioners" in Schifferstadt, it was signed by the (Catholic and Protestant) ministers Gieser, Weber, and Erlenwein—and a certain Dr. Sold. We remembered Hannele and her fate last Sunday at the Catholic service.

Mr. Friedhoff, if you really want to let yourself get upset about the inhuman interactions of human beings with other human beings, then you should read *Medizin ohne Menschlichkeit* [Medicine without Humanity], the records of the Nuremberg trials of the doctors, edited and annotated by Alexander Mitscherlich and Fred Mielke. . . . I read this book in 1947 when it came out under the title *Das Diktat der Menschenverachtung* [Dictation of Contempt for Mankind]. There are no polemics in this book. It simply lists facts, records, and authentic documents about human experiments made by German scientists in the KZ during the Third Reich. During the war, I heard these university teachers give several medical lectures, all of which on their face were completely normal and basic. There was no sign at all of their other secret activities. Whoever wants to study this mentality of contempt for mankind, and whoever wants to know what humans of even educated groups are capable of, will find everything that he needs in this documentation of the Nuremberg doctor trials. He won't be surprised so quickly anymore after reading it. And it doesn't gloss over anything that happened in the Third Reich. All of it took place. It is already such a serious issue by itself that it is actually harmful when journalists seize these things and use them as material to suit their own purposes. It can raise doubts about the seriousness of the events they are talking about.

———❀———

APRIL 30, 1996

Dear Mr. Sold,

Many thanks for your informative letter of April 16, along with the enclosures. The story about Hannele is very touching and shows great compassion, especially by you, for those who were oppressed by the Holocaust. I can very much understand your position. You suffer from what your fellow people did under Hitler, and it doesn't seem that there is any way to erase the shame. But you have to realize that someone cannot be responsible for what other people are doing or have done. It is not your fault that for almost two thousand years they have preached from the pulpits in their churches that the Jews killed their God. In my opinion, that is the leitmotif of antisemitism. The religions have failed to do what was expected of them: love your neighbor as yourself, and lead a good life, so that you will go to heaven. Almost all religions have done the opposite: they hate all the other religions and believe that theirs is the only good one. Yet in doing that, they are forgetting that man created God and not the other way around. As examples we have Moses, Jesus, Mohammed, Buddha, Confucius, Lao Tze, and everyone else whom humanity has deified. Here in America we have close to one thousand cults. The future will tell how many of them gain enough followers to become new religions.

I am pleased that you got the book *Jüdische Lebensgeschichten aus der Pfalz,* and that you read about my youth and where I came from. Although my memories from Rülzheim are pleasant, I still hear the expression *dreckischer Judd* [dirty Jew] going through my head. Then antisemitism became legal under Hitler. I am sending you a page from *Aufbau* [A Jewish-German newspaper published in New York. Founded in 1934, it was intended for Jewish-German refugees in the United States]. The articles speak for themselves. I am also sending you an article from *Der Stern* ["Friendship with an Enemy," an article about Mr. Günzburger, a German Jew, meeting Mr. Dahl, a non-Jewish German, many years after the war] that came out years ago. Mr. Werner Günzburger, who died a few months ago, was my wife's cousin; she was born a Günzburger. Mr. Dahl came to Clearwater in order to see how his "enemy" is living. Among other things, he said that he is ashamed today when he thinks back to the Kristallnacht, how he laughed with every piece of furniture they threw out of the windows of Jewish apartments, as did the other young people in Hitler Youth uniforms. He cannot understand it himself: a belated repentance.

In the meantime I also heard that the book by Goldhagen will come out in Germany in August. I haven't read the book. To the contrary, I was advised that it would be better not to read it. We can just act like an ostrich and bury our heads in the sand.

As for my health, things are going well for me again. I view the world with different eyes; those things that were yellow before are white again. Medicine has made fantastic progress. If I make it, I will be eighty-nine years old on May 17. I am indebted to medicine for that as well. I never expected to reach this age.

Mrs. Gerda Weismann Klein, a friend of ours, received an "Oscar" for a film documentary about her liberation from the KZ and her forced march to Germany. Perhaps you have heard of it or even seen it. The American officer who liberated her became her husband. He was a German Jew and came from the region of Mannheim.

I will have to end my letter with that today. Best regards to you and your wife, from Greta as well,

---

JUNE 21, 1996

Dear Mr. Friedhoff,

On May 17 you turned eighty-nine years old. Congratulations, not only for having stayed mentally sharp at that age, but also for still being able to correct your eyesight—best wishes for the coming years. I didn't receive your letter of April 30 until after my rheumatism treatment in Bad Hofgastein (May 1–22). It helped me again this year, though it certainly won't last in the long run. Yet my ordinary mobility is not seriously hindered, and I'm able to go about my usual tasks and activities.

The themes of the photocopies you sent along, "Friendship with an Enemy," have kept me pretty busy. I see that you knew Mr. Günzburger very well, and that you were able to follow closely the development of his late friendship with Mr. Dahl. As a young boy indoctrinated by Hitler, he could not recognize the atrocities that took place right before his eyes. He grew up in a world where antisemitism had been legalized long before Hitler. For thousands of years anti-Judaism was regarded as a virtue throughout Christendom, a "godly" work. "God wishes it" was the cry with which the European knighthood exhausted itself while persecuting the defenseless Jewish believers in their homes, before it made its way to Jerusalem. As moral authorities, the churches had laid the groundwork for this intolerance centuries before Hitler. So with his racially grounded hatred of Jews, Hitler hardly had any difficulty finding enough "willing executioners" throughout Christendom who were not the slightest bit bothered by persecuting the Jews, even violently. I am enclosing an excerpt from the writing of Martin Luther, which he presented to the people in 1543 with the title "Von den Jüden und Iren Lügen" [Of the Jews and Their Lies]. It could be seen as instructions for dealing with the Jews. Luther had even planned their accommodation in "camps"! So naturally, a Hitler youth like Dahl didn't in 1938 sense the scope and monstrosity of what was happening right before his eyes. Thank God that later his "eyes were opened." It should not be taken for granted that Mr. Günzburger extended his hand to Mr. Dahl, even as a friend, after everything that had happened to him and his family. It is a sign of the hope that despite all bitter experiences, there can still be a path to more humanism, and to better interactions among human beings in the future.

I, too, have seen that the enmity we were taught as youngsters can change into personal friendship. After the long and bitter war against the Soviet Union, I formed a lifelong friendship in 1945 with two former Russian POWs. They had preferred to remain in Germany and not return home. During the war, the Russians were commonly regarded as "subhuman creatures," and were treated as such. We met each other by chance in August 1945 when we were both "agricultural workers" on a Palatinate wine-growing estate. For days and nights, and, in the end, for decades, we talked and discussed things with each other.

One day Oleg asked me about my experiences at the Russian front. As I spoke, we discovered that we had been caught up in the same battles—on opposite sides—both as infantrymen. We were fighting over the fortress Bobruisk, where we Germans had forced the river crossing over the Beresina in 1941 against strong Russian forces. Shocked, I said to him, "We could have been shooting at each other!" Oleg looked at me and said, "No! Nothing could have happened to you. At the beginning of the war I promised my father that I would never shoot at human beings. I only ever shot into the air." I was completely taken aback, and I was ashamed. Oleg's answer had greatly affected me; it still rings in my ears today, for in 1941 I was a well-trained soldier. . . . Oleg died two years ago. Over his grave we scattered a small bag of his dear Russian earth, which he had brought back in small portions each time he went to Russia after the war, and which he had collected in his apartment for just that purpose.

Each of us is born with a blank slate for a brain. During the course of the years, it is filled with the theories and ideas from our chance surroundings. Later, with increasing experience, one begins to think for himself, and then he can critically distance himself from the mould he was provided with— even if it is obvious that it is difficult for most people to make decisive changes and learn to be better. Our future depends on the way our youth is conditioned today. It is crucial that the youth learns to recognize the biases and the chance nature of its conditioning, and that it is capable and willing to correct any detrimental parts of that conditioning. For that reason, I always make a point of talking to young people.

On December 31, 1995, I sent a letter to Otto Landman, whom you know very well:

"You see, here we would both have a subject that would allow our communications to develop even further. Please think about this: if we remain the children of our past, then nothing will change for Jews and Christians. We have to learn to talk with one another if we don't want to reproduce the hostility of before. Those who are capable of talking must dare to begin, and free themselves of the miserable past. But that does not mean to forget it. The sorely afflicted Jews will not be able to, and the Christians shouldn't. For me that means we should learn to talk with one another with respect for and knowledge of the past, and that we should finally make a 'step toward one another,' so that in the end we can get a step closer to a better future."

And on June 2, 1996, I was able to write back to Mr. Landman:

"Many thanks for your letter of April 6, 1996. I want to thank you especially for one sentence in particular: 'We don't want to reproduce the past, but we don't want to forget it either.'

"After almost two thousand years of unbelievably violent 'togetherness,' it is high time that we finally begin to think and reflect on everything together. We need to overcome every fraternal feud that has poisoned our thoughts and actions for generations. In this area, I am trying to do what I can."

The heading *Friendship with an Enemy* expressed precisely the relationship between Günzburger and Dahl. Actually they were not personal enemies—they didn't even know each other then! Both of them, through no fault of their own, had entered a world where their good faith was used for alien purposes; that is, if you disregard Günzburger's self-defense as a later bomber pilot. It is certainly easier to cultivate a friendship when pain hasn't been caused beforehand. It really doesn't happen every day that people overcome the injuries from their past and push the memories aside in order to approach one another and converse as friends. This article made me very happy because it shows that thinking and talking with one another can break down the aversions buried deep inside of us. . . .

July 9, 1996

Dear Mr. Sold,

. . . Your notes on "Friendship with an Enemy" are quite right. Yet you didn't go far enough with them. You wrote about the Crusades, but didn't mention the Inquisition or the repeatedly bloody hostilities among almost all of the religions. You also didn't comment on my remark that every religion had created its own God, and then insisted that its religion is the only correct one. Different religions attempted to spread their opinions with the word, and others attempted with the sword. It is understandable that mankind needs a crutch and reaches for straws when drowning. But that should be a personal thing between the individual and his beliefs. What has he achieved in converting someone else to his religion? Was Goethe right when he professed pantheism? Is God a being by our own standards ("God created man in his own image"), or a power that created the world and now preserves it? Why was Hitler able to kill twelve million people and Stalin thirty-five million? Those are questions that are difficult to answer or that cannot be answered. Your enclosure from Martin Luther's writings is a typical example of how religions can create hatred, and how they continue to do so. It is difficult to find the reason for it.

Your story about the Russian soldier who shot in the air is very moving. It is hard to believe that there was someone like that. But it shows us that there were—and perhaps will always be—individuals who had some understanding of the value of life.

You say that everyone is born with a blank slate for a brain. Hinduism teaches that the soul is the knowledge that the human being acquires throughout his life. . . . Buddha says that praying doesn't help. He teaches that you reach nirvana if you are a good human being and live as one. A friend of mine here says that the best religion is having a good relationship with other human beings. Who is right?

I am enclosing a newspaper excerpt for you that talks about the doctors during the time of Hitler. It and so many other articles speak of the Nazis. Almost one hundred percent of the population voted for Hitler—willingly or because they were forced to—and so they actually all became Nazis = National Socialists. How would you explain that?

Many difficult or unanswerable questions for today. Best wishes and regards to you and your wife, from both of us,

Yours,

———❦———

Dear Mr. Friedhoff,

Thank you very much for your letter of July 9, 1996. Before I go into the (many) particular issues that you touched on, I would like to say that during the evening the day before yesterday, I watched a very interesting discussion on TV. Michael Friedmann and Daniel Goldhagen were talking with one another about the book *Hitler's Willing Executioners,* which can be bought in the next few days. Michael Friedmann is the child of Jewish parents, both of whom survived the Holocaust because of "Schindler's List." He was born after the war and grew up in Germany. Friedmann is politically active in the CDU (Kohl's party), and is the acting chairman of the council for Jews in Germany. I hope that at some point the conversation will come to one of the channels in America. Goldhagen obviously feels misunderstood and misinterpreted by the headlines spread by the journalists. He says that too many people who haven't read the book and understood it for themselves have written reviews about it. He announced that he wanted to come to Europe there and then to clear up any misunderstandings. He narrowed down his "Germans" to the contemporaries of Hitler. I am very sorry that I didn't even record the text of the broadcast, but I wasn't prepared for it. And then, so as not to miss a word, I wasn't able to get away from the television set. Goldhagen introduced himself in the broadcast; he is a voice of the young generation, which very much demands that we listen to it attentively and that we newly reflect on some things. . . .

. . . Your friend whom you wrote about is completely right: the best religion is having a good relationship with other human beings. The goal must be to develop a new world ethos that is acceptable for all religions. Such a world ethos could come, for example, by adopting the covenant that is expressed so poetically in Genesis, chapter nine. It is between the God then, El Shaddai, and Noah and his sons (worth reading!). That would have to be easily acceptable for all religions, for according to legend, this covenant was made between God the Creator and those who survived the Flood, the progenitors of all future humans (Noah, Shem, Ham, and Japhet). So it was long before the Jewish people and their Mosaic God Yahweh: it sets down the laws on how humans, animals, and all of the inanimate world can live together humanely.

You write: "almost one hundred percent of the population voted for Hitler," and you ask me for an explanation. Hitler was not at all "voted" into power by the people! In 1933, he was appointed as a representative to Parliament by President Hindenberg, simply to relieve his unfortunate predecessor for a short period of time. But then with the help of his para-military organizations, he systematically seized power with a coup d'état. Please look in my book *Schifferstadt, wie es früher mal war* [Schifferstadt, As It Was Before], which came out in 1981, to see how all of that happened. Hitler later had ninety-nine percent approval—but the elections weren't held until he already had power. You must be familiar with the similar situations in other countries governed by fundamentalists or authoritarians. I am enclosing a section from the book about our area; it was actually envisioned as a photo album relating to local history and geography, but along with the pictures I couldn't bear to leave out a short text about our Third Reich. At that time, the book was a small sensation.

In my last letter, I wrote about doctors in the Third Reich and the doctor trials in Nuremberg. It should not be forgotten that the Reich government controlled the doctors' existence (that means their financial existence too!). They could only be in business if they bowed to the orders of the state.

The Germans also participated in the Crusades. The initiative came from the pope (Italy). The sermons for the Crusades (in the Speyer cathedral as well) were given by Bernard of Clairvaux (France); the Jewish pogroms in northern France and later in our Rhineland cities go back to the wild group of Peter of Amiens (France); the English knighthood participated dili-gently (Richard the Lionhearted). It was a colossal European and Christian mistake, which in the end wiped out even the Christian (!) sect of the Albigenses in southern France in the cruelest way possible! Originally, everything was directed against the Arabic Muslims, who occupied Jerusa-lem and the Holy Land. In Europe, however, it struck mainly the Jews.

The Inquisition took place in all of Europe, and it was a "Christian" affair. Sectarians and those who had deserted the faith were supposed to be tracked down, convicted, and condemned, and then the punishments were carried out by the secular jurisdiction. The Germans participated just as the other Europeans. The Inquisition was only directed against the Jews in Spain, who followed the advice of Maimonides [Rabbi Moses Maimonides, 1135–1204] and allowed themselves to be baptized, though at home, and in their hearts they remained Jews. . . .

AUGUST 17, 1996

Dear Mr. Sold,

. . . First of all to Goldhagen: I still haven't read the book; my grand-daughter is bringing it to me this evening. He may not always be on the right track, but where there's smoke, there must also be fire. And the smoke was obvious over all of Germany. I haven't seen any German history books, but I am almost convinced that these books will have to be rewritten in order to present the current and future generations with the truth. On one hand it is understandable that people today are ashamed for having followed someone like Hitler; but on the other hand, the Germans should admit—as did Mr. Dahl from *Der Stern*—that a mistake was made, and they should try to avoid making any others. They cannot be like the ostrich and bury their heads in the sand. I am speaking in general, and I know your personal attitude.

Hannele will continue to live on in memory. . . .

In the little book *Wie es früher mal war,* both words and pictures show the population's enthusiasm during the Hitler period. I know that many were only fair-weather followers. But they, too, were happy and laughed when the Jews' furniture was thrown out of the windows. Again we return—without wanting to—to Dahl and Goldhagen. It must be possible to identify the people in the pictures who were throwing their arms into the air. What became of them? How many of them are still living, and what do they say when they are shown the picture? Please believe me when I say I don't understand how human beings are made into murderers. . . .

SEPTEMBER 13, 1996

Dear Mr. Friedhoff,

Thank you very much for your letter and regards of August 17, 1996. Many thanks for the different enclosures as well; the English text about the conversion attempts by the Southern Baptists kept me the most busy. In their current endeavors, the Baptists resemble the Apostle Paul, who must have recognized two thousand years ago that it was pointless to try to convert the Jews. So then he limited himself to the conversion of the "pagan" peoples in the Roman empire.

Depending on the situation, Paul passed himself off as a Jew, a Pharisee, and a Roman citizen. He actually founded two churches here in the West: one that was based on Middle Eastern mythology, from which the future Byzantine (Greek) Christian church and its subgroups arose. In addition, there was the Roman version that Paul, compared to the strict Mosaic God, allowed to be influenced by personal elements and the modified Jewish laws of justice. But even the Jewish interpretation of his teachings on Christ became the root of many subgroups and sects. They number over two hundred today, and the Baptists are one of them.

For several decades after Jesus, a Judeo-Christian congregation existed in

Jerusalem under Peter and Jacob (until the destruction of the city in the year 70). These Christians remained faithful to their temples and congregations as they were before, and they continued to demand circumcision before a Christian baptism (all Christians had to have been Jews beforehand!). They continued to attend the synagogue and appeared there as speakers. But because of their new teachings, they came into conflict with the Pharisees and the Sadducees. Thirteen years after the death of Jesus, the conflict had already escalated to such a point that one of the high-ranking Judeo-Christians (Stephen) was stoned by the orthodoxy because of his "fashionable heresy." It was an execution that Paul took part in according to his written confessions, which we can read today. Therefore, disputes between the Jews and the Christians have existed since the beginning. And since Jesus didn't leave behind any established teachings or written instructions for his successors, disagreement repeatedly opens the door to more discussion even within his own churches. Often there are violent conflicts and wars over beliefs, as there still are in Ireland today.

In 1989 I gave a lecture in which I discussed Christian anti-Judaism. Understanding that is the key to understanding the Christians' century-long persecution of the Jews in Europe. After all, the most horrifying fruit of anti-Judaism was the racially motivated Holocaust. My topic went like this: "Being Jewish in a Christian Land."

I briefly outlined the history of antisemitism up until today. That is a topic, it seems to me, that Daniel Goldhagen has attempted to understand only in the modern age and not throughout history. Virulent hatred of Jews existed long before the Germans entered into modern history! Since it is not irrelevant to understanding the problems we are discussing, I am making you a photocopy of the text of that lecture, and will enclose it.

So now I've already mentioned the name Goldhagen. At the moment, we are still relying on the headlines that have splashed across the big pond. Because of the great uncertainty here about the book, and because we are expecting to hear details that we didn't know before (we even hear from "over there" that history will have to be rewritten!), the German press is "in a flurry" with interviews, conjectures, insinuations, prejudices, and fears that have already led to discussions, even though no one really knows what is in the book. No one has seen an authorized German text yet, but already it's a much-discussed bestseller. Experts—and those who consider themselves as such—have perhaps expressed their prejudices too prematurely, but they have ensured that there is public confusion about it all, and, of course, that they achieve the desired publicity. Now everyone can read in peace and think.

For years now, I have read almost everything on this topic that comes before me. Four big discussions about the book have taken place on TV recently, two of which I was able to record. Afterwards I pick out specific sentences or statements that I want to reflect on. In my last letter, I talked about the discussion in America between Michael Friedmann and [Daniel] Goldhagen. Now I have also seen how Goldhagen has presented himself to his critics here in Germany. As I watched it, it struck me that even on the Jewish side there was a certain reservation about his theories. I got the following impression:

There actually isn't any discussion in the book about the facts and material that Goldhagen collected very exactly and diligently from other authors and available documentation on the Holocaust. Those who still aren't sufficiently informed will be shattered by Goldhagen when they see the merciless brutality of this killing machinery, and the indescribable human misery that the executioners caused with it. Obviously, at the moment there is not a more vivid depiction of what happened during the Holocaust.

Furthermore, whoever had claimed to be an expert before and said that he couldn't discover anything new in Goldhagen, will be completely over-whelmed by the atrocities and details that are passed before his eyes in all of their drama. In a very powerful way, Goldhagen has reopened discussions about these things fifty years after they happened. They were beginning to die out everywhere, but he is bringing back the memories and the facts for all the world.

But Goldhagen has not limited himself just to stating these terrible facts. His intentions reach farther. He contemplates the causes and connec-tions, and the motives and mechanisms that were in effect here, and that first made such a Shoah (Holocaust) possible. But with these thoughts, he departs from the descriptive scholarly portion and the historical "treat-ment" of the Holocaust.

Nevertheless, the result of this attempt to find an interpretation, an explanation, is in one sense a causal analysis of the events and a historicist way of looking at it, and thus is a practical application and thoughtful treatment of what happened. But with such an attempt, we have already gone beyond a scholarly writing of history.

If we want to understand what happened, we must overcome our per-sonal impressions, dedicate ourselves to making thoughtful assumptions, and set up some premises. But since these assumptions are subjective and temporary, we must check to see if they are arbitrary and whether they can stand up to reality.

Deductions that I have made from my thought *processes* can be completely in accordance with the rules of formal logic—that is, they can be logically correct. My *conclusions,* however, cannot be better than the accuracy and cogency of the premises that were set before me. And it is Goldhagen's premises that must be examined for their coherence if we want to judge his conclusions and theories.

Since you are reading the book now, you can be careful to see what premises form the basis for each of his observations, and you can consider for yourself the validity of his claims. I can't spark any written discussion here that goes into specifics, but perhaps I can say what I think by discussing my views on a simple example: on his idea of the "Germans," whom he sees as a uniform and homogeneous mass.

I got the following impression: Goldhagen's presentation of the Germans, which he maintains exclusively throughout the book as the basis of his observations and explanations, is very simplistic (and, in the end, it should not be forgotten that Hitler had no difficulty finding his "willing executioners" throughout all of Europe!). He attributes to the Germans a stereotype that he has invented himself—and by so doing he makes them a "fixed entity" that is no longer worth discussing, and which he uses as a "scientific constant." It is true that such a striking way of looking at everything facilitates the development of simple working models, which are easier for the public to discuss. And the simpler the models are, the more the public likes them. Thus it is strange that until now only a historian from the Hebrew Jerusalem University (Prof. Moshe Zimmerman) has hinted at this weak point, and he did so only casually. I wonder, then, to whom Goldhagen is really referring when he speaks about the "Germans."

Now I don't want to counter Goldhagen with any of my own theories about the Germans, but I would like make a few observations about whether his opinion of the "Germans" has any general validity.

Whenever a guilty party had to be found after the war, the international gaze fixed itself on "the Germans," the inhabitants of the Federal Republic of Germany at that time. The DDR was taken into the ranks of the socialist brother nations. Its inhabitants were suddenly supposed to be considered good and trustworthy Communists—and obviously in the process they all became people who had been "persecuted by the Nazi regime." They couldn't be included with the fascists nor the militarists!

Our Austrian friends, who had faithfully lined up beside us, suddenly in 1945 became a people oppressed and enslaved by the Nazis, who were coming from the prison camps, and who had to be liberated by the Allies. For that reason, there couldn't have been any fascists there either. And since the inhabitants of Austria are not Germans, neither could they have been any "executioners." Accordingly, a denazification was not needed in their country. But think about this: the Austrians made up eight percent of the whole German Reich. Their portion in the SS, however, amounted to eighteen percent. Their portion of the KZ [concentration camp] guard personnel came to forty percent. And Eichmann's staff consisted of seventy percent Austrians! Why then, until today, was it exclusively the fate of the Adenauer Federal Republic of Germany to be the only one charged with the responsibility of the Holocaust—leading to the fact that, until today, it has carried the financial reparations entirely on its own?

Incidentally, in Austria they still wear their war decorations from the German Wehrmacht with pride, which is not possible for us. In Austria, the international comrades of the Waffen-SS still meet today to cultivate their comradeship. In the Austrian resort of Hofgastein in May of 1996 I was able, with great astonishment, to watch the ostentatious funeral procession of a former member of the *Leibstandarte Adolf Hitler* [elite guard unit of Adolf Hitler].

Thus, who and where are Goldhagen's "Germans?" Are they simply and indiscriminately the inhabitants of the postwar Federal Republic of Germany—and these alone? Do the inhabitants of the old DDR (since 1990) belong here now as well? Is the accused Teutonicism therefore a function of today's political country borders?

Or does the accusation apply to a "typical German idiosyncrasy" rather than to an inherent characteristic, which, if such a thing exists, is to be found more or less in the biological genes of an especially reprehensible human race, a race that unfortunately is born that way, and from which we cannot escape due to destiny, even in the long term?

In that case, one would have to expand considerably the circle of blood-related Germans. More than an ample amount of them would be found in Holland, Belgium, Luxembourg, Alsace, and Switzerland. And it would be a catastrophe more than ever: after all, how many of today's United States citizens would then be incurably infected with this pernicious German cancer?

Sometimes plain and simple numbers can stimulate thought better than words, and straighten out prejudices and oversimplifications. I remember an example that is relevant here:

After the war, sixty thousand Nazi criminals were brought to trial by all of the Allied courts combined (including the Soviet Union). Later, after the establishment of German sovereignty, another eighteen thousand were brought to trial by German courts (including the DDR). Thus we can count, with Goldhagen, altogether one hundred thousand active executioners—an alarming number. The Wehrmacht consisted of about eighteen million men under arms. Therefore, that would have been 0.6% (zero point six percent!) of the uniformed Germans actively participating in the Holocaust. Even if an equal number of civilians had been participants—but should one not even consider the large number of vague testimonies?

In accordance with that, you might now ask, justifiably, how I believe something like the Holocaust was possible at all. The participants in the discussion obviously agreed with Goldhagen that, as in other situations, the Holocaust cannot be accounted for by any single cause. Instead, and understandably, we must go back to a combination of many prevailing factors. This is investigated and described in many places, with varied and sometimes even controversial assessments. Goldhagen's view of things is certainly worth considering and discussing. Perhaps in the process, however, with his monomaniacal attempt at an interpretation, he has not quite achieved the precision of a historical account of the destruction of the Jews.

Meanwhile, Goldhagen has attempted to neutralize some of the testimonies in his book. In his discussions, he emphasizes that some of the connections he made have been misunderstood. Many of the people who exhibit this misunderstanding obviously haven't read his book attentively enough. And by the way, I have gotten the impression from him personally that he very well understands how to listen to his critics. To his credit, he is also prepared to think, and that willingness has impressed me greatly—especially since it is something his opponents have occasionally lacked.

What I found lacking in the discussion until now was the answer to another question: was Goldhagen not concerned with the fact that the dreadful annihilation of Hitler's opponents and enemies did not solely involve the Jews? The KZ occupants for the first five years were not really "the Jews." The party-political opponents of the Nazis were doing time there, the homosexuals had been collected there, as well as the clergymen of both denominations who had become unpleasant (who hadn't held their tongues in the pulpit), along with the people who "refused to work," and the Gypsies as well (Sinti and Roma). In some cases, such KZ prisoners were executed in the camp; in the meantime, however, others were released to go home "due to their good conduct." These matters took place outside of the courts. The "verdicts" came from political authorities. Since they took place in public, they were in full view of all the people. They were the means of the Party authorities by which the masses were disciplined and kept in submission and fear. Also forgotten in the debate was the "annihilation of lives unworthy to be lived"—those of the mentally ill. I hardly hear anything about the mass murders of the Russian POWs since 1941 either. And I haven't heard anything at all about effective compensation for the groups of non-Jewish victims, to the people of Sinti and Roma, for example. Obviously these people have no lobby in the world public. The madness of this regime did not at all restrict itself to the extermination of the

Jews! Therefore, with the contempt of all humanity, their actions went beyond the problem of sheer antisemitism!

I know that I am talking about a boundless topic that touches our emotions everywhere, and I know that it is, therefore, very difficult to be able to tackle it with complete objectivity. However, whoever wants to avoid any kind of repetition of the Holocaust, as well as all murder and violence in the future of mankind, has every reason to reflect on the things that can bring a man to torture his neighbor, to take his life from him, to murder him.

This problem is certainly not restricted to the Germans, for it has not stopped since 1945. I do not foresee that somewhere in this world there will ever be a lack of people who are ready to be their neighbors' executioners. But just for that reason, we should continue to study Goldhagen's book closely in the future, and consider the reasons and possible causal connections for what happened.

And so, back again to your and my recuperations, and to the other topics of your letter: . . . The German history textbooks have been rewritten, and the Third Reich is covered in the lessons now (until 1980 it had all been hushed up). Schools have study groups, and together they work hard at mounting appropriate exhibitions. There are always students who pick out topics from the Third Reich for their year-long projects, and over and over again they come to consult me in their search for material.

But this is just as important: people are working together with European school authorities, even across country borders. They are determined to correct the nationalistic conceptions of history that were in the schoolbooks before, and to change them to have a less biased point of view. What is especially necessary and difficult, however, is that Poland and Germany work through their history books together—and together they are correcting what needs to be changed and what is reasonable to change. These are very important steps if we want to save the next generation from prejudices and behaviors that have evolved throughout history.

Hannele's sons, each of whom I was able to meet only quickly in Israel, wrote me a letter after their mother died and enclosed a German translation. For your information I am enclosing photocopies, as well as a photocopy of the text concerning her that appeared in our paper.

Mr. Friedhoff, Daniel Goldhagen (I am back to him again) has really shaken up the nest of historians and everyone else who has been busy with his topic. Everyone has settled himself in his historical armchair and "checked off" the problems in his own way. It is good and proper that everything is stirred up again and being discussed, and that this discussion will now be carried on to the following generation.

I don't believe . . . that Goldhagen always describes "the Germans" as he should. As evidence against his depiction, I point to the development of the Germans in the postwar period. Since no one is threatened with the KZ or execution anymore, the people haven't become the willing executioners on behalf of their current government, and recent changes have included a significant humanization of the public. The Germans are made up of all types of persons, just as all peoples are. Nevertheless, we must remain attentive, and observe and recognize connections; we must arrive at conclusions and deal with the issues accordingly if we want to pave the way for a better future. We are all responsible for doing so—everyone who is living now must be. But those of us who were witnesses are especially responsible. We saw at that time, even if only in our tight circles, a criminal social mistake that has no equal in the history of mankind.

That should be enough heavy stuff for today. So now in conclusion:

How is your and your wife's health now? Watch yourselves carefully, for at our age the "available reserves" are not all that great anymore. You know that if you come to our old continent again, I am counting on you to visit Schifferstadt. People live not only on discussions, but also on friendly conversations. That isn't always successful with every partner; a considerable amount of time should be allotted for it.

OCTOBER 4, 1996

Dear Mr. Sold,

I am sitting in front of my computer ready to answer your letter of September 13, and I do so with a heavy heart. Unfortunately, I cannot agree with your opinion of the Germans in general. I have certainly noted here and there in our previous correspondence how I think back on the Germans. That doesn't mean that we don't have to deal frequently with a large number of exceptions. You are certainly one of these exceptions.

I wrote you that as a young boy in Rülzheim I was called *dreckischer Judd* [dirty Jew] by others of my age. Where had these children heard this expression? Certainly at home, and the parents heard it in the church. But we must make other distinctions: Germany is the only country that didn't have a revolution. By that I mean a revolution like that of France or Russia. In Germany, the bluebloods continued to live on and suppress the farmers and the workers, who took orders and followed them with their hats in their hands and their heads bowed. Those were the remnants of the principalities, and part of it is still stuck inside the Germans today. I still hear the expression today, *"Geh nit zu Deim Ferscht, wenn de nit gerufe werscht"* ["Don't go to your prince, if you weren't summoned"—German dialect].

You are right that antisemitism was not limited to Germany. But only in

Germany did it take the proportions Goldhagen is talking about. You have to have a good stomach to be able to read his book. I've gotten to page two hundred and fifty, and I'm taking my time in finishing it. It makes you wonder whether these people were actually human beings who, without blinking, tortured other human beings and took their lives from them. Again the character of the Germans is reflected here, and in this type of German I certainly count the Austrians and the Swiss-Germans, but not the Dutch. I lived for a year in Amsterdam and got to know those people to be different.

The school system—we've already talked about this—is another reason for the character of the Germans. My history teacher in Speyer gave me the best grades because I knew the dates when each of the kings and kaisers were in power. Other matters were unimportant to him, and nothing was spoken of them. I remember well that almost all of my teachers were nationalistic and right wing, and that they taught the children these beliefs. And now: an article written by a journalist from Berlin and published in *Der Aufbau* doesn't give an encouraging picture of what is happening in Germany today. I hope that these are only exceptions and that the situation in general is different.

Surely I wrote you that I was in Indonesia from 1928–1932. From there I better understood the situation in Germany at that time, and foresaw the future situation in Germany. I broke my contract and returned so that I could take my family to America. We—seven people—set out in December of 1934. No one can imagine the courage of my parents. Their only future was in Rülzheim. They had always lived there, had built a big house, and were successful. But they didn't become victims of the concentration camps.

And then I read about Battalion 101 [Christopher R. Browning, *Ordinary Men: Reserve Police Battalion 101 and the Final Solution in Poland* (New York: HarperCollins, 1992)]. These men were too old to be soldiers, yet they had enough in them to torture and kill innocent people. Those are the ordinary Germans, whose character allowed them to murder. How is that possible? They photographed murders and sent the pictures home to brag about what they were doing. And yet no one knew about it at home?

Goldhagen didn't neglect to mention that others—non-Jews, six million Gypsies, invalids, Russians, and Poles—suffered the same misfortune. Among them were also some Germans (a few) who were against Hitler.

Just as the Crusades and the Inquisition can never be erased from history, so will the Holocaust continue to haunt the German people in the future. In one hundred years, people won't talk about the exceptions. Hitler, his groups, and their followers will still be the ones who are guilty.

I am sorry to have to write to you like this. But we can't change the past, and Germany and the Germans have to learn to live with it. I only hope that the new generations will learn from the past, and that they will forget the German drills and commands and join the ranks of general humanity. That is all for today; it should be sufficiently provocative. Everything is in order here with us. No personal problems to report. With best wishes to both of you, from Greta as well,

OCTOBER 24, 1996

Dear Mr. Friedhoff,

Many thanks for your phone call of the day before yesterday. Since then I have picked out some letters from my two files on "Israel," which should allow you insight into the topics I have discussed with my conversation partners there. The following things are enclosed:

1. A letter from 1991 to Mrs. L., who took our "problem child" into her own family when Hannele immigrated in 1944. During the Gulf War, Mrs. L. took Hannele in again at her place in the country, since in Ramat Gan (Tel Aviv) Hannele was not in the position to leave her fourth-story apartment when the air-raid alarms sounded. The overall view of Hannele's situation with supplies is apparent in my letter. . . .

2. Several handwritten letters of 1992/1993 from Hannele to me, when a young Israeli lived next to me who was nice enough to translate her letters. But he, too, had some trouble reading Hannele's words. Is there anyone near you who is capable of reading and translating *Mameloschn?*

3. A letter to Mrs. N. in Kiron (Tel Aviv) in 1996. It is after Hannele's death and in the letter I am submitting an outline for a letter to Hannele's grandchildren so that she can inspect it. We invested a small capital in an interest-bearing account in an Israeli bank for both of the children. It will be handed over to them at "bat-mitzvah," along with my letter that should tell them something about the history of their deceased grandma.

4. This same letter of summer 1996 to [Hannele's grandchildren], born in 1995/1996. There are things told in it that can't be inferred from our Jewish books.

5. An authorization to you personally to take those parts of our letter correspondence and discussions that you think are of significant interest, and to make them available for research at the Holocaust Museum in the United States.

Please be patient with me in my response to your letter of October 4. I first have to "work myself free" of some other things since returning from my vacation.

With best regards to you and your wife,

———⊗⊗⊗———

Authorization

I hereby authorize Mr. Paul Friedhoff to take those parts of our letter correspondence and discussions which he thinks are of significant interest, and to make them available for research at the Holocaust Museum there in the United States.

Schifferstadt, October 24, 1996

———⊗⊗⊗———

NOVEMBER 12, 1996

Dear Mr. Friedhoff,

You have now been waiting for weeks for the answer to your letter of October 4, a delay that is not only the result of my current workload. I must confess that even today it is not easy to answer you, since I am also affected emotionally—how could it be otherwise! I am no scientist who simply could analyze and investigate the Shoah from a distance as if it were just a historical event. I am also caught in it. I am shaken again and agitated. Again I must overcome the fact that I belong to the perpetrators, and that that won't change. I must live with it and cope with it.

I don't see any usefulness in repeatedly losing ourselves in the discussion of details. The "material" is already so overwhelming that details don't really change the general judgment of what happened. The horror caused by these terrible events cannot be diminished. It is dreadful, and it makes my stomach churn every time I have to look at what happened here. Goldhagen's calm face hardly betrays any emotion, and he discusses his topics with such coolness, but I believe that behind that face I can hear the shriek of his tortured soul. And it forces him to target the generation that has grown up afterwards and to hold the Holocaust before its eyes, again and more completely. He fears that this generation runs the danger of concerning itself only with its own everyday problems, and that it will forget what happened. The new discussions have had an effect throughout Europe, and some have gone beyond a merely superficial level. News is coming from Switzerland [He is probably referring to the discovery that Switzerland turned away thousands of Jewish refugees during the war and acted as a financial broker for the Nazis.] that people claim can't be possible; it was a country so full of integrity before. And in France, Serge Klarsfeld was unable to find a publisher for years, and he relied on hectograph papers [A hectograph is a type of duplicating machine using a large amount of dye and a slab of gelatin treated with glycerin.] for his publications. But now there, too, records that before were never available in this medium are being broadcast on television. I don't know whether the technical specifications are compatible with the televisions from America; if so, you could play the documentation of the French and Swiss documents that I have recorded with my TV. Of course these broadcasts would be in the original, that is, French and partly in Swiss-German, but sections are also dubbed over or furnished with concise German subtitles. If you are interested and able to play them there, I would gladly send you a copy of my video recordings. You will see that Hitler did not have to do all of his dirty work by himself.

I wrote you earlier that in the case of the Holocaust I could not process all the details except on a private, personal, and emotional level. And I wrote you that I have thought about what I could do for my part, and what I must do, to help heal something that for centuries has caused an infinite amount of suffering and misery, and which, in the end, led to the Holocaust. Here is the most important thing: the straight information about everything that happened. And then the reflection about the causes. And then the attempt to counteract these causes for the future. That is, nevertheless, a monstrous task that cannot be accomplished by a single person. The changing of views cannot be decreed "from upstairs." It must put down some roots so that it can spread out over generations and continue to have an effect. I will give you an example of my activities:

On October 22, 1990 it was fifty years since those Schifferstadt Jews who were still at home were taken away to the Gurs KZ. In memory of this day, I arranged that our Christian denominations and representatives from the Jewish community in the Rhineland-Palatinate area come together in Schifferstadt for a memorial service, which was supposed to serve as a remembrance and an examination of our consciences. I compiled the text for the service from historical and available Christian and Jewish sources. For your information I am enclosing a photocopy of this text.

At the altar of the church, which was full to the brim, the clergymen from the Christian denominations stood side by side with the country rabbi Dr. Max Meir Ydit, all of them in complete ecclesiastical regalia. They took turns, along with the readers, in reading the texts and leading prayers. The choir sang songs and the ancient melodies came from the synagogues. Afterwards we went together to our Jewish memorial. And in the end we found ourselves together around the table having conversations for hours. By talking and questioning, we discovered the humanity of the others— and the mutual prejudices melted away more easily.

A certain friendship slowly developed between Dr. Ydit and me. He had survived Auschwitz as a boy. We met in Saarbrücken and held weekend courses for Abitur classes—and we visited the synagogues there with them, which was a very good experience for all of the participants. I believe that these young people will no longer be swayed so easily by demagogic slogans, as could still happen in the schools in my time. Because it's true: the more you know, the easier it is to recognize slogans for what they are and distance yourself from them. Unfortunately, Dr. Ydit, who also held some informative lectures in our area, died of a heart attack a few weeks later. He was mourned by all of us very much, and he was buried in Jerusalem.

Mr. Friedhoff, it doesn't shock me to hear from you that sometimes and in some specific cases we have different ways of looking at things. It is also no surprise, since of necessity we come from different situations, and we must also recognize that we have to correct our own premises. We don't preach any dogmatic doctrines; we think about the things happening in the world around us—and those thoughts depend on the quality of our information. During this process, it is important that we talk with each other as we did before, and listen to the other person, and it is important that we are willing to reflect seriously on any new information. For example, I know right now (according to the information from Switzerland) that my "knowledge" of the first news about the mass murder of the Jews (it had reached London and the Allies with a Polish messenger in 1943) didn't fit the facts. In November of 1941 the Swiss consul, von Weiss, sent out a report from Cologne to Bern saying that a Swiss driver witnessed a mass execution at the eastern front; it was done with gunshots to the base of the skull (this was weeks before the Wannsee conference). On December 8, 1941, von Weiss also reported mass deaths in the ghettoes in Warsaw and Minsk. In Bern his reports were nevertheless filed away as "absolutely confidential," and weren't publicized. In February of 1942, a German deserter showed the Swiss authorities drawings of how the mass executions were carried out. In March of 1942, a Swiss doctor witnessed mass executions as a member of a commission. In April of 1942, a deserter reported mass cremations and supplied photos of dead people who were suffocated in trains. In March of 1942, the Jewish World Congress in Geneva found out about the extermination camps. It passed the news on to the ecumenical church organizations, and also to the Allies. Requests that the Allies bomb these train connections got no reaction. America's failure to act was the result of antisemitism in parts of the American government. So before Christmas of 1942, the Americans and the Russians had confirmed the existence of the mass extermination camps.

In 1938 (38!) the Swiss authorities in Berlin negotiated about measures that would hinder the entry of Jews into Switzerland; Switzerland did not want to be "Jewified." The Swiss suggested that in order to make border controls easier, all Jewish passports should be issued with a big Jewish stamp, "J," and the Reich government promptly agreed with the idea.

After the beginning of the war, no more Jewish refugees were admitted into the Swiss internment camps; Swiss violators were punished severely. Only half of all those who made it across the Swiss borders and were admitted were able to remain in Switzerland after the war. That is a small excerpt from the Swiss records.

Mr. Friedhoff, you wrote me that the Allies knew about the concentration camps from very early on. According to the information I had when you told me, I couldn't confirm what you said. But now I have been taught otherwise. These things don't have to do with personal opinion; instead, sometimes there is just a lack of information that needs to be rectified.

When I think about the future, I don't believe that our dear Germans are so fundamentally different from people elsewhere. It is only that we live under different historical circumstances and were trained very strictly. Nevertheless, that is over. As it is elsewhere, there are all different types of people and characters here in Germany. And the development of the past fifty years shows that even we are not a "lost cause," as the saying goes. But there are a great number of things about us that I could criticize, and there is every reason to be modest and to continue to change our ideas.

But there is also every reason to hope. You have certainly noticed that now and again German Jews find it necessary to defend their fellow Germans whenever Germans are attacked in an indiscriminate way because of international resentment. It isn't just an accident that they do that, and it shows that something has in fact changed here in Germany.

When I tell about a city or a park, I can choose many different viewpoints. I can exclusively praise the sights there, but I could also tell only about the filthiness of the dumps, even without saying something that isn't true. In both cases I am telling the truth, but it is the truth that I wanted to see.

For many years now the Germans have gotten "bad press." After everything that happened, that is no surprise. It is also good if the world continues to watch us. But if you look around the world today, you see that there is no need to be unhappy with life and conditions in Germany now.

And I will conclude this rather problematic letter with a placatory word: I would be very happy to be able to meet you and your wife in Rülzheim, Schifferstadt, or somewhere else in the Rhineland and sit together with a glass of wine and talk in peace. Or would you prefer to go with me the day after tomorrow to our meeting in the Franck Löbschen house in Landau, where the army rabbi Dr. F. wants to introduce us to the Jewish cabala?

Best wishes to you and your wife!

———— ❧ ————

NOVEMBER 29, 1996

Dear Mr. Sold,

Tears came to my eyes as I read your letter. You have no doubt read the book by Goldhagen and were deeply affected by the descriptions of what happened during the time of Hitler, and by the circumstances under which the Jews were killed in the different camps. I understand your feeling about belonging to a people that was capable of such unbelievable deeds. You shouldn't forget that I, too, was a German at one point and was proud to travel with my German passport. My father was the first to hang the flag out the window when the army captured a new Russian city during the First World War. That time cannot be forgotten, and it is surprising how my ancestors could live among people who could be so cruel. And then one remembers that Germany must carry the guilt for the last three wars [He is referring to the Franco-Prussian War, World War I, and World War II.], which claimed innumerable victims. So then one wonders what is hiding inside these people, and there isn't any answer. Were we—the Jews, who lived in Germany for generations—also like that? One wonders and then shakes his head: that can't be, and certainly wasn't the case. Was that the mark that distinguished us from the non-Jews? Perhaps—it is hard to say. There were and still are today many people among the non-Jews who shake their heads exactly as you and I.

Among the guilty are two different groups: those who devise the plans, and those who carry them out. Both should be condemned, and then who is left? According to Goldhagen, almost no one. Is that possible? When you see what happened in Austria, and you read the new reports about what happened in Switzerland, you wonder what type of character the German has, and where it came from. I can only continue to believe that the ordinary German was suppressed by the leaders and executed the commands that were given to him. And therefore he didn't have his own thoughts or feelings. Of course there are exceptions. Exceptions prove the rule.

Many thanks for the offer to send me the publications of Serge Klarsfeld. The television sets in the United States are different from the European ones, and your "tapes" can't be played here. . . .

I knew almost all the information about the Swiss. It was new to me that it was Switzerland that created the "J" in the Jewish passports. The Swiss are intelligent people, and they very much like to have money too.

Germany doesn't have the "bad press" here that it deserves. Only from time to time do you hear about individuals who came to the U.S.A. by making untruthful statements but were really participants in the Holocaust. Then they are sent back home.

My health will not permit me to visit Germany. How would it sound if you came here? If you don't want to fly, you can also come to the U.S.A. by boat. That would be a beautiful vacation. . . .

DECEMBER 16, 1996

Dear Mr. Friedhoff,

. . . As for my being a soldier, in October of 1941 I was lucky enough to be pulled out of that barbaric war on the Russian front. The war rules of the "Hague Land Warfare Convention" and the "Geneva Convention" had no meaning on the eastern front. The Soviet Union never agreed to these international treaties, which protected the wounded, prisoners, medical personnel, and the civilian population. So, for example, there wasn't protection by the Red Cross on either side of the front, which during the course of the war resulted in unimaginable atrocities on both sides. I was transferred to Berlin to study medicine. I was lucky, for virtually no one survived from my former infantry unit. I was commanded to go into action as a doctor at the western front, just when the Allies began to invade France in 1944. To my surprise, the Red Cross rules were valid there. Medical personnel and doctors were unarmed. (My superior staff doctor earned the Silver Medal for hand-to-hand combat in Russia!) I was the army medical officer of the reconnaissance unit of the 116th Panzer division. Our commander was General Graf von Schwerin. He had been a military attaché in the United States before the war, and because of his time there had personal acquaintances among the American generals. He knew some of his immediate opponents personally, which later during the slaughters and bloodbaths (Hürtgener forest with forty-four thousand dead!) led to contacts across the front for humanitarian purposes. These actions, however, brought Graf von Schwerin a court-martial at the command of the führer. We helped to fight back the airborne landing of the Allies at Arnheim, and we were part of the Ardennes offensive in the winter of 1944–1945. After the invasion, our units were put under the control of the 2nd SS Panzer corps, but after numerous investigations, even through the Allied literature, I haven't found the slightest indication that we were involved in any dishonorable actions of any sort. But I regard every war, even legal wars, as one of the greatest and most tragic human mistakes possible. After the war, we discussed with friends what it was like to be a soldier, as well as those other problems of our youth that extended into our present lives, problems that could not be taken into the future unresolved. In 1954, the question was raised as to whether we—as is customary for our French friends and elsewhere in the world—should erect a war memorial during the celebration of our school's four-hundred-year anniversary. The director asked me to say a few words there for our fellow students who died during the Second World War. After a good deal of thought, I decided that I would. In 1991, I also made a speech before our class at the fifty-year celebration of our Abitur. It had to do with our school days in general, and I also mentioned my speech of 1954 about those who had died in the war. Since this text also contains many other school memories from the Third Reich that convey a general impression of the time period and show our viewpoint at the school, I am printing out and sending the entire text to you. I am also enclosing two letters that in past years I wrote to a history teacher at our school. I think that you will discover topics and theories in these texts that could give us a great deal to discuss. Perhaps you will also be horrified that in them I have mentioned almost nothing about the merciless persecutions and exterminations of human beings in the Third Reich. In a similar situation today, I could hardly limit my reflections to the state of health of my classmates, as I did then . . .

Mr. Friedhoff, in your letter there is a sentence that almost made me a little sad. You write that for health reasons you will probably not be able to visit Germany again. For our part, we have never been what in new German is called "travel freaks." We were in Israel three times, and we believed that it was our duty to take those flights and the connected risks. And as for sea voyages: during her childhood, my wife spent a night with her mother on a damaged boat, for which reason she can hardly be persuaded to take a cruise. But for us that would mean there is almost no possibility we will ever meet personally—and I regret that very much. [You and I] have lived completely opposite lives in what are almost contrary worlds, and nothing was ever easy for either of us. Because of our different pasts, we could very easily have developed ideas and prejudices that were miles apart from one another and irreconcilable. Yet after two years of correspondence and despite all the distance that history has created between us, I feel very close to you. I feel as if we are joined in a friendship that is not to be found every day. I think that we should use the time that we both have left to reflect together on a world and a period that we did not intend to create, but in which we must now live. And we must also contribute as much as we can to help the humanization of the present time. When all is said and done, we can do that even if we are not ever granted the pleasure of personally shaking hands. . . .

————❦————

[Friedhoff's son-in-law, David, has been diagnosed with ALS, amyotrophic lateral sclerosis. At this point in the correspondence, Friedhoff and Sold begin a dialogue about the disease and its possible treatments.]

JANUARY 21, 1997

Dear Mr. Sold,

. . . Meanwhile something has happened that brought me back to the Hitler period again, and it worried me. I must think about the time when I was at a furniture fair in Cologne, and I was searching through the telephone book for the name Friedhoff. To my surprise, I found an entire page with my name. I ripped it out, and when I got home I wrote to all of them and asked them to send me their family tree because I was looking for the origins of my family. Since all of the Friedhoffs that we knew were non-Jews, my brother developed the theory that one of these Friedhoffs married a Jewish woman and was converted to Judaism—which was not the case. I reminded these Friedhoffs that during the time of Hitler every German had to have a family tree, in order to show that there wasn't any Jewish blood in the last three generations. I received many answers, among others from Gerd Friedhoff in Dortmund. He wrote that he too was searching for his ancestors and that he wanted to help me.

Gerd found my family in the archives in Detmold. I went there one day with Gerd and found the answers to many questions. My father, grandfather, and great-grandfather were born in Ergste (a suburb of Dortmund). We visited the cemetery there and found my grandfather's grave. We also visited a very nice man, Friedhelm M., a graphic artist and town historian. He was born in the house where my grandfather once lived. He sent me a copper engraving from the house, and we send each other greetings for Christmas and the New Year.

This year he sent me a book that he wrote about Ergste, and he had many illustrations in it—copper engravings—from interesting houses. He didn't describe the Holocaust as a historian at all but wrote things like "Jews sold their houses or emigrated." "Jews died in work camps." Not with one word did he mention why and how these houses were sold, or under what circumstances these Jews died. I was depressed because I hadn't expected this from Mr. M. It took several days before I made myself respond to him. I wrote him that he had immortalized himself in Ergste with his book, but that he only should have written up to the year 1933. When someone writes as a historian, he must report everything truthfully and not leave out the bad and the evil. The SA and the SS certainly marched through the village of Ergste and sang the Horst-Wessel-Lied [the national anthem of the Nazis] as they did everywhere else. I reminded him of the song's words. Since then, Ergste has disappeared; it has become a part of Schwerte and is now a city. It is difficult to see that all of the Jewish cemeteries in Westphalia were turned back into farmland. The gravestones were certainly used for road construction. But that was already happening before Hitler. My grandfather was buried (in 1873) in a small section that was reserved for Jews within the public cemetery. When I was there, there were about seven or eight graves, which is a sign of how few Jews lived in the village. . . .

———— ✿ ————

FEBRUARY 15, 1997

Dear Mr. Sold,

. . . I want to send you this information [about Friedhoff's son-in-law's medicine] as quickly as possible. In my next letter, I will have to discuss the topic of Madeleine Albright—our new Secretary of State. You certainly know that her grandparents died in Auschwitz, and she didn't know that they were Jews, or perhaps she didn't want to know it.

Best regards, to you and your wife, and from Greta as well,

———— ✿ ————

FEBRUARY 19, 1997

Dear Mr. Friedhoff,

. . . To get back to our topics of before, I am sending you some newspaper excerpts that will show you what the papers around here are concerned with. As for Israel, to my consolation I see that "big-brother America" is there to intervene, so that the waves of emotions and unreason don't wash away the tender and vulnerable little plant of peace. It is good to see that more and more conflicts in the world can be eliminated through conversations, even though they are very difficult and take a long time. We should hope that the United States is able to keep a hold on the Israeli and Arabic hawks until the difficult peace talks make everyone recognize that in the long run it is more reasonable to talk than to bomb one another.

Best regards to you and your wife, and best wishes for our patient,

———— ✿ ————

MARCH 4, 1997

Dear Mr. Sold,

That was a great deal of reading material that you sent me. But it is interesting to see that the Germans of our time are looking over their shoulders with a cautious glance to the past. It has taken almost fifty years for what happened to become history. And today one wonders what kind of people were able to commit such crimes. That is the main question for me, but no one can give me an answer.

I believe I mentioned in one of my letters that the biggest wrongdoers were the Germans, the Austrians, and the German-speaking Swiss. What is now coming to light about the Swiss is scarcely credible. But I must say that the French-speaking Swiss were just as guilty as the German-speaking ones. Or perhaps some of them. It is hard to tell. It would be interesting to find out who demanded that the "J" be entered in the Jewish passports. Are there any documents to be found, or did they let them disappear as well?

One wonders why Jews are so hated everywhere. It is certainly not due to genes because too many mixings and rapes during the wars of the Middle Ages kept the Jews from being a pure race. Many Jews are blonde and blue-eyed (my niece was used by one of her teachers to show a class what an Aryan girl looks like). The Italian Jews have somewhat darkened skin coloring, the Russian Jews the raised cheekbones, and so on. That shows that Jews aren't a race, but nevertheless have common behavior that is different from other peoples. We were talking one time about the many bars in Schiffer-stadt and in Rülzheim, and how only a very few Jews frequent them. I believe that I've found a small mark that emphasizes the difference between the Jews and other faiths. The Jew doesn't like to work for others; he would rather have his own business. He hates the punch card, but works countless hours in his own business, has a well-developed sense of family, and is very frugal in his daily life. All of that brings envy along with it, and with envy naturally comes antisemitism. Is this explanation perhaps too simple? We've already spoken a few times about the Church, which certainly carries its part of the blame. One would gladly climb the walls to find an answer for everything that we regard as a hypothesis.

Was Ignatz Bubis right when he said that there is no collective guilt? There are many different opinions. There are certainly many Germans who did not agree with Hitler's theories. It is difficult to say how many of these people were caught in the tumult and didn't find a way out. I always come back to the fact that Germany never had a revolution, and that the Germans were running behind their führer (kaiser, king, prince) like sheep. I hope that this tendency has changed and that the new Germans carry their heads high and have their own ideas.

Yes, so there are also clergymen like Wilhelm Caroli who don't let them-selves be suppressed. But one must ask: how many are there? The only cer-tainty is that not all of the people stood behind Hitler, and some of them valued their lives less than their opinions. Those are heroes who should not be forgotten.

The *Frankfurter Allgemeine Zeitung* talks about a new antisemitism that is caused by the moral turmoil in Switzerland. If that is the case, then one sees that we are close to forgetting the Holocaust or that we never knew about it in the first place. Some claim that Jewish culture is part of all of Germany —but then, why does it seem that melting down gold teeth in order to buy more weapons and prolong the war made no impression?

As for Israel, I have a different opinion. It will never come to a true peace unless the Arabic people stand up and demand a democratic government. It is not easy to negotiate with dictators and find some common ground. We have seen enough of that in Europe, from the Middle Ages to Hitler, and we should have been able to come to the obvious conclusions. I don't think that I will live to see a desirable change.

All the best and best regards also to your wife, from both of us,

———— 🕸 ————

MARCH 5, 1997

Dear Mr. Friedhoff,

In the middle of December 1996, I sent you a photocopy of a speech that I made before my classmates at the fiftieth anniversary of the Abitur of my high school class. It should give you an impression of the atmosphere during the Third Reich when I grew up. I think it was possible to recognize that the values of the humanistic high school then were undermined at the command of the government, and considerably more value was placed on the "pre-military training" of the youth—with great costs to scientific and humanistic subjects. You asked me earlier whether anything has changed in the German schools since the war, with regard to the teachers' attitudes and the objectives of the education. I had said yes.

At the moment we have three grandchildren who are going to my school, now called the Gymnasium am Kaiserdom (since there are two other big high schools in Speyer). The generation of great-grandparents of these children went through these same streets and the same school—has something changed, and what?

Even though the school again sees itself as a model for the "humanistic high school" with an emphasis on languages (Latin, Greek, French), and also includes the necessary scientific subjects, I am not entirely happy with the development of our school system. The ideologically conditioned tendencies of the new period are clearly noticeable. The authoritative way of thinking (stressing obedience!) has been almost completely dismantled, which can only be welcomed. The students move around freely and are allowed to have control over their studies. They publish their own uncensored newspaper, which in my time was unheard of. But that naturally has its dark sides: they stray from a strict principle of achievement, and they believe that one's happiness is more in leveling everything and making it all the same. In the Abitur, they aren't tested on all ten to twelve subjects and on the material as they did before, no! The student can pick out three subjects to be tested on, those that make him especially happy and in which he can expect to perform especially well (= special achievement subjects). But the student can simply give up and forget all of the subjects that weren't his best. And in the last three years before the Abitur, he doesn't even receive instruction in the subjects that he didn't choose. In my opinion, that can be a great disadvantage to one's general education and for later life. So our current Abitur no longer works toward "job preparation on a broad basis." That could prove to be very detrimental in a society that seems to be preparing itself for a more and more professional future, where the jobs are always changing.

Nevertheless, two weeks ago this school of mine surprised me with an event that wasn't in the curriculum at all, and that would not have been conceivable when I was in school: everyone was invited to a huge concert on the two hundredth birthday of the musician Franz Schubert. For this purpose, a huge student symphony orchestra and a mixed student choir were assembled from all the classes in the school. Outside of the normal school instruction and in the students' free time, they were able to make some unbelievable cultural achievements. The audience was just as surprised and enthusiastic as I was. It showed what the school and the students were capable of; they were not at all professionally trained, and the performance was only possible with the willingness of all the participants. But something else made me especially happy: they put Schubert's cantata "Mirjams Siegesgesang" at the end of the concert, which celebrates the exodus of the Jewish people from Egypt and their passage through the Red Sea. The audience demanded that they do it again, and they did. I was deeply moved by the music, but not just by that—you can probably imagine that after the end of the long applause, there was so much about the past that I had to reflect on!

Mr. Friedhoff, I am sending you a newspaper article that reports on an interview with Christopher Browning. Some of the sentences are worth thinking about, since they go beyond the general horror of the inhuman atrocities and show the willingness to reflect further on the background of humanity. His tendency to refrain from prejudices, placative theories, and simplifications seems especially important to me. How could something like the Shoah have been possible?—a question that certainly doesn't permit a simple answer. . . .

———— 🦚 ————

MARCH 20, 1997

Dear Mr. Friedhoff,

Many thanks for your letter of March 4, 1997. You asked who in Germany demanded the stamping of a "J" in the Jewish passports, and whether or not the records and documents were perhaps disposed of. I obtained my information from the Swiss film documentary that was shot in Switzerland in 1995 and was first shown here in 1996.

The film is named *Die Schweiz und die Juden* [Switzerland and the Jews (by Guido Ferrari, TSI, 1995)]. . . . Part of the text of the documentary goes like this: "In order to stop the flood of Jews immigrating from Germany and the annexed part of Austria, the central government commissioned the ministers of state, Motter in the political department, Baumann, head of the police force and the courts, and Heinrich Rothmund, head of the federal police [his superior was minister Eduard von Steiger, Sold's note], to search for a solution with the German authorities. The Swiss intermediary in Berlin was a happy ambassador.

"Switzerland suggested the insertion of a Jewish stamp into the passports of the German Jews, in order to block their immigration into our land. That was in October of 1938. Switzerland therefore approved the racial discrimination, an extreme decision which had terrible consequences. Numerous other countries refused the immigration of Jews because of this Jewish stamp. Rothmund said to the German officials that Switzerland wanted to prevent a Jewification because that would result in an explosion of antisemitism. For this reason Switzerland did not want to accept any Jewish refugees. . . ."

[Here Sold offers Friedhoff an audiocassette of the broadcast.]

. . . Thus, the Swiss documents have not "completely disappeared" by any means, and recently they've become well known in Switzerland. Yet, just as one should not forget those unfriendly Swiss campaigns, one should also remember that there were numerous Swiss (even among the authorities) who did what they could to help the Jews. I can remember the example of a woman from Schifferstadt (Anna Sturm) who was able to send packages of food in very roundabout ways through Swiss citizens to Jews from Schifferstadt (the Levy family) in Gurs and Auschwitz (!) (see *Die Schifferstadter Juden* pages 93, 105, 210).

Strangely enough (according to the Swiss documentary), the conduct toward the Jews also led to big "memory gaps" in Switzerland after the end of the war. Even the organizers of the "defense against Jews," for example

Dr. Heinrich Rothmund, could not remember their anti-Jewish behavior—which indeed has its parallels here in Germany. Who gladly incriminates himself while on trial?

In your letter you ask "why the Jews are so hated everywhere." A few quick theories on that:

1. If there ever was a "Jewish race," there hasn't been one for a long time now. The twelve tribes of Israel inbred very early among themselves, and with friends and enemies. As victors, they also assimilated the women of those defeated and even accepted the children of slaves into their people. Even Abraham's first born (Ishmael) was not a son of Abraham's wife Sarah, but a son of the servant Hagar, the daughter of people who were uncircumcised, for which reason the Muslims see Ishmael and Abraham as their progenitors. Even the men of the neighboring tribes and wartime opponents left their "genes" with the Jews, as the Jews did to those they defeated. In Ethiopia there were even some black Jews, whose bloodlines are certainly far removed from the Israelites. Some years ago they had to be saved from persecution, and in a huge airlift maneuver they were taken to Israel by the Israeli army. From what I hear, today they still represent a minority there and are not very well respected. The (current) Jews are not a genetically defined race, but a people mixed throughout history who have many different types of genes.

2. Even the Nazis' teachings on race were a pure fiction formed by ideological dreams, just as their Aryan cult was also a scientifically indefinable fiction. Today there is no pure "Aryan blood"; it would have to include the Indian peoples as well. The characteristics taught during the Third Reich as being those of the "typical Jew," the so-called "racial characteristics" of the Jews, described an appearance that is also found again and again among almost all the Middle Eastern tribes.

3. Even in their religion, Jews are no clearly defined group. Not even all of those circumcised are Jews (there are infinitely more circumcised Arabs than circumcised Jews). The religiousness of the Jews is broken down into many different factions.

Does someone become a Jew, then, through an actively religious life according to the laws of the Torah? If we assume that, then even in Israel the Jews are an amazingly small minority! And how is it outside of Israel in the worldwide Jewish diaspora? Do you know many Jews in America who really live their daily lives guided by the deep Torah beliefs of their forefathers? Even the rabbis with whom we worked here greatly differed in their beliefs. How many Jewish religions are there in the state of Israel? What, therefore, is a Jew? How many rituals must he observe, how much of synagogue does he need, and how much Shabbat? From this quandary, the state of Israel defines everyone as a Jew who was born of a Jewish mother (since the fatherhood could not be absolutely certain).

4. And how could one define what we are describing as the "hatred of Jews"? Would human hate disappear from the scene if Jews no longer existed? Hatred of Jews is merely the form developed by the Christians for what exists as xenophobia everywhere in the world. A note on that:

If a biologically grown community is observed (even in the animal kingdom!), the following stands out: whoever is part of a community cannot do what he wants. Different social behaviors develop so that the community can recognize who belongs to it. The same languages, views and customs, "uniform clothing," blue jeans, fashion, and hairstyles all show whether one belongs to the group. Whoever wants to be part of the group must be "in." Behavior is scrutinized jealously by neighbors and by the community. Whoever wants to be better, or just different; whoever becomes conspicuous, keeps to himself, or doesn't conform will offend people. He is rejected, fought against, doesn't belong anymore, and in the end is persecuted and banished. This common human behavior, as dumb, awkward, and harmful as it may be on occasion, is an irrational biological trait—and it is in all human beings. It is supposed to protect the community.

An example from Schifferstadt on this point: nineteen thousand residents live here together with twelve hundred Turks. A portion of these "foreign workers" have assimilated themselves. They dress inconspicuously, learn the national language, and have friendly relationships with their neighbors. This group has even founded its own soccer team and takes part in the city championships. It invites people to Turkish festivals so that we can get to know their music and dances. The other group dresses as Turks do in their homeland and have withdrawn into a type of ghetto. The women wear veils. They even forbid their children from attending the German schools, so that they won't be "religiously corrupted." Indeed, our population has also accepted this strictly religious and fundamentalist group, and has helped them to build a mosque and a chapel in which they can meet undisturbed. Theoretically, one should say that there is a gulf between the Germans and the Turks in general. But no: the gulf exists between the two groups of Turks, both of which hold the other at a distance, bordering on hostility. They don't tolerate the differences in their own relatives and they hate them! Some years ago I looked after a Turk who had been badly maltreated by his people because in the month of fasting, Ramadan, he was seen drinking water during daylight. At the same time, the Christian worker could have calmly consumed his meal beside him, eating and drinking, without a word being said about it.

Thus, those who are not accepted into or who are excluded from a community are not only those who grossly contradict the statutes of the community, but also those who are not "in," even if there is no rational reason for it. However, if some real or emotional reasons develop (religious, ideological, or some other type), then a violent hate can result, which under certain circumstances escalates into pogroms. That's how it was in Jerusalem when a few years after the death of Jesus a group emerged in a temple to criticize the congregation's earlier self-righteousness. Its leader was named Stephen. He was kicked out by the remaining devout and faithful temple congregation, and was stoned to death. In the period following, every single group outdid the others in the extent and the methods used to eliminate their hated enemies, even trying to exterminate them—up until the Nazis, who invented a new "quality" of xenophobia: the Holocaust.

5. The hatred of Jews is tied to the presence of Jews. It can be replaced by hatred for Sinti and Roma, New Apostolics, Jehovah's witnesses, homosexuals, Indians—in short, for everyone "foreign." There doesn't have to be any real foundation for it; everywhere in the world a little agitation and clever propaganda are enough to eliminate rational thought and to replace it with catchy slogans (think of lynch laws). It is not difficult to manipulate the masses.

6. Several years ago in my apartment here, I had a conversation about the "special quality of Jews" with Z. P., Professor at the University in Beersheva. I argued that according to the theory of evolution, the hundred-year-long persecution and the difficult living conditions, together with the rules about learning to read early and the continual discussions in the yeshiva, led to the selecting and fostering of the best talents within the Jewish population. P. did not agree. He believed that the Jews are not fundamentally different from other humans. They are prepared to achieve under difficult conditions, as the large number of Jews among American Nobel Prize winners shows. Recently, however (since things are better for them in America now), they have been surpassed by the newly immigrated Puerto Ricans. And in Israel, where the genuine Jews need not worry about their livelihood because they will be well-maintained by the state anyway, almost no Nobel Prize has been achieved at all [This is not true. See note in the letter of November 27, 1994.].

Both of us have reflected on our theories. Perhaps we are both partly right. It is amazing that after the French Revolution, which in 1792 marked the start of the liberation and emancipation of the Jews in Europe,

Jews also took charge of the German universities. And it is amazing that the literary societies in Berlin, as well as the culture there, have frequently been dominated by Jews (which has aroused some defense reactions by the old established parties). Interestingly enough, those long-established "cultivated" Berlin Jews also turned violently against the influx of poor Jewish "pants salesmen" from Galicia, who were not able to enter Berlin and continued to travel to America. It was a repeat of the defense mechanism described above.

What I want to emphasize: there are groups forming everywhere, even Ashkenazim against Sephardim, with aversions to the "other groups." As long as each group keeps its aversions under control, it even could attract a bigger community, bring competition, and there would be nothing to object to. Inwardly strong and thinking people could deal with that easily. But it is bad when the issue becomes emotionally charged; then, uncontrollable and even heightening aggressions can arise. That is where the power of the media comes in. The media can urge people in directions that they hardly would follow on their own initiative. Thus, we must be very attentive and closely analyze the media.

7. Topic of Israel: it cannot be my task to give advice in this area. A German is not entitled to do that. After everything that happened, we have to stand by Israel's side. But it is difficult for me to understand Netanyahu's thoughts [Netanyahu was a hardline Israeli prime minister.]. In a recent letter to an Israeli friend, I cautiously expressed my opinion when I wrote:

"You certainly can imagine that we follow the progress of the peace efforts in your country more than just as interested bystanders. In these parts, we know too well the manifold aspects of such a peace process, which for one side of those involved is happy, but which for the other side can be painful. Since 1945, our people have had to digest inside and outside the catastrophic legacy of the lost war of the Nazis, in which we lost a considerable portion of our national territory at the eastern borders (one third!). Twelve million (!) countrymen were forcefully driven from their houses and homes and admitted as additional residents into the available emergency accommodations and cellars made habitable in West Germany. Thus, the residents inside the private apartments had to stick out the ensuing peace process just as the diplomats did outside in the international community. But it dragged on for decades. Just last year, the negotiations were officially completed with the difficult reconciliation with Czechoslovakia, a long time after people in the private sector had learned to talk with their former 'enemies,' to trade with them, to visit them, to live with them, and to find reconciliation with them. That was a painful and lengthy process for everyone involved; yet there was no other solution if we didn't want to leave the coming generation with the seeds for new clashes and new wars. And look: today after fifty years, it can hardly be imagined that within the European community it would be necessary to resort to violent clashes in the settlement of squabbles. So I imagine and hope that in the end this is how it will be in Israel, if not for the current generation, then for the next. At some point, both sides will come to their senses and work for peace. It will always be the question—how many deaths and what havoc are necessary to make politicians and peoples capable of peace in their hearts? Netanyahu is obviously a tough negotiator. That can serve the interests of his people very well. Indeed, the speed of the peace process doesn't matter; instead it is the soundness and lasting ability of the discovered solutions that do. It is certain that sometime in the future, these problems will be solved—and I don't give up hope that the price of blood and soil, which will pay for that peace, will bear a tolerable relation to the result."

As a German I am not entitled to introduce moral views in this "game for the land of Canaan." But in the long term, it is inconceivable to permit the suppression of hundreds of thousands of people within their own borders with force of arms, and to allow them to go to work or not, according to Israel's own needs and situation. The barbed wire, the locking up entire countrysides from their outside world with guards (Gaza, the West Bank), who even shoot when they deem it appropriate, and the execution of rigorous occupation "laws and regulations" in the captured areas call to mind even for me very unpleasant memories and fateful comparisons to situations in partisan warfare, which one had hoped had once and for all become an inconceivable notion in a civilized world. At the same time, I am amazed by the political skill of the current Palestinian leadership, which has obviously been successful in a few short months at keeping its own hotheads in check and remaining moderate. On the other hand, I stood on the Golan Heights and can understand how difficult it must be for Israel to give up such a strategic position. Also: how difficult it must be for everyone involved to reduce to a common denominator the many-sided ideological claim to Jerusalem. All of that can only be resolved with negotiations—or it ends up in a bloody battle for survival, the extent and end of which cannot be determined beforehand.

I won't forget the scene when two days ago the King of Jordan kneeled before the parents of an Israeli girl who had been shot by Jordanian guards. He expressed his sympathy and asked for forgiveness for a deed that could have been committed only by a madman. At the same time, it came to my mind that all expressions of sympathy by the international world were directed only to the Israeli president and other representatives. Netanyahu was skipped by everyone. We will see how well the United States will come to terms with the failure of its policy of peace that cost so dearly and that Netanyahu is gambling away so skillfully.

8. Now to the topic of Albright. What is her current "Jewishness" actually supposed to consist of? Is it supposed to be founded in some intractable genes?

It can be said that among the Jews—just as with all other populations—there are very intelligent but also less intelligent people. No one has spoken of a special gene that identifies one as a Jew or determines his specific biology. Only racists could have a problem with this question.

Or was that supposed to be her religion? And yet, as we have read, she has chosen a denomination that is completely different. It would be best if she is accepted as a clearly intelligent human being who has been placed with an important task for which she can prove her diplomatic and human qualities. Earlier on TV she made a good impression. She will do her work, and we will see whether she can bring the Israeli "hawks" to their senses.

Mr. Friedhoff, during these days of Pesach I think of the Egyptian Pharaoh who one day was so understanding that he freed his slaves, the people of Moses, from their bondage. And I think of the Jewish people, whose journey through the deserts of this world—as one can see—has not yet come to an end. And of Israel and Netanyahu, who in the long term cannot succeed in keeping the Palestinian people under Israeli rule without doing serious damage to themselves.

To you, your wife, your entire family, and everyone who feels close to the Jews, a shalom that comes from the heart.

———— 🦋 ————

MARCH 22, 1997

Dear Mr. Sold,

This week, after the article by Henderson appeared in the newspaper, the telephone just didn't stop ringing [when the National Holocaust Museum first preserved a portion of their letters, a columnist (Henderson) for the *Clearwater Times,* Friedhoff's local newspaper, wrote an article about Sold and Friedhoff's correspondence]. Coincidences seem to be an ordinary occurrence: a Jack Mayer called me up and told me that he had been born in Schifferstadt, that his parents moved to Speyer when he was a small child, and that his family emigrated to America when he was eight years old. After the war he visited Schifferstadt, and you were the one who showed him his ancestors' graves and their old apartment. You see how small the world is. Jack Mayer lives here in Clearwater, and we have promised each other to get together when he returns from a trip. He is visiting relatives somewhere.

A retired doctor of eighty-nine years of age called me up, and it took him a while to tell me that he studied medicine in Frankfurt from 1930 to 1935 as an American. He said he even attended a meeting where Hitler spoke, and that he wouldn't have had any problem as a Jew. He must have been blind or deaf and dumb.

Then a Romanian phoned me who had served two years in the Romanian army and three in the German army. He told me in detail that he didn't know anything about the Holocaust until he came here to America. He was wounded three times, perhaps even mentally, because he didn't know anything about the persecution of the Jews. One often hears unbelievable things.

Your comments on the present school system are very significant. It is not only important that the schools replace the idea of obedience (command!) with individual decisionmaking, but also that all Germans make this change. I have mentioned that on occasion before, and I even maintained that the German character is strongly affected by "commands." As an example, when in German one says *"Rauchen verboten"* [smoking forbidden], we say "no smoking." Every once in a while we hear that Germany is the country of commands. The Germans could have been made subservient with these commands, and they would have followed a bellwether without any thought. Perhaps that is a small part of the explanation why Hitler was successful in manipulating the masses.

. . . I still haven't received any response to my letter [to Friedhelm M., who wrote a historical book about the village Ergste but didn't mention the Nazis or the Holocaust]. You see, perhaps I am too sensitive and shouldn't have pointed out the bad times to him again. But how can they be forgotten?

All the best to you and your wife from both of us,

APRIL 7, 1997

Dear Mr. Friedhoff,

Many thanks for your letter of March 22. Henderson's article in the *Clearwater Times* briefly outlines the background and course of our communication—and I am very happy with it. What Henderson of course could not have noted is the important role that our letter correspondence has come to play for me.

All of my previous contacts with Jews were from the outset extremely friendly and accommodating. I have always been surprised at how easy it was for those on the Jewish side to communicate with me, and how completely they overlooked my ever-present pangs of conscience that come from being German. Finally, I informed myself fairly well and learned about what had happened. I was always strangely moved by the enormous hospitality and friendliness with which I was met in Israel, and by the obvious fact that everyone was careful to avoid talking with me about guilt or participation, etc.

From the beginning, my encounter with you was of a different quality. Even more quickly than with Otto Landman, I had the impression that here was someone who still was suffering from all that happened then, and that he, exactly like me, would never be finished dealing with it. And that he doesn't talk like someone who, although he was a part of it personally, is content not knowing anything more about what happened. For that reason, I want to thank you today for the sometimes brutal frankness with which you have countered my arguments. . . . Only in this way can we talk with one another sincerely, and, if it is necessary, also contradict each other's theories. It may be hard to swallow the dissent sometimes, but it is the only way that we can reflect together at an honest level and, by doing so, lead to a better future.

I feel that our relationship, which is able to withstand these disagreements, is rare and remarkably friendly. Indeed, in old age when the mind begins to narrow, one seldom encounters a relationship like this anymore. Yet something like this is necessary for those people who in old age are still pursuing a goal, who are searching for improvements and solutions for common problems.

For that reason I would like to begin my letter today with a new salutation, in which I say,

Dear friend Paul,

I was very happy to read that you had a telephone meeting with Jack Mayer; I wrote about his visit to Schifferstadt on page 125 and 126 of the book about our Jews. Please send him my regards. It made me extremely happy to see that decades after that horrible time, and despite everything that had happened, it was still possible to have an encounter with the "other" as happy as mine was with Jack Mayer. I believe that we both enjoyed being able to communicate so excellently in Palatinate, even though Jack didn't learn German script when he was in school. I hope to be able to see him here again sometime.

With regards to German society's "relationship with commands," I would like to speak about a peculiarity that for a long time has been more pronounced with us than in the rest of Europe. I want to talk about a "sovereign rule," a type of rule that was not seen as "beautiful" at all, but which had to do with the "sovereign" at the time. [The German word used here for "sovereign" is *landesherrlich*. The irony is that *herrlich* means "beautiful," but the adjective *landesherrlich* actually derives from the noun for "prince" or "sovereign," *Landesherr.*] Since the Reformation in 1518, Luther had broken away from the religious supremacy of the pope in Rome with his own form of Christianity, but he had assigned the function of spiritual head to each political sovereign, who then was also promoted to the spiritual leader of the country's Protestant church. That is called the "supreme ecclesiastical authority of the regional sovereign." You can hardly imagine today what that meant then. Each political sovereign was always also the spiritual leader of his subjects—and, therefore, he was also justified in making decisions about the type and content of their beliefs. Moreover, it followed that many countrymen who didn't want to submit to this arrangement were forced to leave their homes. Schifferstadt at that time, for example, was divided in this manner: Greater Schifferstadt was politically in the possession of the Bishop of Speyer, who also carried all of the secular power, even when it meant going to war. Since he remained Catholic, we are all still Catholic here today. The village part of smaller Schifferstadt, however, was in the possession of the Chur ruler of Heidelberg, who declared his support for Luther. Thus, all of his local subjects became Lutheran. The successor of this prince declared his support for Calvinism, with the result that all of his subjects in Schifferstadt had to become Calvinists. That meant that they had to change their religion a second time because of an authoritarian command. Several years later the new ruler supported Luther again, which resulted in a third change of denomination for the subjects. Therefore, each sovereign completely determined the religious denomination of everyone beneath him. A small story about that: in our neighboring town of Dannstadt lived a shepherd named Isselhard with his flock of sheep. Electorally, Dannstadt was governed by Heidelberg. Therefore, Dannstadt automatically made each change of denomination along with the ruler there. But the pasture of Dannstadt became too unproductive for the flock of sheep, and the shepherd tried to move to Schifferstadt. But since the Protestants of Schifferstadt didn't have any appropriate pastureland available, Isselhard had to become Catholic so that he would be accepted by the ruler of Greater Schifferstadt, the Bishop of Speyer, all because of his flock of sheep. The Isselhards, who had already changed their denomination three times, were forced to change a fourth time, and then as "newcomers" in Schifferstadt, they had to prove themselves as Catholics. And so they became—as is customary for converts throughout the world—especially good and dependable Catholics. That is the reason why my wife Elli—born in Schifferstadt as Isselhard—is today Catholic, for example. Here it is popular to say, "he who pays the piper calls the tunes," which is an indication of the deep influence each ruler here has exerted on his subjects. The sovereign governed even the innermost soul of his inferiors. Whoever was unable to endure that had to leave the country, which, along with all the other reasons, led to a good many emigrations.

But there is also an additional point: for the Protestants, the greater portion of the Germans, each ruler was also the leader of the Protestant ecclesiastical administrations. They were accountable to him, were controlled by his officials, appointed by him, and promoted by him through official channels—or they weren't. And at the same time that the German unification was taking shape, forming the German Empire under Bismarck, Kaiser Wilhelm was the religious leader of the majority of the Germans. He made rulings on the controversial questions of his civil servants; they had to justify themselves to him for everything. It was the same even after the First World War, when the general of the army, von Hindenburg, became the German president—and later as well, when a certain Adolf Hitler came to power, even though his denomination from Austria was Catholic. From the outset of the Third Reich, the German Protestants lived in a Catch-22 situation: their ecclesiastical administration officially supported the sovereign, so to speak—thus his "Reich bishops" could only turn against him with great difficulty. That was one of the reasons why the Protestant Church was effectively silenced during the Third Reich, and why oaths of service and oaths of allegiance played such a significant role up until the last days of the war. "I swear this holy oath before God that I [will remain faithful] to the Führer and German Chancellor Adolf Hitler . . . ," a ritual oath that was maintained very solemnly up until the end, and with many of the Germans, it didn't miss its target.

That is another one of the reasons why the German hierarchy of commands was effective even down to the prison camps—and why after the war the Allies could depend on the effectiveness of the German "chain of command from top to bottom." It was effective since the refusal to execute an "official command" called for the death penalty (I hereby give you the official command!), and following these types of commands became second nature, "an inner attitude." However, before the completion of the oath of allegiance, "official commands" were not possible. This "organized function of commands" in our "authoritarian state" was first dismantled during the "student revolution" of 1967–1968. Since then, we have departed from "authoritarian education." A liberal spirit has seeped into the population—and, as so often, perhaps too much good has been done in some areas: some things are too disorganized now, too chaotic, and obviously it is somewhat difficult for us Germans not to sink to extremes and remain at a healthy equilibrium. Yet, in any case, the population has finally said farewell to its former authoritarian state.

Time and industrial air pollution are gnawing away at the gravestones, most of which are made from sandstone. It is happening in the Jewish cemeteries as well, which number several hundred. The inscriptions are becoming more and more illegible. Therefore, some people are taking stock of the inscriptions in the Jewish cemeteries and conserving them. Several have already been completely catalogued. Thus, I have looked after the cemetery in Rülzheim, which could not be included in the program this year (it is a long-term operation). I found the cemetery in order and very well cleaned up. Perhaps it was done too thoroughly, for all of the little remembrance stones [In the Jewish tradition, small stones are left on gravestones to show that people have visited.] were removed from the gravestones, so I had a difficult time finding a single little stone in the cemetery. Presupposing your permission and acting in memory, I placed the stone on the single grave that I found with the name Friedhoff (as you will see in the photo). Did you have a personal relationship to the "good mother, Mrs. Julie Friedhoff born Jakobs"?

I also noticed that in the cemetery there was not only the grave of Arnold Feibelmann of 1972, but also very recent graves, a sign that there are still Jews who today seek their final resting place in Rülzheim.

For today, best regards and best wishes to you and your wife,

APRIL 15, 1997

Dear Emil,

Since you declare me as your friend and I value that very much, I assume that we can call each other *du.* [*Du* is the informal "you." Until now, the correspondents have been addressing one another with *Sie,* the formal "you."] That may be the first time that two people have come into a true friendship without ever having seen one another. The written word has the same power as the spoken word. I hope that we can continue to enjoy this friendship for a long time.

Your letter of March 20 contained many things to discuss. Yet I want to say first that I was invited by the Schiller University to give two lectures on the Holocaust. Because of Henderson's article, a German professor phoned me (he comes from Heidelberg; his name is Dr. Peter L.) and asked if I would speak to his two classes (History and Philosophy). Even though it's a whole new field for me at my age, I immediately accepted the offer. In doing so, I thought about you, and like you, I want to help to ensure that the Holocaust isn't forgotten.

Now to your letter: I would very much like to have the tape cassette so that I can hear more about our Swiss friends. One always wonders what the next surprise will be. Whatever bad things can be said about the Swiss, it is also true that my brother with his wife and daughter escaped to French Switzerland and were welcomed with open arms. My niece and her husband (a doctor) are coming in May to celebrate my ninetieth birthday with us. Dr. B. is a non-Jew and a deep-rooted Swiss. Even though he completed his Abitur in German-Switzerland, he is no friend of the people there. The French part is his home.

Both books about Schifferstadt are now in the Holocaust Museum in Washington. Perhaps at some point you could send me replacements by the slower surface mail.

Emil Fackenheim was born in Halle in 1916 and became a philosopher and rabbi in Jerusalem; he said in an interview: "the Germans of the younger generation are not guilty; there is no question about that. But they have to carry a special burden, whether they want to or not. It goes without saying, at least for some, that even if one isn't guilty, he still has a responsibility. The German youth has the responsibility to see that the future is different from the past."

I agree that the Jews are not a race. It is their religion and their tradition that tie them together.

In my opinion, Abraham was not the "great" man whom the Jews and Muslims worship. There is no doubt that he was influenced by his wife Sarah when he sent Hagar and Ishmael into the wilderness. In all religions, honoring certain people can be linked perhaps to their ability to speak to crowds. We always see that in cults, which are appearing out of the woodwork everywhere. Some are successful; others disappear, like the thirty-nine who took their own lives in San Diego [The "Heaven's Gate" cult: the group believed that a spaceship was hiding behind the Hale-Bopp comet and would deliver them to their salvation if they killed themselves.]. People allow themselves to be manipulated. Both the yearning for security and the desire to go to heaven are very strong. In almost all human beings, there is a compulsion to find something to lean on.

The splintering of the Jews could prophesy the end of Judaism. The orthodox Jews have salvaged their religion in two thousand years of persecution. Emancipation leads to conversion and mixed marriages. The children from the mixed marriages usually take the religion of the "other," since usually it is the mother who is the non-Jew. They keep her religion, especially if she is Catholic.

You write that the Jews suffered from xenophobia. That could only have been the case when the Jews appeared in Germany for the first time. But that was a long time ago. The Jews were already living in Germany during the time of the Crusades and the German-French-Italian Inquisition. How could they have been regarded as foreigners? When I stepped onto American soil as an immigrant in 1935, I saw myself as an American. I turned my back on Germany, and when I became a citizen five years later, every trace of Germanness in me disappeared. Indeed, those were special circumstances, and it was understandable how I felt. Hatred against Germany and the Germans also played a role in it. But even those who leave their fatherland for, let's say economic reasons, say goodbye to their native country. And very often the next generation doesn't even speak the language of its parents. And yet the Jews were foreigners in Germany and had to suffer and die from xenophobia? This view cannot be correct, or it can be justified only when it is shown that this hatred was ignited again and again for centuries. By whom? I will let you answer that question.

It is certainly not the difference in clothing that could create the hatred. Hatred is the leitmotif of all the big religions. They cannot comprehend that there could be a God different from the one they believe in. For that reason, they send missionaries across the world to move others to what they consider the only correct path. It is exactly the same thing as the princes and the kaisers who forced their subjects to adopt their religion (your letter of [April 7]).

The quality of the Jews: it is a common view that human beings become lazier mentally when they are doing well financially (with exceptions of course). When the state supports them, or when they inherit the money of their parents or grandparents, they often lack a personal drive. And perhaps in that way, talents are squandered. The eastern Jews who came to America at the turn of the century were motivated to use their talents. They were successful in all areas of art, medicine, economics, etc., and of course they helped to bring America to the level where it is today.

It is not the Puerto Ricans who are so successful today in the schools here; it's the Asians. On their island, the Puerto Ricans can be divided up into three classes: one class of those who are successful, a small middle class, and a large class of the disadvantaged. These classes haven't changed in the last fifty years. Because of that situation, crimes have increased.

That brings me to a delicate topic: Israel. It seems as if you have gotten lost somewhere with regard to your opinion on this topic. How can you compare Israel with Germany, and how can you believe that a piece of land will guarantee peace? Let's consider Germany first. It began and lost two wars. Alsace-Lorraine, the greater part of the East, and all of its colonies were taken away from Germany, and it signed the peace treaties anyway. The Russians took several islands from the Japanese. The "victors" have never returned land to the "losers." Now Israel: the Arabs began and lost all of the wars against Israel. The victors gave some land back to Egypt to bring about peace. They gave a section of land back to the Palestinians and there is no peace. Historically, I can't remember any case where the victors had to beg in order to receive a peace treaty. Israel is trying everything possible to bring peace to the region, and because of its attempts, it is punished with stone-throwings. A war has been avoided because the Arabs suspect that Israel has the atomic bomb. The ultimate aim is to throw the Israelis into the ocean, and only Israel's military readiness is keeping the Arabs from pulling their swords from the scabbards. And peace will only be possible when democracy deposes the dictators. I wrote you about that earlier.

I completely agree with your letter of April 7. Just one sentence was missing: religion is the primary reason for all hatred. Even though everyone prays to the same God, they follow different paths and believe that paths other than theirs just aren't acceptable. The Baptists here say that you can only go to heaven through Jesus. That causes a great deal of trouble as well as more hatred. What can be said about that?

Many thanks for the pictures of the cemetery in Rülzheim. Yes, Julie Friedhoff is my grandmother. I was seven years old when she died, and I have only good memories of her. . . .

APRIL 26, 1997

Dear Paul,

"I hope that we can continue to enjoy this friendship for a long time," you write at the beginning of your letter of April 15, 1997. The way we approached one another really was an unusual way to establish a friendship. Normally friendships develop out of common experiences. They are emotionally motivated. You have lived with each other, laughed together, sung together, endured fate together, and cried together—and in doing so, a strong trust develops for the other person, which permits you to be less cautious and break down the distance that is supposed to protect you from unpleasant surprises caused by others. It was the nature of our correspondence that brought us closer to each other. We have common problems that on both sides are very charged emotionally and are not easy to digest. But each of us searches to find a path to get the connections straight. And together we reflect on how this type of situation can be healed. Even when we are starting from different premises, we can agree that first of all we must discuss in detail what happened in the past—and that we should reflect on what steps could be taken to overcome the existing problems. Not all people are interested in our problems. They go about their own tasks and that gives them enough to do. Thus, it is all the more important to have good relationships with people who have the same intentions about the same issues. Friendships can be created that way, as we both have seen—ones that cannot be easily replaced.

The part of the sentence "enjoy for a long time" introduces the factor of time into our relationship. Naturally I, too, have known for some time that your ninetieth birthday is coming and that this day cannot be reached by everyone with the mental vigor that you still have. Due to our great distance, it is not certain that my birthday greetings will reach you at the proper time. Therefore, I would like to ask your dear wife Greta to make sure to deliver my best wishes, on schedule, on the 17th of May. May we all be granted several more years worth living! . . .

Miracles still happen!

The Torah curtain (*Parochet*) of the synagogue in Schifferstadt, destroyed in 1938, has been found. After sixty-nine years, it has now appeared in the German History Museum in Berlin (during the period of the DDR, the German National Museum). It is the last remnant of our former synagogue. No one knows yet how the *Parochet* could have made it there. I heard about it once years ago in a DDR correspondence, but I was unable to find out any details and finally believed that it had been an error or a misreading. But now it's really there! The *Parochet* presents us with a mystery. Not only do we not know how it got to Berlin, but its text, which can be easily read and translated, also hides a riddle. We read that the curtain was endowed in the year 5680 (=1920). We read the names of the donors: Baruch, son of Michael and his wife Chana, daughter of Alexander from Schifferstadt. But who is concealing himself behind these religious names, and what are these persons' regular names? I asked the surviving Jews in Schifferstadt: not one person still knew the Jewish names of his ancestors. . . .

Now to the topics of your letter of April 15.

1. Where is this Schiller University that has invited you to speak? At first glance, I hoped that this German professor Peter L. had invited you to Germany to give lectures. But after reading your letter several times, I came to the conclusion that L. indeed comes from Germany, but that he invited you to lecture at an Institution in the U.S. If it is in Germany, however, that would be a chance for us to be able to see one another personally. If that is the case, I invite you and your wife to stay with us for a while, so that we could speak in peace about our pasts and our common interests.

I came to the following realization while speaking with the rising youth: they have gotten some vague ideas about the Holocaust from their education and the press, and without really knowing what to do, they have ignored the things they heard because they themselves had nothing to do with what happened. It is all beyond the limits of imagination. They also refuse to accept that afterwards and for generations to come they can be held responsible for atrocities that they didn't have anything to do with personally. Therefore, they must be given the opportunity to ask their own questions about the topic. Then conversations materialize about subjects they can identify with—and they recognize their task to inform themselves and reflect on the past—and to feel responsible for ensuring that the same things are not repeated in the future.

2. I am happy to send you a copy of a tape (the soundtrack) of the Swiss videos about the problems of the Jews in Switzerland at that time. It also aired on the television here. Naturally, all of the pictures, texts, and documents shown in the video are missing; my tape player only recorded what came out of the speakers. I am keeping the real video (from which only a few beginning sentences are missing) here at home. You have to listen closely to the words, since sometimes the Swiss, French, and the German translation overlap. Since then I have heard that the last "gold washing" [As bankers for Germany during the war, the Swiss held a large amount of Nazi gold.] between Berlin and the Swiss banks took place in March of 1945 (!), when the end of the war was imminent. In spite of everything, it should not be forgotten: there is not simply a group called the Swiss. There, too, as everywhere, there are and were all types of people—and that's true in all cantons of the wonderful country. And there, too, the guilty have long since realized that they committed a huge and, for many people, disastrous mistake.

3. The books that you wanted, as well as one with a collection of notes from diaries of Schifferstadt citizens of the last hundred years, are coming to you by boat. The diaries were written uncommissioned and come to you untouched; I've passed them on without making any corrections; even the occasional typos stand as they were. You can see from the diaries how little the persecution of the Jews during the Third Reich was reflected in the day-to-day thoughts and feelings of our average citizens.

4. I am enclosing a photocopy from the Confessio Augustana, the "Augsburg Confession," with which the Christian faiths attempted to make peace with one another in 1530. It is still the creed of the Lutherans today. In my last letter, I talked about the "rule of the church by the sovereign," which is based on article 16 of this creed.

5. When I spoke about "xenophobia" in my last letter, I used a word that at the moment is frequently in discussions in our newspapers with an expanded meaning. But what I meant was only an "aversion to everything foreign and strange," a quality that is common to all naturally evolved and self-contained human (and animal!) communities. Perhaps the North America of conquerors and immigrants is an exception. Two hundred years ago, the United States was a melting pot for very different kinds of peoples and all types of individualists. A multicultural society developed there, which must have made it easier for those arriving to fit in inconspicuously—especially when they all had reasons to escape their former homes. Nevertheless, the American Civil War developed there. There is the racial

problem, and the "equality of everyone under the law" can only be accomplished in reality with a great deal of effort. Militant groups are formed there that prepare themselves for violence against others—even if in the long term that should be limited to verbal discussions and threatening gestures (as we can only hope).

6. We completely agree about the role of aggressive religions in the motivation of hatred toward one's neighbors. It seems to be a pot that has inexhaustible resources. Yet my problem is reflecting on it by boring small holes into the pot so that it doesn't overflow again one day. You can't speak sensibly with people fighting for their religion because they don't listen, and they already have answers to questions that weren't even asked.

Humanity learns best from painful experiences—and even that is still a difficult process. The Third Reich was such an experience for our people. The changing of views never could have taken place without total defeat; I just hope that it will be a self-propelling process that has an effect in the future and leads to true changes. Here I also see our personal task: passing on to the following generation the knowledge from these experiences, so that after the death of our generation, the following generation is not cut off from what happened and, in order to collect its own painful experiences, is forced to start again as Adam and Eve.

7. Israel: you write: "How can you compare Israel with Germany, and how can you believe that a piece of land will guarantee peace?"

You know that at the last Israeli election almost fifty percent (!) of the Israeli citizens agreed with me and voted for the exchange of "Land for Peace," knowing well that this solution would not automatically pacify the hotheads on both sides. Perhaps to be successful, the peace process will have to be forced into their minds for two generations. . . . The solution lies in breaking down the hatred; it lies in the negotiations of Rabin and Peres and Arafat. They must give each other a chance, truly, and they must let each other live—in a joint democracy or in a separately governed neighboring country. A settlement of this Israeli-Palestinian conflict would not fail to have its effect on the neighboring states (I point out the development in Europe). So now I come back to my comparison with Germany: I wanted to show that a nation must be prepared to control emotions and take on some burdens if it wants to create conditions for a successful future. It isn't important to us anymore whether Breslau (today: Wroclaw) is governed by Germany or Poland: it is only important that it is governed well, that the people can travel in and out as they wish, and that they can trade and live with one another in peace.

You speak about the behavior of the victors and the losers. I think that those categories are from the time of nation-states, and that condition never led to a true peace. It would be valuable to change that way of thinking. Did returning Sinai harm the Israelis at all? By doing so they won over a predictable neighbor, Egypt, many years ago, even though in many places this was regarded initially as a strategically incomprehensible risk. . . .

8. Neither you nor I have an instrument of power that would enable us to change the course of the world. But we both must free ourselves from inherited ideologies and thoroughly think through everything that moves the world. And we must be willing to contribute our share and make sure that the people in our small personal surroundings are thinking about these things, and that the number of these people grows, so that finally there will be an improvement of the conditions in our world.

In doing so we must, as the rabbis demand of a yeshiva student, join together with a *chaver* who questions our thoughts and leads us to additional and better reflection. You play this role of a good *chaver* for me in many issues—for which I thank you and, at the same time, I hope that it can remain like this for a long time. . . .

Best wishes again for your ninetieth birthday—and best regards to your dear wife Greta,

---

MAY 29, 1997

Dear Emil,

Above all, many thanks for the fax with the good wishes on my birthday. It was just another day for me. Our son-in-law's illness weighs too heavily on our hearts to celebrate. . . .

When we came back from Virginia yesterday, we found your books. I paged through *Von Bauern, Bomben und Besatzungszeiten* [Of Farmers, Bombs, and Periods of Occupation]. It is more a report of events than anything else; hardly a mention of the reactions of people who actually make history. It is certainly a reminder for the town and will remain just that. Its tone was similar to the book by the man from Ergste; perhaps you forgot to answer me about that. I must read more about the "farmers, etc.," however, to get some idea about them. In any case, Otto L.'s childish crying doesn't belong in the book. He should have been in a concentration camp for a month to see how his countrymen dealt with the "enemy." The word "enemy" is in the book too often. The occupation period was loaded with the desire for "revenge," and the troops didn't know—after everything that had happened—what they had to expect from the population. L. is a pedant and a true stickler for detail, and was perhaps a clerk in some minor position who didn't have anything to do except write down unimportant details.

Also many thanks for the cassette, which is especially interesting. I assume that with time more facts will come to light. The Swiss are just clever people. My niece and her husband came here from Switzerland for five days to "comfort" me on my ninetieth birthday. Neither we nor they mentioned the Swiss reports. It was better that way.

To return to the Rülzheim cemetery again: yes, it seems as if it's well cared for. What isn't seen are the stones that were used for road construction. The remaining stones were separated into pieces, and parts of them were placed on the graves that had no stones. My grandmother is not buried where you took the photo. The headstone of my niece, who died at the age of four, can't be found anywhere. And so on.

Neither did you react to the report that the German army took part in the killing of unarmed and innocent people. An exhibition in Munich is supposed to prove that. In Munich of all places!

The Torah curtain: it was certainly endowed by a Jew from Schifferstadt. It is hard to determine how it got to Berlin. Perhaps it was a present from one Nazi to another. As you know, before 1845 the Jews didn't have any last names. Baruch was the son of a Michael. But that doesn't mean that the first name of the donor was Baruch. They frequently tried to choose a "common" name somewhat similar to a Jewish name. My Jewish name is Uri, the son of Abraham Halevy. First my name was Paul, and then my father chose the name Uri, perhaps because the "U" appeared in both names. The person who donated the Torah curtain lived in Schifferstadt in 1920, and who he was will remain a huge question mark. . . .

Schiller University is international and can be found throughout Europe. The students who heard my lecture came here from everywhere and represented all possible races. The university is about ten kilometers from our house. The students' reaction was positive. On May 17th I gave a lecture to a group of teachers, who didn't have any questions after I finished speaking. That bothered me a little bit afterwards. They had certainly had enough of the Holocaust, for they saw a half-hour film about the same subject before my talk. . . .

We haven't found any common basis for the comparison of Israel and Germany. The rights of the "victors" are not the same as those of the "losers." In any case, that was the norm in the past, which we can still see today. The time will come—we don't know when—when Germany will put that on a poster, show it to the world, and deal with it accordingly. Germany is not a country that will forget very easily. Israel, on the other hand, gave back some land in order to establish peace. How much land is necessary to achieve that? And—the main question—with whom must one negotiate who is trustworthy and believes in the text of a treaty? The Arabs are always of the opinion that the Israelis should be driven into the ocean and that would bring peace. Peace among the Arabs? That sounds absolutely ridiculous. . . .

———— ✿ ————

JUNE 8, 1997

Dear Paul,

Many thanks for your long letter of May 29, 1997. It showed me that you had successfully made it through the burden of birthday celebrations. Because of my occupation, I have often observed that for older people those kinds of days are full of stress. Sometimes it's such a problem that they don't sleep well for days on end, and afterwards they are happy that it is over and that normal life can continue. . . .

"Of Farmers, Bombs . . . etc." wasn't claiming to do anything but collect the diaries of individuals from Schifferstadt from the last one hundred and fifty years. The articles assembled in it have no common thread; it is only that they should not be forgotten and should be offered for personal reflection. Just as you immediately and justifiably hooked into "schoolmaster L.," other citizens have also related his petty-minded and exaggerated nationalistic views about the French occupation period to the later behavior of the German occupation forces in the regions captured by the Wehrmacht, and they arrived at similar conclusions. There were many conversations following the publication of the book; they were different according to each individual's views and ability to remember. Yet they went beyond a mere interest in local history. And they also showed how personally biased and full of gaps the memory of an individual can be. By the way, Heinz Mängen (book of Jews page sixty-four) [his book, *Die Schifferstadter Juden*], who emigrated to Scotland in 1935, told me that contrary to his colleagues, the teacher L. never said a single disparaging word against his Jewish students. Students today read L.'s writing and are greatly astonished by the views that existed then. They have learned well how to make distinctions.

My familiarity with the book about Ergste is from your comments. When the book about our Schifferstadt home came out in 1981, my report about the seizure of power during the Third Reich was still regarded as a sensation. Perhaps today Mr. M. would no longer ignore this topic if he were writing about Ergste.

Switzerland: right up until the last days of the war, the fuses for German bombs and shells still came partly from Swiss production.

The cemetery at Rülzheim: it was already clear to me that the meticulously clean state in which the cemetery appears today could not be its original condition. The local authorities have obviously attempted to conceal their guilty consciences. Something similar happened with us too when the gravestones were found under a road surface after the war: the stones were set up in a decorative semicircle at the place of the old Jewish cemetery, and they were equipped with borders to put flowering plants—as is customary in Christian cemeteries. At my intervention, the city administration removed the floral decoration, and then the question arose as to whether the gravestones should be oriented toward the east. I pleaded that they leave them in the semicircle, which they did. As it is, there isn't one gravestone that stands anywhere near the graves themselves, and we no longer know where the graves were originally. Secondly, I didn't want any more damage done to the gravestones. And thirdly, everyone who knows can today recognize in the "stylistic incongruity" that here was a cemetery that was desecrated and then improperly restored. Thus, the Jewish community in the Rhineland-Palatinate took over the possession and management of the cemetery, which earlier was the property of the city, and left it unchanged as a "memorial."

Exhibition in Munich about the German army: these records were shown before in a string of cities without incident. It is appearing in Frankfurt at the moment, and will be shown in additional cities. It doesn't introduce any new facts. The material was collected many years ago by the research section of the German armed forces in Freiburg, and was published as a book. It included both written articles and visual material, and I have had it at my house for a long time. It is a documentation of the guerrilla warfare, how it developed behind the front in Russia and in the Balkans, and how it was maintained by both sides with incredible fierceness and cruelty. It was supposed to cut off the German front from contacts in the rear—and, since it was conducted with ambushes with explosives and handguns, it was quite successful! The German reprisals (executions by shooting, public hangings of the imprisoned perpetrators, and later also hostage-taking and hanging of hostages, since the real perpetrators couldn't be caught) increased the scale of the conflict month by month toward Stalingrad and into "total war": the deaths were initially in the proportions of 1:5 and 1:10 (the murdering of hostages in the Ardeatic caves near Rome), yet in a number of places it rose to proportions of 1:100, including the extermination of entire towns. This "war of ambushes" was conducted by the entire army. Though there were certainly overlaps, originally it had nothing to do with the Holocaust. In 1944, guerrilla warfare was initiated in France as well, prepared for by the Allies long before, through the jettisoning of weapons and the construction of a resistance organization (Résistance) behind the German front. The war was conducted and managed there by the task forces of the French Vichy government, and not any less fiercely than by the Germans—but it also led to the disaster of Oradour sur Glane, where, in retaliation, the entire town and its inhabitants were exterminated by the Waffen-SS. On the occasion of the Ardennes offensive in December of 1944, the German army also tried to install the means for guerrilla warfare behind American lines (the English-speaking sections of the "Brandenburg Division" were dropped in by air and put into action partly in American uniforms, which defied the regulations of the Hague Land Warfare Convention). Just as mercilessly, the Americans sent all of the undercover German soldiers whom they could catch to the firing squad. And perhaps you remember the American solutions to this problem in Vietnam?

The exhibition shows nothing but the truth, but only one side of the truth, and that has upset many people. The public is very much impressed by the documentation and horrified by the pictures, especially those of guerrilla warfare—all of this, as with many other things, was hidden from the eyes of the public and was mentioned in the army reports only occasionally. Everyone who sees the exhibition is shaken by the atrocities that people could and did commit then. It would be almost comforting if only the "evil Germans" were capable of such excesses. Then there wouldn't have been any need for the Geneva Convention in 1864, or the Hague Land Warfare Convention in 1899, in which twenty-six nations attempted to humanize their wars so that they were somewhat humane and "chivalrous." It was also attempted by Rommel and his opponents in Africa, for example, and I remember the notion quite well from my time in the army. But even "humanized wars" are horrors, and I hope that one day the coming generation of humans will be dreadfully ashamed of any war.

The Palatinate Jews have had last names since November of 1808 (see the book of our Jews, pages nine to eleven). A corresponding documentation can certainly be found in the French language in the register of births in Rülzheim.

You write about the "laws of the victors." The ancient Romans spoke about that two thousand years ago: *Vae victis* = woe to the defeated. "The law of the stronger" starts from the beginning and affects all of biology; it therefore plays a part in the entire history of mankind. The victors are even usually successful in choosing how to write history. Victorious generals are the heroes of human history.

Thus, standards have developed for interhuman conflicts that are supposed to apply to everyone in the state, the victors and the losers, the strong and the weak ("Roman law" two thousand years ago, the Bill of Rights 1789, Napoleon's Code 1804). So one day there will be a supranational law that also protects the weak on an international level. Until then, it is obvious that humanity must pay dearly with the toll of lives. That cannot prevent us, however, from thinking about a necessary international law and fighting resolutely for its development. In view of what is happening today all around the world, you and I may be regarded as dreamers and fools. But if actions like ours do not succeed in changing the general views and achieving international rights for the weak, then we can be nothing but pessimistic about the future of humanity. It comforts me that you write: "In any case, that was the norm in the past . . ." That shows that we are not so far from agreeing with one another, which you fear on the issue of peace in the Middle East. I am Israel's friend, and therefore worry when their interpretations of the laws are limited by ideologies; *that* once led our people to great tragedy. I am frightened by how much some of the fundamentalist ideas there remind me of the way of thinking in Germany when I was young. People without space, ancestral legacy, blood and soil, law of the stronger, acquisition of land, the subjugation of inferior national traditions. Doesn't that sound damned similar to fascism, like Alfred Rosenberg? In the long run, it is impossible for one people to keep another people in submission. Please, let's think out this issue in the way the "man on the street" or at the bar does.

Naturally, I am unhappy with quite a few developments and events in Germany, particularly as they are presented in the *Aufbau*. What I miss in the newspaper excerpts is the effort to find a common path toward a better future. I recently saw an exhibition in the Jewish center at Mannheim with the topic *"The Fools" in Israel.* This compilation has been making the rounds in Germany since 1995. It doesn't conceal anything. Yet the material does not continually overwhelm and crush today's youth with its fathers' guilt— it even praises young Germans for having helped with the kibbutz for years, and its says that the youth in both countries are making a welcome progression toward understanding each other. You could also read that after the United States, the German Federal Republic has become Israel's most important partner, and that the collaboration has made some very good progress. Every once in a while it would be good to read of such small rays of hope in the *Aufbau*. The editors of the *Israel-Nachrichten,* the Israeli counterpart of the American *Aufbau* (I receive excerpts of it from my Israeli partners), could lend the proper assistance and show the *Aufbau* how to do this. Unfortunately, the *Israel-Nachrichten* will have to cease its publication in the foreseeable future, since its subscribers are dying off slowly but surely. . . .

The "law of the stronger" should not be the standard of behavior for the future, just as it should not have been so in the fascist state of my youth. Obviously, the law of action and reaction is also valid outside the world of physics. If we continue with the thought patterns of the past, we will only reproduce the events of the past! . . .

———⚙———

JULY 3, 1997

Dear Emil,

Just quickly today. We have decided to move closer to our children. We see the time coming when Lynn (our daughter) won't be able to leave Dave (her husband) alone anymore, and there are only so many days that we can travel. Our house has already been sold, and our day of departure is August 15. We have rented an apartment in a home for the elderly, where we will also receive one meal a day. We have two bedrooms, a living room, dining room, kitchen, and two bathrooms. That should be enough for us. Enclosed is the new address; we still don't have a telephone number.

It is incredibly difficult work to give up a house, and to bring everything that's been collected over the years to a new life; work is often mixed with tears.

For today, best wishes and regards, to your wife as well, from both of us,

———⚙———

JULY 11, 1997

Dear Paul,

Yesterday I received your letter of July 3rd, which informed me of your forthcoming move to Williamsburg into a "home for the elderly." Obviously you will have a perhaps smaller, though still respectable apartment there, and so despite everything, congratulations.

Naturally I can well imagine the serious reflection that resulted in your decision. We plan for our old age—and then suddenly something that we hadn't reckoned on at all comes from an unexpected side. And we see ourselves forced to change our ideas completely. At the sight of this "force majeure," which is obviously involved in your situation, it makes me a little sad. Yet also: your daughter Lynn will need you more and more in the future, and you will have to bear that in mind.

We have all arrived at a phase of our lives at which it can be helpful to withdraw occasionally from the bustle of everyday life, and reflect on things anew. In these periods, one's bearings can often be found in the "quotations of the fathers" (*Pirqe Avot* of the ancient Hebrews). The life experiences recorded there have helped people overcome their difficulties for thousands of years. They are maxims that can help us rediscover our temporarily destabilized equilibrium. It's certainly worthwhile to read. . . .

Paul, even though the situation of the world offers new topics for conversations every day, perhaps for the moment we should discontinue our conversations about the past in favor of your current situation. If it were possible, I would very gladly help in any way I could. If you feel as if you want to return to earlier topics or bring up new ones, then please let me know. At the moment, however, problems have imposed themselves on you that demand your entire attention. I am convinced that after a little while you will also overcome these difficulties, and that everything will be straightened out. . . .

JULY 30, 1997

Dear Emil,

We are in the process of reducing the number of our important possessions, since we can't bring everything to the new apartment that for many years we were able to keep in a house. It is often difficult to give up things that you had regarded as a part of everyday life. We must wait and see how life will be with everything smaller, and we must get accustomed to more restricted movement. . . .

I don't have enough time today to take up your topics, but I am sending you some newspaper excerpts that may be stimulating. The views that are expressed in these excerpts are not always the same as mine. But they are often stimulating. I hope that the German today thinks differently and doesn't have much to do with previous generations. Yet is it possible to change the people from one generation to the next, so much so that other countries lose their fear of the "Germans"? This is certainly a topic for discussion.

Work is waiting for me. Best regards and wishes from both of us to both of you,

---

AUGUST 2, 1997

Dear Paul,

. . . The campaign on the Swiss accounts is running worldwide now. We can only hope that in this way a portion of the generation of injustice against the Jews will be atoned for. There is the old saying: "ill-gotten gains seldom prosper." Since I can get Swiss radio and parts of their television broadcasts, I have the impression that the Swiss authorities and even the population are no longer trying to hush things up, but that they now have the intention of bringing everything to light and putting it all out on the table. And there are also many people discussing the topic who are quite concerned with the moral side, not only the belated "recovery of a stock exchange." A new generation is at the helm in Switzerland. And in the meantime, many surprising things are coming to light: until now, I hadn't heard that temporary volunteer Swiss medical units were in action at the German eastern front, and indeed under German command (the "Swiss Red Cross on the Eastern front"). There also are investigations going on at the moment about the profitable Swiss commerce that utilized art objects confiscated from the Jews in Germany and France ("Jewish art and Switzerland"). People have also been talking about the fact that portions of "Nazi Gold" are still in the hands of some of the Allies. In case you are interested, I can send you a document about it from Swiss television (soundtracks); it is recent, but the context has already changed. Yet, before the entire world directs all of its emotions against the Swiss, it should not be forgotten that the Swiss actions are a matter of peripheral importance compared to what the Germans are responsible for! After all, Auschwitz is not in Switzerland! Switzerland tried to save its own skin and was partly successful, and those responsible took on the role as Germany's partners, an arrangement that was useful to both sides. It is certain that very few people at that time even suspected that it would be seen differently today, a half century later. However, if one did not want to be so lenient, one could cite the behavior of the bankers in the period after the war.

I recently read a book by Liana Millu, *Der Rauch über Birkenau* [The Smoke over Birkenau], first published in 1997, and it kept me very busy. Mrs. Millu, an elementary school teacher and journalist from Pisa (Italy) who today is over eighty years old, was deported in 1944 and sent to the women's concentration camp in Birkenau. She survived until the liberation of the camp at the end of the war, and up to now she had been completely silent about her time in the camp. Her book is remarkable in many ways, since by showing individual fates it demonstrates the psychological mechanisms that allow oppressed people to imprison and torture one another. How is it possible that prisoners become the merciless "bosses" of their fellow prisoners, themselves becoming the oppressors, maltreating the other prisoners, and in the end sending them to their deaths? Yet the book contains many examples of interactions between humans that are comforting, instances of solidarity and the willingness to make sacrifices—and the hardly comprehensible Hanukkah celebration among the imprisoned women, where, for an hour, the "bosses" even took charge of the religious events, and for as long as it lasted, everything was even humane—though immediately afterwards, the everyday, inhuman whip was swung again. . . . In the end, human behavior must be judged according to what humans have, in days of better sense, acknowledged as world opinion and set before themselves as a necessary goal. That is how one should judge what is actually being done today. "You should recognize your offenses."

Why am I reflecting in this way? Israel is surrounded by enemies. There are agreements with Egypt and Jordan, and there is no reason to think that these agreements are in jeopardy. Neither of these two wants to take the chance of a war, in an attempt to "drive Israel into the ocean." Israel's military and international political position is too strong for that—unless suddenly in an ambush they fire off modern weapons of mass destruction.

However, the situation within Israel with the Palestinians remains unresolved. There are obviously strong, emotionally controlled powers on both sides, which, with secret uses of force, attempt again and again to shift the outlined "claims" in the difficult peace process to their own favor. At the moment, threatening gestures are escalating on both sides, and there are new killings. If both sides are not more restrained and more cautious, permanent guerrilla warfare will develop as before, conducted with ambushes. Neither will be victorious, and again life will be poisoned on both sides. The past reveals very clearly where such a running battle will lead. It will last a long time, until, because of mutual exhaustion, there comes a state of affairs that makes an agreement possible—an agreement that with a little bit of thought could have been reached many years before, if they had been capable of talking with each other reasonably and uncontrolled by emotions. For that reason, the negotiations must make further progress right now—and everything that stands in the way of that goal is nothing but damaging.

Paul, a couple of days ago I got hold of a newly released book and I "devoured" it as quickly as possible: Avi Primor, an Israeli Ambassador in Bonn since 1993, put it on the market with the title . . . *mit Ausnahme Deutschlands* [. . . With the Exception of Germany]. It is about the notation in Israeli passports that for decades now was supposed to bar Israelis from going to Germany. Primor conducted himself accordingly and avoided Germany in every way conceivable—until finally he was forced to examine for himself, as the ambassador to this hated country, the reality of the aversions he had acquired. I can't find out if there is an English translation of the book available. Therefore, I am sending you several excerpts. . . .

Perhaps I should say a few words about Primor's book anyway: naturally, for everyone involved, it does great good to search for better relations between Israel and the evil Germans. He breaks the earlier automatism with which all humans were put indiscriminately in pigeonholes: on one side there were those who are unquestionably good—and on the other side (according to Goldhagen) the irrevocably bad, who have been so for generations and will be in the future. Indeed, humanity will also have to reckon with their corrupt genetic material in the future. Primor, however, shows a certain enthusiasm for having discovered, to his surprise, that there are also all types of people here with us, even those with good intentions. In his view, it is precisely the experience of the last fifty years that has been missed, for during that time a certain consciousness and changing of views could have been achieved. Today he is dealing with people who have slept off their historically incited "German frenzy," and realized with horror what they have caused with this frenzy. And he is dealing with the descendants of the generation of perpetrators. Primor's contribution is that he encourages the powers here that have devoted themselves to changing their views. But today there are still powers who want to ensure that fascist thinking and the accompanying antisemitism don't fall into oblivion. Strangely enough, these groups and political movements are mainly in foreign countries (see Juri's letter about the Russian fascists). . . . Primor's book is going down well here; that is in keeping with the current situation in our country. . . .

It is not possible to change in one day the mentality of a population. Something like that happens most easily after painful experiences and after the failure of plans. For us, such an experience was the complete defeat and utter destruction of our country in 1945. Yet such a changing of views happens with the course of time. It cannot be driven out of someone's mind with force. There must be a long-term restructuring within the mind. Thus, all of us must start at the beginning. The Germans had been warned and had seen how easily their own dreams could come to ruin. Everyone must think through everything, examine the conditions, and account for himself. In addition, those set in their views have begun to die out, and their descendants have acknowledged their responsibility. They keep their eyes open now, and, just as importantly, and with the assistance of foreign countries, they carefully observe current developments in the country. I was recently reminded that with regard to the Jews, the Danish and the Swedish, who are just as much Teutons and Lutherans, conducted themselves differently than the Germans and their henchmen throughout Europe in the last war. But also: that today, strangely enough, the Danish have become the primary supporters and frankly a European bridgehead for the activities of the Nazis in the United States, who try to reactivate the fascist demon here in Germany, especially in the youth of the former DDR. . . .

August 27, 1997

Dear Emil,

Your letter of August 2 reached me the day after our arrival at our new home; many thanks. Nearly all of the boxes have been unpacked now with the help of our granddaughter, Nancy. We naturally brought too many things along, some of which found a place at our children's homes. . . .

Now to your letter: concerning Switzerland, I am less surprised by what they did during the war than by the new generation's refusal to try to correct the evil in any way. Acquiring money that doesn't belong to them is actually theft and should be dealt with as such. I haven't heard that the Swiss matter has been regarded in that way. Certainly the thieves are no longer at the helm, but the heirs should be responsible for what they did. It is outrageous to accept that kind of position. Now we must wait to see what the future will bring.

The book by Liana Millu could be interesting. But for a while now two things have disturbed me about those concentration camp inmates who survived for a long time: the first point is understandable for me: the bosses obtained slaves in order to save themselves. Yet it remains a mystery to me why so many who came out of the hell alive needed fifty years to tell of their personal experiences. Is that perhaps psychological?

As far as Israel is concerned, I stay with my old opinion: there is no one among the Arabs with whom Israel could negotiate a peace agreement. Our "cousins" have developed differently from the Jews, and not to their advantage. It is tragic and difficult to change. Perhaps future generations will understand that peace is good for both sides. They must first learn that the Israelis will not allow themselves to be driven into the ocean.

As regards Germany, I have developed two new ideas that can be discussed. I am nearly convinced that the Jews would have put up their hands like everyone else if their extermination hadn't been part of Hitler's program. Imagine if Einstein had written that famous letter to Hitler and not to Roosevelt. [In August of 1939, Albert Einstein, a refugee from Germany, wrote Roosevelt to tell him of the potential of creating an "atomic bomb" by using the fission of uranium.] Hitler would have had the atomic bomb and been able to rule the world. He would have had people like Bohr, Franck, Born, and many others at his side. You can certainly remember that it was Fritz Haber who helped the kaiser lengthen the First World War. When you think about all of that today, you get goosebumps.

The second point is a little more difficult: the German people were enthusiastic about Hitler's ideas. He would erase the peace treaty of Versailles, protect the dignity and honor of Germany, and conquer more land in the east. For all of that, the German people happily overlooked the question of the Jews and gave Hitler the Jews like candy to a child. Why not? Only five hundred thousand Jews in Germany, with a population of sixty-five million, I believe; they did not even represent one percent. Something like that could easily be overlooked if, with Hitler, Germany regained a leading position among the nations of the world, and could even become the leading nation. The good outweighs the bad; it's a compromise. Is this theory useful? And if so, how can the Germans be judged in general?

Primor's book is the standard view of the generation that didn't live through the Holocaust. When I speak with my children about the Holocaust, I always hear the same thing: "Dad, that's history." It seems as if one had to live during the time period to understand it properly and know the consequences. Perhaps it is better that way, so that the young people learn to live with one another and give up hating. But is that really how it is? . . .

—— 🦋 ——

SEPTEMBER 12, 1997

Dear Paul,
    . . . We really don't need to think anymore about Switzerland and its connection to the past. It appears as though everything is being resolved, as far as is possible. Nothing can be changed. However, we should hope that the related financial problems are settled to the satisfaction of the victims. If you are still interested, I could send you the soundtracks of the broadcasts "The Swiss Red Cross at the Eastern Front" and "Jewish Art and Switzerland."

Liana Millu: I will send you this book by surface mail. It isn't a report of the author's personal experience; in fact, she doesn't appear in the book at all. The *New York Times* writes in a review of the book: "Literature about the Holocaust has a heavy burden to carry. It is supposed to be authentic, and yet also literature. Liana Millu's stories about the life of women in the KZ succeed in both in an exceptional way."

You asked a question in this context that I can't answer without some qualification. First of all: "The bosses obtained slaves . . ." Possibly several "reliable" bosses from the ranks of the prisoners were able to survive because of their efficiency, and, therefore, were silent afterwards. Yet I would have great problems assuming something like that in an individual case. And why were other, "normal" prisoners just as silent afterwards? Even my father-in-law, who was arrested by the Nazis in 1933, didn't say anything later. Other political prisoners from Schifferstadt, who were taken into custody at Dachau, were also silent after being released. Now in this case it could be assumed that in being silent, they wanted to protect themselves from being arrested again (since they were under continual surveillance by the secret state police, the Gestapo). But I met and looked after a whole string of German POWs who returned home in miserable condition from Russian imprisonment after the war, and many of them, too, had suffered a change in their nature during their imprisonment, had become quiet, and never wanted to talk about that time period. They would "immediately be sick" if they were merely asked about it. There are, as with brainwashing, obvious defense mechanisms against bad memories, but that does not mean

definitively that the person must have a bad conscience. It is certainly—
as you say—psychological, yet the cause of each individual case must be
examined.

Israel: I am very unhappy about the current developments there. Both
sides have obviously driven back the peace efforts in their single-mindedness.
They haven't suffered enough to be capable of peace. . . .

The Jews were good Germans! And perhaps they would have become
good Nazis partly, if . . . One day I was a guest in Israel. After we "got to
know" each other, my host (after a short discussion) went up a floor and got
from the closet his father's war decorations from the First World War! And
he proudly showed us photos from the western front of World War I. See
the book of our Jews, page sixty-seven under "Kurt Joseph Mayer." And the
contemplative game: "what would have happened if" . . . is, after what has
happened, useless to consider in many situations. Yet some people also say:
the idea of a true "national socialism" would not have followed the same
course perhaps, if it had been paired from the beginning with the idea of
humanity and a democratic way of thinking. And in the long run, that
certainly would have proved preferable to the current way of thinking—the
brutal maximization of profits in a merciless capitalistic society. The current situation, where the rich and powerful people of the world can exist due
to the continuing impoverishment of the rest of the world, conceals a huge
potential for explosion in the future. In the long run, this problem cannot
be solved with the methods of today, by continuing to supply the "third
world" with more weapons so that the manpower there can massacre themselves and thus pose no threat.

I don't see any problem with your second point: the initial success of the
Nazis on the international stage (the 1936 Olympics, and America's admir-
ing appreciation of the Nazis' system!) silenced a great number of critics
around here. My father, who was wounded several times at the front in the
First World War, was filled with consternation at the outbreak of the war in
1939. When, contrary to all predictions, Verdun and Paris fell into German
hands in 1940, he could only shake his head. He didn't understand the
world any longer. Hitler's initial political success on the international
stage, and then his military success, seemed to make him [Hitler] right,
even in the eyes of his critics. His propaganda machine functioned excellently. The people could be fed with news of success for a long time. And
whoever heard any news from foreign countries was taken to the KZ. . . .

The extermination of Jews took place out of the people's field of vision,
and often completely under cover. Today you can still read the appeal to the
Jewish population, where they were asked to take along all hand tools (for
the women, even their sewing machines!) for labor duties in the East!

I am certain that Hitler was of the opinion that after a war, all the dead would be attributed to the conflict, and, in the process, no one would even ask about the whereabouts of the Jews. Indeed, that had been a common way of proceeding for centuries. If even for your own people the view was supposed to be "Live high, oh fatherland, and don't count the dead: there could not be too many killed, if it is for you, beloved . . . !" [from Friedrich Hölderlin's poem "Der Tod fürs Vaterland" ("Death for the Fatherland")], then who could ask about the "enemy" casualties after a war that was won? For centuries, the memorials to war heroes have been built over the remains of an anonymous soldier! Your theory on point two corresponds so perfectly to reality; it shows the corresponding practice of all peoples. Or were you not thinking about the "body count" in Vietnam, which became customary, or the collection of scalps in the Indian pogroms? The survivors always stand on the shoulders of the fallen—and say that now everything is good. If the Nazis had won the war, I can well imagine the way they would have written history—also: which side would have been "evil." . . .

OCTOBER 14, 1997

Dear Paul,

  Perhaps this letter will cross your next letter over the Atlantic, as has already happened—but I have to write today so that I can get this topic off my chest: Israeli-Palestinian relations. Naturally, I have been following these things closely—but they were happening far away and without any direct affect on me. Yet this time it was right before my eyes and ears: I received an invitation to be a guest at a public discussion between Israeli and Palestinian intellectuals and journalists; in fact it was here in Speyer. Topic: "Where Does Man Live? Home Among Reality, Memory, and Hope." . . . Where do the Jews, and where do the Palestinians have a home, and do they need one? . . .

  Lea Fleischmann was born and raised in Germany after the Holocaust and emigrated to Israel "because I cannot live in Germany." The reasoning will interest you: she got to know the German civil servants and became convinced that they were capable of and willing to serve faithfully any government that came along! "This is not my country!" She writes, thinks, and works in German, but "I am not a 'German in Israel'; I see myself as an Israeli."

  Sami Al-Kilani from Nablus spent years in Israeli prisons as a Palestinian terrorist and suffered a miserable fate. Yet he recognized that terrorism could not lead to a better future. He dealt with his grief with all of his heart; he is fighting for peace, so that there can be a home for everyone in the land of Canaan, and so that they will be able to enter and leave unhindered and freely. He found his "principle of hope" in the German-Jewish philosopher Ernst Bloch.

Martin Lüdke, German journalist from Mainz, recognizes the Nazis' political misuse of the term "home"; they gave this traditional term bad connotations. Thus, we would have to redefine the term in a roundabout way: with the mobility of modern society, "home" can no longer be any definitive geographical place, but an "imaginary sanctuary" that everyone must create for himself. Only in this "roundabout way" can we define a "home."

There were many high-ranking party supporters in the audience. The moderator had a hard time keeping the speakers on the actual topic of the evening, since for the most part they were constantly using common complaints to reproach the other party, and everyone wanted nothing but to present loudly a list of atrocities committed by his opponents. Hardly one of them spoke about the actual topic of the evening. Quite a few of the people there left the hall before it was over after seeing the hopelessness of the initial discussion. At the end, the moderator finally said that the planned "discussion about home" had not taken place at all, that no easy answers had been discovered for the Israeli-Palestinian dilemma, but that "to continue to speak with one another" was seen as a necessity—and that the intellectuals and levelheaded people on both sides had a duty to do so.

Lea: the Israeli population is, in contrast to its government, tired of conflict. The radicals on both sides should be banned, as well as their families.

Kilani: invites Lea and her relatives to Nablus to visit him in his hometown, so that they can speak with one another in peace. She could look around there without any problems. Both sides must forget about the gigantic lists of atrocities, as well as the constant charges of guilt. They must finally enter into a competition to build a common future. The Israelis should finally have a right to a home, but the Palestinians should as well. No one should rob the other of his freedom.

The party supporters (Israeli and Palestinian) among the speakers often threw out very harsh words of political agitation, which was difficult for the moderator to deal with. One Israeli's call of protest filled me with consternation. He refused to hold such discussions at all if they were outside of Israel, "and certainly not in Germany: you can't talk about the rope in the hangman's house!"

Lea: Netanyahu obviously must be voted out of office at the next opportunity—however, he is meeting with Arafat now, which was inconceivable beforehand! Recently, Israeli society has also made great progress in its views. The cultural and religious similarities between the former enemies must be acknowledged.

Kilani: the change would begin by preventing the hostile indoctrination of the young generation. They must learn to play together.

Uri Avneri (who sat in the audience) made a very good impression on me: "I think it's good that this discussion is taking place in Germany." After the Shoah, there had been two diametrically opposed theories: "Israel should allow itself to do anything now . . ." and: "after the Holocaust, Israel has a special obligation to ensure peace." There must be something in between the poles.

The moderator: "Whoever wants to go a long way, must at some point begin with the first step!"

The changing of views is a difficult process; it often takes a long time and can take generations. That evening, I had expected everything but the avowal of friendship, and I am very happy that it was decided that they should continue to talk with each other. Lea, who (for me) is also a young Jewish German, was a good listener, made a good showing in the company of men, and represented her ideas very successfully. Whoever is willing to talk with the other, loses him from the "crosshairs." Perhaps a people can even convert its rulers to another path, one that doesn't lead to bloodshed (as became possible in portions of the Eastern block). I, too, maintain Ernst Bloch's "principle of hope," and I'm not giving up. . . .

------- ✿ -------

OCTOBER 9, 1997

Dear Emil,

. . . Now to something else: who is this Röder Wuppertal? [see below] Is he speaking only for himself, or for the entire party? I told you earlier what I am telling you now. My landlord in Homburg was a good Catholic and when he heard Hitler speak one time, he became a good Nazi. Both were acceptable to him, and one can only wonder whether such a man didn't throw his hand up in the air in church and end his prayer with "Amen— Heil Hitler." What can we learn from that? We learn that well-presented theories that also please people are highly successful. You can condemn Hitler however you want, but he was certainly a good orator. His ideas were the same as those of his listeners, and they were presented successfully. His voice inflamed the masses. My landlord believed that he could serve both— his religion and Hitler. He, like so many, did not know what Röder Wuppertal had in mind. Were not all Nazis Christians, and didn't the majority of them go to church? How can that be reconciled? The rally [mentioned in the Wuppertal material] is dated June 4, 1937. I left Germany with a portion of my family in December of 1934, for I knew then that Hitler and the German people should be taken at their word. I say the German people because the people accepted him and saw their ideas fulfilled by him. When I say "the people," I know that certainly there was a small group that did not agree with him. The small group was afraid to declare its views publicly and was overrun by the masses. When Wuppertal says that the Christians were worse than the Jews, I must assume that it was just easier to eliminate the minority first, and that the followers of Jesus had to wait until the time was ripe. For me, these are new ideas with which the Nazis meant to replace the Bible, and if that were to have happened completely, it would have brought the world to chaos. The possible consequences of that are indescribable.

It would be interesting to study whether these stubborn Swiss were only German-Swiss, or whether all of the Swiss believed and still believe that money is God and that human feeling has no place in their activities.

Germany still hasn't forsaken the Nazi way of thinking. Now there are the immigrant workers instead of the Jews. In Lübeck things are going horribly. Even the local TV reveals what is happening there. If it is in Lübeck, it will certainly appear in other cities as well—perhaps to a lesser extent. Germany seems to be a restless country that is never happy with what it has. Wilhelm II's desire for expansion remains in their blood. That must also be the reason why other European countries fear Germany and keep it under a watchful eye.

It is difficult to understand how the bosses could have survived four or five years in the concentration camp on the meager amounts of food there. Did they receive better rations, or did they steal from the others? And how did they overcome that mentally? Those are questions that we're not supposed to ask. I can understand and accept your other explanations. . . .

. . . With regards to this general topic, I only want to say that the Jews in Germany were good Germans. For example: four young Jews from Rülzheim willingly followed the kaiser. Among them was my cousin, the first violinist of the symphonic orchestra of Karlsruhe. He was killed his first day at the front. At that time, there was a small memorial in Rülzheim near the town hall to the seven Jews who died in the Kaiser's war. Naturally, I don't know what became of it.

OCTOBER 19, 1997

Dear Paul,

. . . You ask about "Röder Wuppertal." A patient of mine found this leaflet for me in 1944 when, during an air-raid warning, he fled into the cellar of an abandoned house near the train station in Frankenthal. He was bored there and by chance found a pile of leaflets that were anti-government and took them because he thought that keeping them would cost the owner his life, were they to fall into the wrong hands. He gave them to me several years ago; I then handed them out to historians, in copies as well. There were also secret messages that arrested clergymen (among others Pastor Niemöller) had smuggled out of the prisons and KZs in order to teach the outside world about their fates.

At the beginning of his activities, Hitler first calmed the world and gave signs of good behavior. And he cleverly conducted his "putsch" through unofficial channels so that often the man on the street could say "If the führer only knew that . . . !" The elimination of his political opponents (and later also the Jews) was not at all done with claps of thunder, but bit by bit, although with brutal consequences. Thus he quickly succeeded in driving a wedge in the clergy of the Protestant Church, splitting it up into "religious parties" and weakening them. Many ministers, who were already disposed to German nationalism from the time of kaisers, joined the party. Out of them developed the "German Christians," who also began to glorify the führer religiously, for as their ruler, he was their superior anyway. Beyond that, I haven't encountered Röder Wuppertal anywhere else. Yet I assume that he belonged to the "preachers" of the propaganda ministry. They were supposed to fuse Christian ideas and the ideology of Rosenberg (*The Myth of the Twentieth Century*) [Alfred Rosenberg was the chief architect of Nazi ideology. His *The Myth of the Twentieth Century* was an attempt to prove German racial superiority.] into one and make a new religion for the "German people." That was called the "German religious movement." They didn't want to bother the Christians with such bothersome things until after the imminent war because they relied on them to be soldiers (the Nazis really weren't as stupid as they are often presented. After all, they still remembered the consequences of the cultural war under Bismarck). But after the "final victory," they would have also "done away with" the political conservatives, especially the Catholics—and the necessary "instruments" had already been developed in the extermination camps—if they hadn't been able to send them to be slaughtered effectively in another "profitable" way at (even in the coming peace) the continual front in the Urals. . . .

On the Catholic side, a quieter yet more tenacious resistance developed among the bishops and the people, more in thought than in actual deeds. It was watched carefully by the Gestapo, and over and over again, with the help of imprisonment and the guillotine, the resistance was robbed of its civilian leaders. They didn't dare to go near the bishops (its head: Cardinal Graf von Galen, Münster). . . .

I have no documentation as to whether the majority of the "stubborn Swiss" were Teutonic. Nevertheless, the head of the Swiss general staff, who was accused unjustly and excessively of friendliness to the Germans, was "Henri Guisan," which is a French name. He came from Mézières. He withdrew the Swiss army from the borders and occupied only the "Réduit," the fortress in the Alps. The men from the army who were released as a result of his measures were put into weapons factories. In doing that, the Swiss earned a great deal of money from both the Germans and the Allies. After the war, Guisan was accused in a trial of having acted in secret agreement with the Germans.

As for the mentality of the Western part of Switzerland, one should consider that the recently published material in France clearly reveals that one did not need to be Teutonic to distinguish himself in the persecution of the Jews. The current French government made it public that the searching out and extradition of French Jews to the place where they were assembled on the transports, and even the deportation of Jews who were minors, were the tasks of the *French* police. Thus the Germans in Drancy were provided with trains that were already filled with Jews. By the way: the ancestors of the French, the Franks, are also counted among the Teutons! I don't have any idea as to whether the partly French blood of the Swiss occupies a special position in their being. In any case, all Europeans helped to bring about the Holocaust under the instigation and leadership of Nazi Germany. And there were very few exceptions, which we have already discussed. If I remember correctly, the active antisemitism, in Europe and in other places, was not purely a thing of the Teutons. Erica Jong [contemporary poet, novelist, and essayist] confirms that in the interview I sent you recently. In no way does that detract from the fact that the Germans instigated the crime; it merely straightens out, to a certain extent, the earlier "version" of the matter, which effectively focused the Holocaust on the West Germans and cleared the other participants of their part in it.

There is a huge difference between the persecution of Jews and what you call the current problem of "immigrant workers."

The persecution of the Jews arose from a harebrained religious, later racist, ideology. There was really no reason for it. Since their emancipation one hundred years before, the Jews were completely integrated into our people. They earned their own livings, were economically integrated and self-sufficient, and were a major cultural element of German life, especially capable in the arts. Socially, they were even exemplary due to their health insurance and their association providing for burial arrangements, all decades before German social security! They belonged. Economically they were no burden to any German, and they had long since found their place in the German leadership. Even their expulsion up until 1939 was a great economic loss for Germany. By no means was everything balanced out by robbing the Jews of their property, as you well know. Nine hundred years ago, the Bishop of Speyer had taken Jews into his country to "boost the reputation of the city" as it says in the documents! You yourself name the consequences of losing a well-known Jewish physicist before the war.

The group of "immigrant workers" is a completely different problem and must be distinguished.

During the war, there were first of all the "foreign workers" who were gathered to be a work force, often with very dubious methods, from the occupied territories. They were given communal accommodations, had a supervisory staff, received a small minimum wage and sufficient communal provisions, yet had very few liberties. They wore badges that indicated their origin to the public. Day after day, they worked together with the Germans, in factories or on the farms. It is true that friendly relationships with Germans were not looked upon kindly, yet they did not have such serious consequences as a friendly relationship with the "Eastern POWs." The workers were free after the end of the war, and they returned to their homes. Or they went to the U.S. army as Displaced Persons (DPs) to be guards, etc. —or they preferred to remain in Germany, where they since have "merged" into the population.

"Immigrant workers" are something entirely different. After the war, from about 1960, they were brought here because of the lack of workers in our rising industries. After health exams, and until they found themselves apartments, they were accommodated very respectably and without supervision in communal housing. They immediately had all the obligations and rights of a German worker. They paid the normal taxes and normal social security, pension, and unemployment contributions. If they wanted to, they could become union members, and they were advised and looked after by the other members. They had all the civil rights that weren't directly connected to citizenship (therefore, they did not have the right to vote, did not have to do military service, etc.), and for the most part, they retained the citizenship of their homeland. These people have long since settled in among our people; they are club members. Their children are completely integrated and have married mostly Germans. The greater portion of them, however, have long since retired, and well situated with their pensions, have returned to their home countries. They took their cars with them and are now envied by their own population as well-to-do "Germans" because of their social security. Often they are even proud of their partial "Germanness." For some years now, "immigrant workers" have no longer been necessary because of the restricted economic situation, and so they haven't been recruited. There were no problems with this group as a people. Yet these follow-up costs have resulted:

As is common with us Germans, we set no reasonable limits. In Switzerland, which also recruited "immigrant workers," there was a strict regulation in effect from the beginning: the immigrant worker could not bring along his family. He had to return home after nine months, stay there for three months, and then, if he had proved himself and could still be used, would be able to return to his workplace in Switzerland for an additional nine months. He saved money and sent it to his relatives at home. Thus, this arrangement aided both parties. But he could not bring his family into Switzerland, and he couldn't get an apartment there either. Accordingly, he received no "child allowances." His family in Switzerland was not insured.

Here in Germany, however, the immigrant worker had no difficulty receiving rights of residence and social support for his entire life. The family members in the distant hometown were also supported. Whoever found himself an apartment could bring his family here. All of them had health insurance here in Germany, but could also be treated on our insurance in their own hometowns. Even the grandparents could come to Germany and be cared for on our social security. If a hometown mayor confirmed in writing that someone had additional children abroad, then the immigrant worker also received complete social support for those not living in Germany. No one objected at all to their completely equal status with German employees, who for four generations had formed a unified community, the same that their ancestors had taken part in. And why should anyone object, when our social security believed it could afford this expenditure?

Socially, Germany is referred to worldwide as a land of milk and honey: . . .

But now there are also citizens who have never had a normal job at all, and therefore were not insured anywhere (single or divorced women, people who have been sick for their whole lives, those incapable of working, but also alcoholics and addicts, etc.). These people are supported by the state, that is, by taxpayers via the tax office, for their entire lives. This group is called "welfare recipients." The money for this does *not* come from an insurance that the people have paid; it comes from the pockets of ordinary taxpayers, who by law must pay for that, in addition to the contributions for their own insurance. Along with the employees, individuals who are independent, self-employed, and middle class are also in this situation.

The welfare recipient not only has the right to money from the state, but also the right to the objects necessary for daily life—winter clothes, television sets, subsidies for rent, heating, etc.

As can be determined easily by anyone, our social support systems have run into some huge difficulties in the past several years (unemployment, economic depression), since more and more non-workers must be taken care of. Thus, social contributions must be raised repeatedly, and the payments should be cut back simultaneously, but naturally, everyone involved fights against that. I saw it coming a long time ago. The problems are too big. . . .

Legally, our social system is supposed to assure the absolute welfare of every single person! Corrections to that law could be effected by parliament but only with a two-thirds majority, a complete impossibility in the world of lobbyists and continual battles for votes. It is a situation that probably could only be resolved if there were a serious collapse and something had to be done.

The financially ailing DDR had to be taken into this social system, which still functioned at the time, without any preparations made beforehand. By raising taxes, the western part of our country spent more than a trillion German marks to help redevelop the eastern part! Our fellow citizens there are cared for (almost) as if they had been in our system (= each group of young people pays for the elderly) since the beginning, and had been putting money in the Western banks for the past fifty years. That has completely destroyed the basis of calculation for our system.

In this regard, the island of Germany has been a solitary beam of light for decades. It alone has had this kind of attraction, and nonetheless it is perceived incorrectly by the peoples of the world. We are, despite our otherwise bad international reputation, the legal and illegal refuge for many who consider themselves needy and who do not have a home on this earth. Asylum-seekers from all over the world want to reach Germany, where they are free of all economic worries, for you will be taken care of by the state without doing anything. Even the flow of refugees from Yugoslavia poured hundreds of thousands into our country. More refugees from there came to Germany than to all the other countries in the world combined. Our eastern borders have been left almost completely open for organized groups to bring people in. The Asians pay twenty thousand dollars for a passage into Germany; they are flown to Warsaw and escorted until they set foot on the other side of the border. If they are then picked up by us, they must be received and cannot be sent back. They count as immigrants or refugees or asylum-seekers. By law, they obtain the status that is characterized as "welfare recipients." The expenses for all of this must be raised by local authorities who have been designated by the government to care for the immigrants.

To determine whether they can be sent back to their homeland requires an individual trial, which can take at least two years! In the meantime, they live among us with all of the rights that we have. They are assigned to accommodations, often against the will of the owner, but are also accommodated in hotels at the expense of the state. They receive food, clothing, and furniture, including monthly allowances that are often higher than the pensions of some of the locals. And yet these locals have worked their entire lives for that money. It is especially harmful that by law the immigrants are prohibited from pursuing a job or earning a living without first receiving permission from the state. Yet the state won't give its permission until the legal proceedings concerning their residence have been closed. In the meantime, they are at the mercy of their boredom and populate the streets with all the consequences of their lack of commitment to the local society. . . .

. . . Our government is the prisoner of its own laws, which were passed during more favorable periods. There is no way to distribute the refugees more evenly among the European countries so that the social expenditures connected with them become more tolerable. From the outset, our dear Switzerland has spared itself from such burdens with its very "effective" legal measures (see above).

An exception to all of the legal regulations here are the "immigrants" from Russia who can prove that their ancestors were Germans, and also those who claim to be Jewish. I say this with caution because these "Jews" come from Russia uncircumcised and often without any knowledge of the religious traditions. They are supposed to be accepted into the existing congregations—and then the problem with Jews is transferred to the Jewish community itself. Severe difficulties often arise because these newcomers outnumber the Jews who were there before. The immigrants in both of these groups, the Russian-Germans and the Jews, immediately receive all of the state's support and financial benefits, as I have noted above in talking about "welfare recipients." Thus, it is not any surprise that many Eastern Jews who at first had emigrated to Israel prefer to leave there and emigrate into Germany. That has led to much conflict and anger in the long-established Jewish communities here, since they are inundated with a huge number of mostly young and dynamic immigrants. They are driven against the wall, and it has sometimes led to grotesque clashes within the communities. The new, Russian-speaking members of the community easily win all of the votes and occupy influential positions in their community. Because of these clashes, the newly founded Jewish community in Speyer was *not* accepted into the Jewish religious community, and therefore formed its own, more fundamentalist "organization." The leadership of the

Heidelberg community and the "Jewish university" there have also fallen into the hands of the young fundamentalists. In Mannheim, as I've heard, the old leaders were still able to win. I assume that you have different sources and are better informed about these problems, which even came up at the recent Zionist Congress in Basel.

I have attempted to outline for you the background, both financial and otherwise, of the protectionist position that has arisen here recently against a continued "foreign infiltration"—that is, against an additional increase in the financial social problem, and I have attempted to show the various focuses in our country. It has nothing to do with the normal aversion of people against everything "foreign," but has originated out of a precarious situation that has developed in a number of places, and which the government has not yet figured out how to correct. All groups in the society give their opinions. As bad as it is on the individual level, it nevertheless shouldn't be generalized. It is not a "national movement." It must be acknowledged that despite horrible events of the past years, the willingness of our population to help is among the best of other leading nations fighting for a practical humanization of the conditions in this world.

Treatment of the "foreigners" and suggestions for resolving this burning issue have become campaign topics for next year's election. Our government has been powerless with regard to a reasonable regulation of this problem. We will see next year what kind of "blooms" sprout from the emotions on this sociopolitical topic—and then we will be able to recognize what is actually in the hearts of our people! Those who have already been victims of our "nation's heart" have an especially important role in closely watching this process! . . .

———— 🐚 ————

NOVEMBER 17, 1997

Dear Paul,

. . . I am sending you some pictures from Rülzheim. You wrote me recently that you didn't know whether the old war memorial, which begins with the name "Feibelmann," was still standing outside the town hall. We drove there on a Sunday afternoon to look. We took several pictures, which show you the current condition:

The old town hall was demolished and has been replaced by a brand new modern building. The memorial still stands in its old place. It is dedicated to the memory of the members of the community who died in both world wars, but it has also been dedicated to "The Victims of the Tyranny: 1933–1945." The list begins with the name Feibelmann.

In the photos, you see the western part (entrance) of the old synagogue, and the northern view with the windows tapering toward the top. Within the synagogue, a bronze plaque is mounted on the east wall, commemorating the synagogue and its desecration in 1938, but also calling to memory all of the Jewish families of Rülzheim who were affected by the terror at that time. The restorers have closed the alcove for the *Aron ha Kodesh* [holy ark where the Torah is kept] (probably in ignorance of its function and meaning). On the north wall, there is a picture with a psalm; I have enclosed the German translation for Psalm 126, which is probably what it is.

Today the synagogue holds all of the usual cultural events: lectures, concerts, and exhibitions. When we were there, a water color exhibition had just been opened, which gave a general idea of the former function of the building. For about twenty years now, smaller synagogues are also being restored whenever enough remains still exist and the corresponding expenditure is possible. The Jewish community of the Rhineland does not take these buildings back into its care, contrary to its practice with the old Jewish cemeteries. Very probably, however, they watch to make sure that these buildings are connected with cultural functions. The synagogues could only be rededicated if there were a *kahal*, an active Jewish community, at the location. The Torah cannot be left alone in a closed building. We spoke recently about the cemetery in Rülzheim. . . .

I still haven't been able to gather all my thoughts about a topic that you touched on in your last letter: the question of why some camp inmates survived so long as bosses, and even lived to see the liberation of the camps at the end of the war. Perhaps they survived because they turned into "valuable workers." But who of us, who lived through very different situations, would want to pass judgment on them today?

I came across a related topic recently when I saw that prominent Jews had been discussing whether it was an error that during the Third Reich, so-called "Jewish officials" were willing, especially in the big cities like Berlin, Frankfurt, etc., to help the Jewish communities that still exercised freedom of "self-administration," and, as a German assistant so to speak, deliver their communities to the KZs in an orderly fashion—down to the tracking of the last member of the community, who kept himself hidden in some basement. I read in something by Hannah Arendt that without the preliminary work and the service done by these Jewish self-administrations and "Jewish elders," it would have been impossible to carry out the Shoah in such a precise and well-ordered manner. Indeed, without these well-functioning and cooperative "self-administrations," there would have been chaos everywhere, and very many lives could have been saved. There are people who have "calculated" that at least one million more Jews would have survived. Who knows?

Of course, today we can lean back in our chairs comfortably and discuss such things. Yet these discussions cannot consist of throwing around more assignments of guilt; rather, the purpose of such discussions should be to search for practical applications for one's own future. . . .

NOVEMBER 17, 1997

Dear Emil,

My answer is coming a little late; there is a reason. Greta had her hip replaced (October 29th); her old one was worn out. She was in the hospital for a week, and I was with her every day. Then she was sent home and three different nurses came daily to treat her. She was already on her feet the second day after the operation. . . .

I owe you an answer to two letters. There is so much to write about the different topics that it almost makes me dizzy. First to your letter of October 14: it doesn't seem as if a solution for the Israeli-Arabic situation will be found any time soon. The King of Jordan didn't think about giving the Palestinians a home when he controlled the region. His own country is populated for the most part by Palestinians. I think a better solution would be for Israel to give Jordan a portion of the West Bank so that the Arabs could settle there instead of creating a whole new country again. The Arabs are already spread out among too many countries. The more Arabic countries there are, the more hostility there will be among them. I mentioned once that it is difficult to deal with dictators—and we shouldn't expect to see any democratic governments among the Arabs in the coming years.

What is the meaning of the word "home"? The Jewish refugees from the time of Hitler made their homes wherever the boat landed. I became an American overnight, and at that moment I only had mixed feelings about the country where I'd been born. Europe is taking a step forward. In the foreseeable future, the populations of the different countries will all declare themselves Europeans with different languages (Switzerland), and will learn to live peacefully with one another. In contrast, we see the Arabs: they live in different countries, each of them with a führer who would gladly devour the other countries. The obsession with power and land often proves to be the misfortune of an entire nation (Kaiser Wilhelm II and Hitler).

A growing young man accepts as a matter of course that he was born in a certain country (home) and with a certain religion. Both of these things are the basis for later hatred. Especially religion will soon rear its ugly head. The young man will be convinced that his religion is the only correct one, and that only his God exists. Of course, there is no proof of that, but since the speaker is a good orator, he can convince his listeners. And anyway, he is saying what they want to hear. They need this guide, for without him they would be unable to find the path through life. Contrary to that, we have also seen that there are people who have converted from one religion to another—finding the religion that is convincing for them. Yet they find only human ideas, not their God. So they go through their lives empty. The "New Europe" unites the different nations politically, but as far as religion goes, they could never all be placed under the same roof. Tolerance is only possible for the individual; it doesn't exist for the masses. These are harsh words, but I don't know any other way out. Was it the Nazis who moved me to think like this?

The apology of the French Catholics came too late. This tardiness causes one to doubt any guarantee for the future. And thus we will continue, in order to give life some meaning. I don't know where and how everything will end, and at my age, I am certain I won't see any changes.

Your letter of October 19th is very instructive with regards to the "foreigners" in Germany. One day Germany will wake up from its socialist dream, shake its head, and regard economics from a different viewpoint. I have watched this state of affairs through a friend in Dortmund. Gerd Friedhoff (not a relative) started out as the president of the labor union in his company. Then he represented the company with respect to the employees, and now the company has stopped its operation—Gerd lost his job. He is not worried. He receives so much support that he can hold on until he starts getting his pension. I once wrote an article about conditions in Germany: how good it is there and how well the workers are treated, and how it nevertheless remains an economic power. The article was published, and I hope that no one remembers it now.

My son-in-law is not doing well at all. The progression of the disease [ALS] can be seen almost day by day. We cannot talk much with him about it anymore; it is too painful. I have the feeling that he has come to terms with it, even though he sometimes speaks of medicines that don't exist yet. The drowning man reaches for straws.

Best regards to both of you from both of us,

DECEMBER 6, 1997

Dear Paul,

Hannukah and Christmas are just around the corner; the year 1997 is drawing to a close. So before all else, I would like to thank you for your willingness to engage in an honest exchange of thoughts, even on issues that are not at all our expertise—even when we are not the active subjects, but only spectators of the events in the world—and even if in the end we cannot escape the effects of these events.

People often use the end of the year as an opportunity to exchange best wishes. In our case, we naturally think of health as well. The older one gets, the less one expects hopes in this area to be fully realized. We begin to deal with advancing physical restrictions. The preservation of the ability to perform the necessary vital functions of life becomes the foremost objective, even if one has already learned slowly to accept one or another limitation and adapt to it. It is a universal wish that we may remain exempt from any avoidable pain.

Business concerns no longer stand in the foreground. It is good when we are able to set the pieces on our economic chessboard in such a way that we no longer need to make decisions that weaken our nerves. I have already expressed my deep respect for your decision to give up your home because of your family, and in their interest dare to start again. I hope that you will be able to maintain your old, close friendships, and that at your current home you will be able to put down some new roots. I am also thinking about your daughter and son-in-law, both of whom must walk a very difficult path to deal with their fates.

One of the most important factors in maintaining our mental health is the acceptance of the circumstances that we are dealt. We must be prepared to say "yes" to them, even if we were only partly able to choose them ourselves. Therefore, I look into the future without any great apprehension; it will be my future, and I will have to accept it, insofar as I can't change it.

I wish both you and your wife Greta all the best for the New Year, and especially that you can be together for a long time and enjoy both nimbleness of mind and body—and I hope that I, too, will continue to gain from the discussions that your health will make possible . . .

In conclusion and instead of any new problems, I would like to add some news that would perhaps be interesting to both of you:

My son-in-law Christian, who has also taken over my practice, was born in Lyon in France after the war in 1950. He was the child of a German student who later became a secondary school teacher, and who raised her son as an only child without a father. Thus, Christian grew up "fatherless." He went to a high school in the United States as an exchange student for a year, and studied medicine in Germany—and long ago became an undeniable part of our family. After all, he is the husband of our daughter Martina, and father of our grandchildren Ulrike, Rolf, Simon, and Jochen. You can pick him out, along with his family, in our family photo.

Several years ago, Christian began searching for his lost father—and in 1997 he was successful, which made all of us happy: father and son could finally, with a blood test, prove their relationship to each other. Since then, they have seen each other several times and gotten closer. Elli and I are very happy that I am no longer the only acknowledged grandfather of our Stabenow grandchildren! And what will be interesting for you to know is that my newly gained partner in the role of grandfather is of Jewish descent, and survived the Holocaust in very complex ways: he is the writer Edgar Hilsenrath. As a twelve-year-old in 1938, he was able to leave Germany in time. He then went to relatives in Romania (in Bucovina), and was sent with them to the ghetto of Moghilev-Podolsk in southern Ukraine. He dealt with his fate there, and was liberated from the KZ by the advancing Russians in 1944. He lived in Israel for several years after the war, went from there to France (Lyon) in search of his own family, and met a German student—Christian's mother. He left and went to the United States without knowing about the child, and came back to Germany in 1975 where he has lived ever since as a writer in Berlin. He wrote several award-winning novels about his Jewish life and experiences and his corresponding outlook on the world. Edgar Hilsenrath is several years younger than I am, but he is not that healthy anymore and, therefore, not capable of traveling too often. I haven't spoken to him personally; only Christian and Martina have met with him. They have done so several times and have talked to him frequently on the phone. We hope, therefore, to have him visit us at some point in Schifferstadt. I know him from the television, where he appears every once in a while as a witness from the KZ generation. All of his books, even those written in the United States, were in German. I don't know whether they can be found in English. I am very impressed by his books, which in style and content are completely different from what one would expect. I am looking forward to speaking with him personally soon.

Since this discovery, I have seen Christian and Martina's family with different eyes. Occasionally, I stroke my grandchildren's heads and imagine what fate they probably would have been forced to expect if they had been born during our Third Reich! If you would be interested in any of the German editions of Hilsenrath's books, I would gladly send one to you. As surprising as it was for me, it is also satisfying that I cannot only feel a mental and spiritual connection to your people of the Old Testament, but that it has also turned out that I have some actual ties there, even if they came in a roundabout way—and completely without any effort on my part. . . .

―❀―

DECEMBER 20, 1997

Dear Emil,

I almost fell from my chair when I read the story of your son-in-law. It sounds like a fairytale. It proves that reality can often surpass the imagination. And in this case, that is exactly what it has done. That could also be material for a book. Where does the name "Hilsenrath" come from? Was that the original name, or did he Germanize his possibly Romanian name? Did he assume the name to save himself during the Holocaust? Or did he take on the name as a writer? I am eager to hear all the details. The entire story is hardly conceivable, and I can't stop talking about it. I wait in anticipation for your meeting with the new member of your family. What do the other members of your family think about suddenly finding Jewish blood in your clan, and, especially, how does Christian feel after discovering that he has a Jewish father? In these types of cases, it often happens that the person who searched for his ancestors regrets that he had ever been curious enough to do so. In one instance here, a well-known woman said that it was bad enough to be a refugee—and that one did not need to discover he was a Jew as well. Life is difficult enough as it is. Our Secretary of State also knew where she came from, and was quiet about it until a newspaper wrote her story. The mayor of the town where her grandparents lived had told her about it years before, and perhaps she stuck the letter in some drawer so that no one could find it. As you see, it is not always pleasant to find skeletons in the closet. . . .

JANUARY 3, 1998

Dear Paul,

We've all made it to the New Year. I thank you for your greetings and wishes for the New Year—and for the letter with questions about Edgar Hilsenrath, which reached me on New Year's Eve.

Let's stick to this topic today, which, I think, is a completely happy one. It is too terrible to think about what would have happened if the slightest detail of this story had been any different from the way it actually is: then Martina's current family wouldn't exist at all! Christian and his children would not be here—something that we shouldn't even bother thinking about!

We knew from the beginning that Christian had grown up without a father. Christian's mother never spoke of the details; she bore her fate on her own, raised her child with an enormous amount of love, and took care of his education. She had given up investigating the whereabouts of Christian's father, who knew nothing of Christian's existence.

For Christian, the only part of his father that was tangible was his name; he knew neither the whereabouts and address of "Edgar Hilsenrath," nor his fate. He didn't even know if he was still living. But one day, he discovered a German writer who had the same name as his father. His books reflected a difficult, Jewish fate—and Christian began collecting publications of and about Edgar Hilsenrath, which provided him with an insight into his thoughts and career. In one of his books, Edgar described his stay in Lyon, and the time coincided with Christian's birth.

One day I picked up a video in which I saw the real Edgar Hilsenrath wearing a beret. I was thunderstruck when I saw Edgar's face: it could just as easily have been Christian's face. The video covered a discussion about the still unconstructed memorial to the Holocaust for the city of Berlin. I got in contact with Lea Rosh, the leading journalist of the discussion. She gave me Edgar Hilsenrath's address. I was already as good as certain that he was Christian's father because of the physiognomy. For his whole life, Christian hadn't known whether his mother had told him the entire truth about his father; he therefore got in contact with Hilsenrath with a great deal of caution. Father and son began to approach each other with small steps. They met, spoke with each other, and easily got used to the idea that they were possibly related. Finally, they decided to be certain by obtaining a blood test, which had a clear, positive result: Edgar is Christian's father.

Edgar hadn't married until he was older, and doesn't have any other children. Edgar's brother is married in America, and doesn't have any children. When Christian got in contact with this newly added "uncle," the uncle became almost immediately jealous of his brother Edgar, who suddenly, without really having had a hand in the matter, had gained with Christian a complete and easy-to-handle extended family!

I have the impression that everyone involved is very happy with the familial development. The "genealogical gap" in our well-mixed family is now closed: originally, we were all Catholic. But: Guido's wife comes from old Prussian nobility and is Lutheran; their children were admitted into the Protestant Church (that was available where they are) [Guido is one of Sold's sons]. But Guido's family has no problem participating in a Catholic service if the situation arises. Markus [another son] found a wife from Bulgaria who was raised Greek Orthodox. Owing to circumstances, their children are Catholic. Gisela [one of their daughters] was Catholic, but is completely indifferent about religion. She has two children with her husband, who doesn't profess any particular denomination either, and whom we regard very highly. The children's denomination would probably be called Protestant. Also, Gisela and her husband haven't actually performed the civil marriage ceremony (imagine it: they are "living in sin"!). Martina's husband Christian was raised as a Protestant, but now we know for certain that he was the child of a Protestant mother and a father who in some way feels as if he belongs to the Jewish denomination. Their four children are Catholic, three of them are servers in the Catholic parish—and their (as we found out for certain a few weeks ago) "half-Jewish" father (following the Nazi nomenclature) has no problems accompanying his children to Catholic mass on occasion.

As you can see, our family is completely tied up in the historically evolved succession of the Mosaic monotheistic tradition. My wife and I have no problems accompanying our grandchildren to their different places of worship. Two of Martina's children who have remained in the Jewish-Catholic tradition play trumpet and English horn. At the service the evening before Easter, they played their instruments for the glory of God in the Catholic church. On Easter morning at six o'clock, they did the same thing at the Protestant service. When one keeps in mind the source—historically—from which individuals receive their "religious convictions," our family can hardly have any problem with Christian's father's religion. These convictions, as I wrote you earlier, were mostly the result of "sovereign decisions" and by no means the result of one's own thought. We are completely content with our clan (*mishpacha* [family, in Hebrew and Yiddish]).

Paul, there is neither Christian nor Jewish "blood" in our clan. Such ideas stem from the ideology of the Nazi race mania, which has obviously etched itself deeper into the memory of other peoples than one could think possible, and which strangely enough shines through again and again between the lines of the newer Jewish literature. It is true that in human biology there are different physical predispositions that become apparent in the phenotype of the person. Mental and spiritual predispositions, however, are more individual, can be acquired, and cannot just be assigned to a phenotype. Religious convictions and dogmas have never been determined by one's biological gene pool. At most, "racial skeletons" haunt only a few old-fashioned minds. . . .

DECEMBER 30, 1997

Dear Emil,

. . . The holidays are over and the tumult has passed. Thus, from year to year we celebrate the same festivals and believe in our reasons for doing so. In my opinion, it is really more tradition than it is belief. The human being's level of development two, three, or four thousand years ago was very primitive. People believed more in prejudices than in a faith. These biases led to cults, a few of which survived and became religions. And that continues today, for there are always people who are finding new paths and followers. It is the same old story that I have mentioned several times before: people need a crutch to help them through their lives. And in the process, they become the slaves of their beliefs. People in America are well known for their generosity and for financially helping the underprivileged. It is now coming to light that most of these donations go to churches and synagogues, which use a large amount of the money themselves. During the Middle Ages, the churches constructed luxurious buildings (gold on church cupolas) and supported artists. In general, the churches were the rulers of the land during the Middle Ages. It was recently said on TV here that in four thousand years, the churches hadn't achieved anything good. I just read a book by William Manchester with the English title *World Lit Only by Fire: The Medieval Mind and the Renaissance.* Since the book has been translated into ten different languages, I assume that it can also be found in your library in German. It describes the power and sin of the Church (especially the pope), how many Christians were killed by Christians, and how little a human life meant. The book also explains the grounds for Luther's Reformation.

Many thanks for the pictures of Rülzheim. I helped design and pay for the plaque in the synagogue. Near the town hall, there used to be a plaque with the name of the Jews who died during the First World War. It doesn't seem as if this plaque can be found anymore. Oskar Feibelmann was a neighbor and one of my mother's relatives. He died in the Kaiser's war and not under Hitler. His wife was a victim of the Holocaust, and his only daughter—Karolina—died a few years ago in America. I still remember when she was born. Mrs. Feibelmann began a grocery store in her living room to make a living.

The book by Liana Millu is more difficult to read than the one by Goldhagen. The one is more personal, the other objective.

I know about the vices of fanatic radicals from any religion, and I have no sympathy for them. The time will come—certainly after us—when science will find developments that prove the majority of religions to be incorrect. It took the Catholic Church three hundred years before it agreed that the earth was round. And how many people had to pay with their lives for believing that? And how long will they be convinced of the infallibility of the pope? There are too many miracles carried over from olden times when there was little reasoning, and which are nonetheless still believed today. (Moses spoke with God!) . . .

JANUARY 16, 1998

Dear Paul,

Your letter at the end of the year, December 30, 1997, was very thought provoking and expresses perfectly the mood of those of us who have grown older. As I was reading it, I had your picture from November lying next to me, in which you are overjoyed great-grandparents with your great-grand-child on your lap, looking down with complete admiration for your next generation. What will be in store for our descendants? And can something be done to affect their future?

When our first child was born, we first thought about his physical and intellectual development. But we also wanted to impart our life's experiences to our children's generation. We were able to assure that all of them received a good education, and we were very happy with the scholastic successes of our children. But even during the time of their schooling, I recognized that along with what they received at home, there were other factors that contributed to the molding of their character: their classmates, the teachers, the "spirit" of their scholastic community, and the rest of their surroundings had a huge impact on them. I was amazed one day when one of my sons said, "By lecturing us, you want to spare us from having painful experiences, yet why won't you just let us have our own experiences, even if they are harmful? Nothing makes one more cautious than when he burns his own finger!" I responded that an intelligent man shouldn't want to repeat all of the painful experiences that had already been suffered by humanity. It is more advantageous to observe carefully, and draw conclusions from the experiences of others. But as I have seen in my own life, "collecting experiences and utilizing them to your advantage in the future" is not only a difficult task for the individual. It is just as difficult in the sphere of relations among different peoples. And it is most difficult when, as you have written so correctly, the thoughts of people are held captive by ideological or religious dogmas. Obviously, our former rabbi Max Meir Ydit was right when he said that during the course of his life, the individual can only change his way of thinking with a great deal of difficulty, but he can do it. True changes in the thoughts of entire peoples, however, require the development of two generations—if their ideology is not severely shaken by timely catastrophes. As you see, even the viewing of kind great-grandparents who are happy and proud of their great-grandchild automatically returns me to the topics that fill both of our hearts—and whatever makes the heart full, should also make the "tongue speak" in God's name. . . .

We can all see the power of religious and ideological dogmas in separating people and groups of people, but I do not have any exaggerated hopes that the natural sciences will provide any intellectual element that will tie peoples together. As in the past, the sciences serve mostly their sponsors, and, protected by espionage and counterespionage, they help the powerful of the day exercise and strengthen their power. However, what we need is something that can be denoted as "a humane way of thinking." But that would require the renunciation of revenge, of egoism, the renunciation of exercising power against one's neighbors, and the development of a public spirit that watches out for the well-being of the other just as much as for one's own advantage. The best-developed example of such a mode of conduct, I believe, is in the teaching of the well-known Jew who critically examined the theories of his fathers ("*Auge um Auge . . .*") [Eye for an Eye], which he knew very well. About some of the opinions in the temple, he said: "You have heard that the 'elders' (the 'writings') say . . . but I say to you . . ."! Naturally, with that statement he distanced himself from what the temple-servers denoted as their "law," and thus had to suffer the consequences. I am speaking here about the "historical" Jesus, not about the religious sects that people created afterwards according to his alleged teachings, and that then became the fundamentalist groups that are found and continue to be found in all types of religions. The search for a true teaching, as far as can be made out after the blurring and misinterpretation of over two hundred Christian denominations, is the motive of my religious studies, the reason that for years I have been going to relevant lectures where I can have these types of conversations with other listeners.

The human necessity for some type of spiritual security cannot be satisfied by any type of science. It can correct some flaws in reasoning and mistakes that have arisen during the development of religion, in that it uncovers objective correlations among things. Then, within this researched area of the faith, "knowledge" is possible, "belief" no longer necessary and, in fact, no longer appropriate. Scientific knowledge is conclusive for everyone and then the discussions are over. But can modern science give our lives meaning? The increase of the number of sects and new, often comical, religious groups in the last decades suggests the opposite. . . .

A little while ago, I wrote some words about *Der Aufbau,* in which I complained about the collection of purely negative reporting on Germany. I would like to change somewhat this assessment today. Since then I have read some articles with a balanced judgment. . . .

Regionale Schule Rülzheim
76761 RÜLZHEIM

DECEMBER 15, 1997

[Composed in English]
Dear Sir Friedhoff,

During a visit of the greatest library in Speyer (Rheinland-Pfalz) we found your book "My Story, Paul Friedhoff." We read in this book and we found that it was very interesting for us, because we are working just now about a documentation which is called the Jewish cemetery in Rülzheim. We would like to translate some chapters of your book and use them for our documentation. If you allowed that, we could be very glad. Please give us an answer as soon as you can, because we want to begin with our work.

Yours sincerely,
Class 10

Paul Friedhoff

To the Tenth Class of the Regional School
76761 RÜLZHEIM
Germany

JANUARY 10, 1998

[composed in German]
Dear Students,

Your letter of December 15 was forwarded to me. My wife and I have recently moved to Williamsburg in the state of Virginia. We wanted to live near our children.

Rülzheim is the town where I was born, and where I hoped to lead my life. Yet, you know why we had to leave our home prematurely and with tears in our eyes. Only the memories remain.

I will gladly give you authorization to translate part of my book, *My Story,* and use it in the documentation about the Jewish cemeteries. I hope that you will then send me a copy of it.

With best regards,
Paul Friedhoff

[postscript composed in English]

P.S. Your English letter was very well written, a compliment to your teacher.

———✿———

FEBRUARY 6, 1998

Dear Emil,

Yes, retired people are the busiest people in the world; thus the somewhat belated response to your letter. I also had to work on my lecture that I am giving here in the home next week. Naturally, it is about the Holocaust. I don't know how the older people will take the topic. There are about three hundred people here, from the ages of about sixty to ninety-seven. On February 17th, we will see how many of them are interested in the Holocaust. I will tell them how I was affected personally during the Hitler years. I will see whether it turns into a discussion afterwards. I will give you a report about it.

Your letter with the commentary on your family and the expansion due to Edgar Hilsenrath reads like a fairytale. Otto Landman was here to visit us, read the letter, and made a photocopy of it. I also wrote to *Der Aufbau,* which on August 27, 1971 had a review of the book *Der Nazi und der Friseur* [The Nazi and the Barber, by Edgar Hilsenrath. It is a satire about the Holocaust in which a Nazi mass murderer takes the identity of a Jewish friend he killed in a concentration camp during the war.]. I just finished reading the book in English and now have an understanding of his attitude toward God. He wasn't there to prevent the Holocaust either. The book is well written, even though I find that the metamorphosis from a Nazi mass murderer to an innocent Jew is not very well explained and appears to be impossible. The main themes of the book are excellent, his style acceptable, and the section from his autobiography very striking. Another of his books is supposed to arrive here in several days. In the meantime, I am reading a very detailed book about the history of the Jews, going back to the year 2000 B.C.E. [before the common era]. It seems as though I'm in school again and learning something new. As in the Middle Ages, there were constant wars and I can't imagine how the Jews are still around. The eternal hostility among Jews, Arabs, Greeks, and Romans had less to do with religion than with land. At that time, there were just as many gods and cults as there are today. The cults that enlarged and became religions had better "minds" than the others; they had heads of state who introduced religions into their countries and said that theirs was the only correct one. And again, people believed that the religion they grew up with was the only correct one. A few became critical and doubted what was presented to them. They realized that superstition was the foundation of most religions. I often say that if Houdini had lived two thousand years ago, he would have been declared a god. In those days, whatever people didn't understand or couldn't explain became "divine." In many cases, that hasn't changed much today. Again and again, new prophets will emerge who know everything better, and who will find followers for their new ideas. Man can be manipulated very easily, and needs help to come to grips with life. In Clearwater, we had the headquarters of the scientologists, who are so popular in Germany! . . .

I am going to a doctor here who told me, the first time I went to him, that he was an Arab. And I said to him that I was a Jew. That initiated a friendly discussion. He said that a person is successful if he leads just one other person down the right path. That is very wonderful, I told him, but how many single people can one convince?

And then on TV, we again hear the tirades of different clergymen, and you wonder, who could believe in that? And when you hear about how much money is going into their pockets, you wonder if their followers have any sense at all, or if they just blindly let themselves be convinced. Have we made progress since the time when every person had his own God? Has the development of the religions helped humanity? It is often said that more people have died in the name of God than for any other reason. Why? Then we can come back to Hilsenrath, when he asks where God was during the Holocaust. And God came down from his throne and said, you are right. . . .

Greta is completely back on her feet again. The operation is forgotten, and now she is doing water exercises as additional therapy.

Best wishes and regards to you and Elli from both of us,

FEBRUARY 10, 1998

Dear Paul,

Your news about the correspondence with "Class 10" from Rülzheim made me very happy. I see it as an important piece of the puzzle in our efforts for better mutual understanding, and as a step in the direction of a better future. It is true that the class can be told everything possible about the Holocaust during regular instruction; but then, the next hour they have math or gym, and the topic of the Shoah will have disappeared beneath the river of everyday impressions that a student must continuously digest. But if the students make such a subject their own topic, they are thinking about it more. They discuss it with one another, they want to organize something themselves, and the topic grasps them on an emotional level. And then it won't be so easily forgotten. During this class's inquiry, it is certain that no new facts will be discovered about the Jewish cemetery in Rülzheim. The class "works out" the topic for itself and by itself. It then becomes theirs, and they will no longer fall quickly for any slogans given out by anyone.

My initial impulse was to get in contact with this class. Therefore, I wrote them a letter, but after some thought decided not to send it. Young people (they should be about sixteen years old in Class 10) should not have the feeling that someone from the outside is trying to guide their thoughts in a particular direction. As for me, I am very anxious to find out how they are dealing with such a topic there today. But I will wait until a few weeks go by, and then I, too, will ask the class for a copy of their work. And then I can reconsider whether it is appropriate to intervene with help or corrections—or to speak with the teachers. Above all else, we "old people" can talk about what once was. But it will rest with the youth everywhere to determine what will happen in the future. For that reason, I think more about the future than about the past.

In Germany now, it is a year for elections. They are taking place amidst very unfavorable economic conditions. Perhaps this will put the nation to a test. The population is unhappy with all of the political parties. Instead of completing the important tasks on the agenda and facilitating solutions, they block one another for tactical reasons having to do with the election. Kohl and his people have been unable to run the government for two years now. The unemployment rate has risen to close to five million. The welfare state is not being maintained, and the people are not being told the truth. Not a soul can be seen, not even in the opposition, who has offered any solutions to the problems. Reunification caused a change in the world economic situation, and the continuing ramifications that we will have to deal with in the future cannot be predicted absolutely. In addition, our state financial reserve has already withdrawn more than one trillion German marks. Coping with reunification has proven to be much more difficult than expected. The youth in the old DDR, who were accustomed to being occupied and drilled every single day, like during the Third Reich, and who had to fulfill their marching duties and other duties to the state, are now on the street without work or prospects (twenty percent unemployed!). It is fortunate that no führer has emerged today (yet?), who can inspire the masses and tell them "what's what." And I'm not forgetting that the old DDR completely backed the Arab countries and was against the West; many of the people here haven't reconciled this. The radicals from the right are recruited mainly from the East; they are even supported from abroad and send in their mobile troops everywhere they think their "deployment is worth it." Thus, they get more attention than befits them. They have also begun (according to the teaching of Mao's "March through the Institutions") to infiltrate the government institutions, which is not easy to control in a free country. I still haven't seen the personality who can break the news to the public that the "seven fat years" are at an end—and that we're at a point where we finally have to make a tremendous change in the way we think about things, and that even mentally, we'll have to adapt to the new situation in the world. On the other hand, I hope for the "powers of necessity," which have made sure that the trees don't grow into heaven—that they may cause a general change of views that makes possible a good existence in the future.

Hilsenrath's brother is living with an extended family in America. He also got in contact with us and sent us his family tree, which went centuries back, as "proof of his Jewishness." We learned from it that there have hardly been any changes of faith in the family caused by marriages. . . .

(February 17, 1998) Dear Paul, your letter of February 6, 1998 has arrived recently at my desk, and is also waiting for an answer. I want to begin with it right away:

Today is the day that you will be speaking to your fellow residents in the home about the Holocaust. I would be very interested in their response. I would imagine that today people are no longer easily shocked by facts that would provide them with news. But it is certain that the personal consternation of some of the listeners will reawake painful emotions, and that those emotions will have to be overcome again slowly by the problems of every day. It is somewhat different for us, the "perpetrators." For us, the Holocaust is more than a permanent, unpleasant topic because it is always conveyed with severe, generalized reproaches, pointing toward the past and the future, for everyone without exception, whether or not he had something to do with it himself, and whether or not it took place during his lifetime. Certainly, one must make sure that it is not simply pushed away and forgotten—and something must be done for that. But if one intends that the "perpetrators" seriously reflect on these events and change their way of thinking, and if one thinks about how such things can be made impossible in the future, then he shouldn't go too far. At the very least, he should encourage and help those who have good intentions. It should also be realized that by approaching the situation without making distinctions, we are doing the same thing that the "Christians" did to the Jewish people a long time ago. And now, two thousand years later, the grandchildren of these Jewish people are still supposed to pay for the fact that their great-great-great-great-grandparents were once accused of being involved in the execution of a founder of a religion. Certainly, none of us should complain about being dragged over the coals for "our deeds." But sometime, sometime, sometime, there should be an end of these generalized reproaches, which extend even to the generation of the grandchildren. We have to get together and reflect on possibilities for a better future. And to begin that, we must dare to take small and cautious steps toward one another. I hope that in the long run, it will be recognized that everywhere, in Israel as well as here, the voices are getting louder that are speaking of a peaceful coexistence—and that, to this end, we must also be willing to participate in working toward a "reconstruction." The good intentions for doing so can certainly be found here.

Hilsenrath writes: "God was not there to prevent the Holocaust."

You write, "the eternal hostility among Jews, Arabs, Greeks, and Romans had less to do with religion than with land." I must admit that both you and he are completely right.

I see it this way: ever since there have been people on this planet, they have been trying to defeat their rivals. And so they have waged war on each other, for sources of water, for land, and for livestock. It was about means of power that could assure one's own survival. Later it had to do with "colonies," their exploitation, riches, and the black people as work slaves. Today it is about outdoing one's rivals economically, about oil, even about the water from the land of Canaan, which flows out from Mount Hermon; without that land an expansion is not possible for that religion. Throughout the world, millions of people have massacred each other because of these problems.

The development of "religions" in this "game" became influenced by an additional factor. Originally, religions were the intellectual achievement of developing human societies. Man felt the necessity to think about himself and his environment. That happened in different ways, which we have already discussed in detail. For reasons of stability, the führers of such groups attached great importance to ensuring that all subjects submit to the same religious rituals. Securing a common ideology is indeed an important aspect of leadership; it makes it easier to manipulate a group effectively. Then, on a certain spiritual and national level, it is possible to feel threatened not only by the guns of one's neighbor, but also by his way of thinking and his ideology. This scenario has led to many religious and ideological conflicts, even if, for the most part, those things could not be separated from real, substantial interests in power. The actual reasons for such wars are often concealed by propaganda. Now we are fighting for God, for the king, freedom, the fatherland, democracy, justice; recently we were fighting against any "isms," but it is always for something higher, good, "intellectually worthwhile." So everyone carried his "god" on his banner—regardless of how it was misused.

"The war" didn't have anything to do with God himself, even if people were appealing to Him. War is a completely human invention and achievement. It would be an entirely greater achievement to consider how one can finally cope with this problem, which is founded in general human nature, and get out of this misery.

The construction of the cathedral in Speyer began in 1030. The first Jewish settlements were documented between 1070 and 1080. The Jews were from Mainz, where they were being persecuted at the time. They fled to the protection of the Speyer Bishop, who expected, as it says in the documents, to build with their help ". . . a cosmopolitan city out of a small town, and to boost even further the honor of our town. . . ." Actually, the Jews were the only ones in the country who had the right to lend money on interest. Because of religious reasons, it was not legally possible for the Christians to demand interest of borrowers (and, actually, it is still not legal today! It is still considered sinful according to the teachings of the Church). It is also very probable that the Bishop of Speyer had finished building his dome with loans subject to the payment of interest.

But in many places the regulation arose stating that debts were dissolved when the lender died, which meant that during pogroms the debtor was often well on the way to giving in and killing his former lender to relieve himself of all debt. (The indebtedness to Jewish lenders was a main cause for the eternally strained relationship between the impoverished population and the Jews.) I still haven't been able to find out how much such "disencumbrance mechanisms" played a role in, for example, the case of the Speyer cathedral. At any rate, it was stated in the documents that the Bishops of Speyer had a good relationship with their (!) hard-working, tax-paying "refugee" Jews, whom they even allowed to settle on the land outside the city wall and use for their own community, which they afterwards included within the protective realm of the city wall. . . .

Your contact with the Arabic doctor pleases me very much. It reminded me of my first encounter with a Jew. Before 1978, I had never exchanged a word with a Jew! (Finally, it was Fritz Löb. He was visiting Schifferstadt from Buenos Aires, and I was called as a doctor to look at him. Beginning there, I became interested in the Jewish problem.) Sometimes people get in touch with others, come to realizations, can check their own thoughts by talking with others, and might possibly have to modify their way of thinking. Such a changing of view cannot come from outside and certainly not from commands from "above." Loud arguments seldom convince anyone. Something must first happen internally with a discussion partner that reprograms emotions into the correct direction. That cannot happen in huge masses of people or globally; it takes time and patience. Inner knowledge can only grow slowly. It is a difficult path that demands patience. But that doesn't frighten me. In the end, even the mass of humans is composed of honorable individuals with whom one can talk. The masses can be reached with public relations and megaphones and thus be made to be enthusiastic for something, but they can also be incited to cause great damages. A true reconstruction or rebuilding has always demanded time and patience. You obviously realized in your interaction with the Arab that at the bottom of it all he is a human being with the same feelings and problems that all of us have. . . .

---❀---

MARCH 5, 1998

Dear Emil,

Your last letter was very far-reaching and comprehensive. You explained many of the thoughts that you had touched on before, but at the same time also introduced many new topics. It especially surprises me that until 1978, you had never spoken with a Jew. You must have sat at the same desk with Jewish students in high school or at the university. How did it happen that you never got into a conversation or discussion with them? Or was there, at that time, something to the extent of a Jew-free school or university? Or was it the Hitler period then? I don't know how old you are so that I could figure that out. I assume that between 1945 and 1978 there were no resident Jews in Schifferstadt. Then where did you meet the first Jew?

I haven't heard anything else from Class 10 of Rülzheim. I am happy that you are interested in their project, and hope to hear about it via you.

Is it, therefore, the Kohl administration's fault that Germany has so many unemployed? Someone has to take responsibility for it. I am only happy that it is impossible to make the few Jews in Germany responsible for it. Or are there, in fact, some who do that? With its socialist views of the past years, West Germany was only a few steps away from the East German practice of guaranteeing workers a permanent job. Indeed, I, too, was once enthusiastic about German socialism, but I didn't know that in the process the government's purse was being emptied. That doesn't get recognized until afterwards. The situation is ripe for another Hitler. It is the same way in South Korea, where the workers are in the street, loudly holding the president responsible for their problems. . . .

It seemed that my lecture about how the Holocaust affected me was well received. More than fifty people came to hear me. Several wanted a copy of it, since they couldn't understand everything. Many people in our home have problems with their eyes and ears. The questions afterwards were not surprising. I left out the horrible details as much as possible.

You are right: sometime, sometime, sometime, everything should be better. May one hope for it? Christians say that Jesus was the Messiah. If I remember correctly, all wars were supposed to stop with the arrival of the Messiah. All swords were supposed to become plowshares. The opposite is happening. It is incredible how many people had to give their lives in the name of God. Most religions—especially the big ones—are founded on myth. Spinoza said that the Bible is a work by humans. The intention of the authors was to tell history. Each person can regard the Bible however he wants and doesn't need any higher approval for doing so. Until recently, superstition had been a part of every religion. Among other things, superstition spurred the Inquisition and held the Jews, in particular, responsible for many things—for example the plague, which killed exactly the same percentage of Jews as Christians. Everything that didn't go properly was the fault of the Jews. This was happening two thousand years ago, and no non-Jew fought for the Jews. During the time of Hitler, even the pope remained silent. Why should he also protect the Jews! They could even have been considered a thorn in his side. And thus it continued, and still continues, in the minds of many people who are full of hatred. And hatred doesn't die out. Am I a pessimist?

It is true that the Jews lent out money on interest. They had to do that for two different reasons: because of the guilds, they were forbidden to become handworkers, and they needed the money to buy security and accommodations from the nobility. It is not known how much they had left for themselves after that.

Best regards and wishes to you, your wife, and the whole family,

---

MARCH 11, 1998

Dear Paul,

Your letter of March 5, 1998 arrived today; it made me very happy and I will answer it immediately. It would be best to start at the beginning of the list.

1. Contacts with Jews: I was born in 1920, went to elementary school in 1927, went to Speyer in 1934 for boarding school and high school. Only a few Jewish families lived in Schifferstadt. There were only two Jews on the boys' playground: Heinz Mängen, four years older than I, and Hans Michael Bender, four years younger than I. I had no relationship at all with either one of them. Heinz Mängen emigrated to England in 1935; he visited me in Schifferstadt around 1980 in connection with my research for the book about the Jews from Schifferstadt. Hans Bender's father, Oscar, emigrated to the U.S.A. with his family in 1938–1939, after his release from the KZ in Dachau. Hans now calls himself "Mike," to avoid a German name.

Because of a compensation issue, I have corresponded with him several times in the past years, but have never spoken with him personally. We had no Jews in our high school class in Speyer, and I can't remember any Jewish students in any of the other classes either. Yet I will clarify this issue next time I meet with all my classmates (insertion after meeting with friends: according to our school's yearly report, in 1933 there were four Jewish students at the high school, none of whom are mentioned in the following years). Almost all of the Jewish students in Speyer went to a different high school where the subjects were oriented more toward business occupations. The (few) older Jewish girls from Schifferstadt went to school in Mannheim. Certainly I spoke with Mr. Rubel as a child when I had to go to his store to buy some little things; he always asked my parents about me, yet that was no real conversation. After Kristallnacht in Speyer I saw the shards of glass on the path to school. I knew the photos and stories from the "Stürmer" [a Nazi newspaper, founded in 1923 and characterized by its harsh antisemitism] very well; it was plastered everywhere. I didn't see any Jews during the war, nor for a long time afterwards. Yet I must correct myself here: the former orthopedist from Heidelberg, Professor Dr. Weil, Jewish, came back from emigrating to America and reclaimed his chair. I heard him lecture and took exams from him, but didn't have any other contact with him. I also sat at the feet of the philosopher Karl Jaspers and the surgeon K. H. Bauer, whose wives were Jewish, but whom I didn't know. These professors lost their chairs during the Third Reich, and were placed back in their positions in 1945. On a walk with Juri [his Russian friend, mentioned May 8, 1995 and August 2, 1997] in the seventies, I got to know his daughter's boyfriend, Ralph Giordano, a radio and television journalist from Westdeutschen Rundfunk [West German public broadcasting]: that was my first true, though short, conversation with a "half-Jew" (Ralph wrote the story of his family's survival in the Hamburg underground, *Die Bertinis* [The Bertinis], several parts of which have been made into films). In 1978, I was awakened personally; I became sensitive to the topic when I was called as a doctor to look at a Jewish man who used to be from Schifferstadt. He had come from Buenos Aires to visit his old hometown and became seriously ill here. It was Fritz Löb. In the following years, Fritz has taken every opportunity to come back to Schifferstadt. I became friends with him, and began to write down whatever he could tell me. That led me to the archives where I was able to fill in the gaps in my knowledge, and I decided to record everything that had happened in our houses then, and to become more active about pursuing the topic. Much of the information in the book about the Schifferstadt Jews came from Fritz Löb—and that book is what finally led me to you.

2. "Class 10": I got in contact with them. The Rülzheim municipality

has had this piece of class work printed; it is one hundred and fifty pages long and will be introduced to the public in the middle of February at the Rülzheim synagogue. Within a few days, I should be receiving a copy (certainly you will also).

3. [Sold answers Friedhoff's question about unemployment, writing that the issue is very complicated and that any particular government has only limited control over the state of unemployment.]

4. Hilsenrath: two weeks ago, Edgar held a book-reading in the casino of a small, nearby city. Christian took this opportunity to arrange a family meeting with him for the first time. Elli and I went along as well. At first, we both sat in the audience without acknowledging ourselves, since we wanted to let the young family meet their new grandparents alone at the beginning. During the break, however, Hilsenrath came over to us. We could only exchange a few words, since as an author, he had to be there for the audience. At the end, we took the Hilsenraths back to their hotel and went home to Schifferstadt. The Hilsenraths stayed with Christian and Martina in Schifferstadt for the next two days, and we didn't really get involved in that either. We drove together to Speyer one evening. Because of the amount of time they had, it was a very jam-packed tour that only could have given them a very superficial impression, since it soon became dark. At the time, the Speyer Mikve [ritual bath] was being restored and has now been closed for weeks. Even during dinner, we only engaged in very cursory discussions, since they mainly had to do with topics of the family. Edgar is already physically restricted, but mentally he is very sound and a very sharp observer. He uses every minute to write. The next day we were with both of them in Worms: Jewish cemetery, synagogue, the Raschi house. We led him around in a wheelchair. After two days, they flew back to Berlin. They are coming back again soon. We had a good impression of the encounter on both sides, and will certainly meet with one another again.

5. My colleague from Kassel with ALS is also confined to a wheelchair and no longer leaves his room. He has to use the artificial respiration machine more and more. The initial depression has slackened somewhat, and again, to some extent, he is willing to eat. His voice is very weak. I talk with his wife on the phone to keep him from overexerting himself.

6. The Jews await their Messiah at the end of time. He will straighten out everything on the earth beforehand, even the political situation of his people.

The Christians, on the other hand, have developed the idea that Original Sin, which has come into the world because of the disobedience of their ancestors in paradise, and which will be passed on as an inheritance from person to person for all of eternity, was first made redeemable by the crucifixion of Jesus Christ. Christ's messianic deed has, therefore, already taken place. The human being can only be blessed with this redemption in one way: by being baptized. After his death, he will be held responsible for the course of his life at the Last Judgment. Both very different ideas about messiahs are the contents of a faith. They are interpreted and realized in very different manners by their respective followers, which has led to dozens of contradictory versions and denominations. All of the religions that I have gotten to know so far try to push a certain order (ethic) into the private and social lives of their followers. That is always only partially successful because all religions suffer from the inability to change the basic tendencies of the human being who has evolved from "primeval life." The animalistic quality always breaks through the surface. The emotions natural to a human being—love, hate, jealousy, greed, the aspiration for power, egoism, irrationality, chaotic thinking—can be found in the individual and the society in varying amounts. With every infant, they are reintroduced into the world in their original condition, and it is then the task of a long education to make both that individual and the human collective adapt to the current conditions and be compatible with one another. But wherever one looks, and during all periods of history, human beings have been guilty of "inhumanity." Human intelligence is obviously not sufficient to allow people to consider the welfare of their neighbors if it is disadvantageous to themselves. On the basis of our thousand-year-long experience, we have ample reason to be pessimistic about this issue. Nevertheless, one could take this situation and pull out the morals for himself, and begin to change his own way of thinking and his own behavior (in the language of the Torah: to reforge one's own (deadly) sword to a useful plowshare).

7. Private or real causes due to surrounding conditions laid the foundations for the greater number of all the wars in history. It was first the missionary (monotheistic!) religions and political ideologies, who tried to force their own religion and way of life on their neighbors, that began wars because of ideological reasons. In the process, the commanders quickly realized that it was profitable to fill up their warriors with religious emotions, for it made them more willing to fight. Nowadays there are more solid considerations (self-interest) behind the decisions for war. Ideals are still always used as a pretext in order to motivate the soldiers psychologically. However, since the courses of wars can be simulated at least partly on computers that are somewhat incorruptible, I harbor the hope that in the future, at least the big world wars can be "rationalized away" beforehand. In this respect, computers could prove to be important thinking aids, though they would nevertheless not be able to rid the world of murder and manslaughter on a small scale. . . .

———— 🦢 ————

APRIL 3, 1998

Dear Emil,

. . . I am happy that you are now in contact with Class 10 of Rülzheim. I haven't heard anything from them yet. . . .

As I once wrote you before, I, too, went to the high school in Speyer. I was the only Jew in my class, and I felt at home. I don't know what was happening behind my back. Yet I did have the feeling that I wasn't quite welcome. What came later proved it. . . .

I see that you are keeping me up to date on the situation with Hilsenrath. . . .

My niece brought me the book *Geschichte der Deutschen* [History of the Germans: From Their Origins until Today] by Joseph Rovan. [The full title is *Geschichte der Deutschen: Von ihren Ursprüngen bis heute* (München: Deutscher Taschenbuchverlag, 1998).] It is from their beginning up until today. It is a thick, eight-hundred-page book, and as of now I have gotten to page fifty-two. I think it's too bad that this history isn't taught in the schools. The word "barbarian" appears very frequently. I'll give you several lines that struck me in particular: "German antisemitism was a great historical ingratitude." "The Germans are colonizers, assimilators, and rulers." "Not only the Romans, but also the Jews (who came with them as Roman citizens) lived in the Rhineland long before the 'Germans,' and that means the Germanic 'occupying forces,' settled down there. Germany and the German people, and all of German culture, would not exist without Rome and Israel." I am very excited about what else I will find in the book. I will let you know about it. . . .

———— 🦢 ————

APRIL 15, 1998

Dear Paul,

. . . Both the word and concept of "barbarian" come from the Greeks. *Barbaroi* or *balbaloi* means stutterer or stammerer. The Greeks gave this name to everyone who came to their country and was unable to speak Greek. The Palatinate *babble*, the French *balbutier* for "talking incomprehensibly" come from this Indo-Germanic etymology. *Barbaroi* were all of the uninvited intruders into the Greek region who, as is probably still the case everywhere today, conducted themselves in the same way, and there were never any people who should elicit our sympathy so justifiably.

Here, too, things are repeating themselves that already happened in the past: the foreigners and the immigrants are being excluded. At least initially, they are barred from associating with the locals. Even the group of

German Jews is unhappy about the further immigration of Jews from Eastern Europe. They are repeating the history of almost one hundred years ago, when the established Jewry of Berlin called the arriving immigrants from the east "pants salesmen," and in the end made sure that the immigrants continued their migration and went to America. The established Jewish community of the Rhineland-Palatinate, with a seat in Neustadt, which has managed the Jewish property that still remains since the war, is in a constant battle with the immigrant Jews in Kaiserslautern and Speyer for many reasons. And because they cannot agree with one another, they are letting the German courts decide the matter! Because of their rejection by the existing congregations, the young congregations have set themselves up as separate and independent organizations. They even had to fight a legal battle for their names, though the German authorities stay away from the difficult question as to who can be regarded as a Jew. In Israel it works thus: the child of a Jewish mother is Jewish. But is someone still a Jew who, because of the conditions in his authoritarian homeland, could neither be circumcised nor have acquired any knowledge of the Torah and its religious applications, nor has any knowledge of Hebraic writing? The German authorities stay out of this issue. They pass over to the Jewish congregations the responsibility of judging the ethnic origin of such a person. For the Jewish authorities, someone is Jewish if they are acknowledged as such by a Jewish community—and here is the true reason for many clashes. Must one's Jewishness be acknowledged by the old Neustadt congregation, or can the newly formed groups of arrivals make out those things among themselves, without asking Neustadt? In this situation, it doesn't have to do with religion alone; these issues also have a considerable financial backdrop because of the state support that depends on these things. At any rate, the Jews from Kaiserslautern and Speyer have since separated from the Neustadt community and founded independent religious "organizations," which hasn't exactly made resolving the clashes any easier. In addition, the young Speyer congregation is demanding that the city of Speyer construct its own Jewish prayer room in the area of the historical Mikve of the city, which is being renovated now. This issue has also led to problems of jurisdiction with Neustadt. Not much of the internal, emotional discussions among those involved reaches the public; nevertheless, the battle is being conducted with considerable fierceness and in all possible ways. . . .

There is a psychological rule that says nothing can weld together a community as much as an outside threat. Naturally, the opposite also holds true: if such a threat vanishes, then the feeling of community diminishes. The individual members go their own ways—and the community dissolves. This principle can also be studied easily in the example of the

Eastern bloc–Western bloc, as well as with the current Gulf coalition. And it is also true: a country disintegrating domestically loses its strength beyond its borders. There is reason to worry about the current domestic situation in Israel. What will become of that country if one day the Arabic threat were to disappear? . . .

MAY 8, 1998

Dear Paul,

Happy birthday and congratulations on your ninety-first year. This time my greetings might not be on the exact day, as they were when I used the fax machine, for I also wanted to enclose a CD. And in any case, the letter is being sent from Bad Hofgastein, where we are spending three weeks rejuvenating our bodies again. Throughout the year, you and I both occupy ourselves with the problems of our unfortunate pasts, and we suffer from them. And we think about the reliably uncertain progression of our world. Both things are legitimate and necessary. On a birthday, however, we pass our whole life in review and consider our assets and liabilities. We know that a generally pleasing balance in our accounts is not the only thing that makes our life worth living. If we reflect only a little bit, we notice that along with the material necessities, there is also a spiritual necessity to find a meaning for our existence, a necessity to find balance and a type of inner happiness—something that the successful bustle of every day cannot provide by itself. It was also like that for our forefathers, since ancient times. Besides their violent past (violent in land acquisitions) and civilizing past, they have left us with cultural assets such as poetry, art, philosophy, and religion, creations that can reconcile us to their primitive state of humanity. And that remains true even when we no longer agree with their religious ideas and feel provoked into a constant conflict with their earlier world of thought.

As an example, I am sending you a CD for your birthday with two-thousand-year-old poetry and music, reproduced by the Collegium Musicum Judaicum Amsterdam. I've heard it several times "in real life," and it's also shown up in the Worms synagogue on occasion. With the exception of the conductor Chaim Storosum, the performers are all young people who are extremely dedicated to what they're doing. When you listen to it, you can shut your eyes, forget your everyday worries and daily realities, and understand the worlds of ideas from past generations. You can realize that despite all other adversities, we are not so completely alone on this earth with our feelings.

Even if we can no longer really share our ancestors' views of the world, on your birthday I hope for you the pleasure of being able to enter, in an hour of contemplation, that river of questions and longing that induced our ancestors to devise a world more lofty than the one we encounter every day. Music of the synagogue, passed on from person to person for thousands of years, could first be written down only several centuries ago, and today with recordings it is available to us at any time. It is good that there are not only the melodies, but also, above everything, some texts. One, for example, is Psalm 23, "Adonai Roie." It is very comforting to older and sick people, and it can help one deal with the course of life.

For today, happy birthday again, and best wishes to you, your wife Greta, and to all of your relatives. With a shalom that comes from the heart—and in friendship,

------❧------

MAY 8, 1998

Dear Emil,

. . . I received two books from Rülzheim. They wanted me to send one of them to the Holocaust Museum in Washington, which I have done. The museum has already thanked me for it. The children and their teachers have created an unbelievable memorial for Rülzheim with this booklet. It seems as if a consciousness of guilt is perceptible in one part of the youth, whereas the others shave their heads and act foolishly. The percentages cannot be determined. I have enclosed a copy of my letter to the mayor and the teacher.

Joseph Rovan adopted his name in the resistance. His name was Rosenthal. My niece in Switzerland who brought me his book about the Germans knew his parents. He was Jewish and later became Protestant. In the end, that religion didn't suit him either and he became a Catholic. . . .

Somewhere Rovan says that the German population at this time was ninety to ninety-five percent peasants. A smaller portion of the populace was in commerce, the Church, part of the nobility, and perhaps some were Jewish. Jews were also sometimes peasants. And then later he writes:

> The faith of the sixteenth century held that God had shown humans different, apparently incompatible, ways to reach him. . . . In both their minds and their hearts, rational thought was eclipsed by a tremendous amount of superstition. In the truest sense of the word, the fear of God frightened and horrified the people. The love of God, the rapture, and the grateful admiration of him were constantly forced into the background and overshadowed by the dark fear of hell and powers of the devil that

could take possession of people, especially women. Was it necessary for
them to throw the poor souls to the cleansing flames in order to protect
the general public—and to save themselves from the fires of hell?

During this period, apparently superstition, hell, and the devil out-
stripped religion. Thinking back, I felt something like that during my
youth in Rülzheim. I can agree with him that the peasants of my time were
still living almost in the Middle Ages and knew very little about the
progress of the world. They lived on a small portion of land that they had
inherited and never let go. Going to church was their only opportunity to
put on better suits and better dresses; perhaps also they dressed up for the
church festivals. Instruction in the schools was minimal, and was almost
completely forgotten during the difficult years of work. But they heard in
church that the Jews had murdered their God, and this caused a hatred that
was not forgotten. This type of person formed the majority of the population until modern times. As a young man, I didn't realize any of this. I
accepted our and their way of living as a matter of course, and I couldn't
imagine that life could be different somewhere else. This view was also the
result of my minimal and provincial education.

Until about 1930, Rülzheim didn't have electricity or plumbing, but
open sewers. I saw peasants pull a plow through the field with a horse and
a cow (forbidden in the Talmud), and today I think that it must have been
like that during the Middle Ages as well.

George Will—one of the most well-known journalists in our country—
wrote that ten percent of the population in the Roman Empire was Jewish.
If we had the same proportions today, then there would be two hundred
million Jews. The direct and indirect persecution of the Jews by the Church
has seen to it that today (1998) there are only thirteen million Jews in the
world.

This thought caused me to start an investigation about ten years ago. I
wanted to know the ratio of Jews to non-Jews among Nobel Prize recipients. It turns out that 547 Nobel Prizes were given out to Europeans and
Americans (thirty-eight to other countries). Of the 547, 107 went to Jews
and 440 to non-Jews. At that time, the population of Europe and the
United States was 932 million, of whom twenty million were Jews (the six
million murdered by Hitler included). One out of 224,000 Jews and one
out of 2,073,000 non-Jews won the Nobel Prize. You think how much
further humanity would have come if in the last two thousand years the
Jews hadn't been decimated.

If three million of the six million Jews killed in the Holocaust had been
children, then possibly thirteen potential Nobel Prize winners lost their

lives. We come to these figures when we try to transform the cruelty of human beings into statistics. And why must something like that have happened in Germany, in the country where I was born and once called my home? I cannot understand it. Rovan opened my eyes in some respects.

When one compares the Jews with the development of the Germans, it can be seen that the Jews—the people of the book—could read and write much earlier than the Germans. That is also the case with France. The Germans, on the other hand, were more intimate with the sword and conducted constant wars during the Middle Ages and in our time. By "our time" I mean the wars of 1870–1871 and both world wars, all three of which were started by the Germans in order to get revenge on their "archenemy" for invading Germany in earlier years. And always with the goal of conquering new land—a remnant of century-old thoughts and plans of princes, kings, and kaisers. Castles are memorials to their capabilities and power (for the most part, they resulted from a series of robberies). The nobility didn't read the books that the Church burned. Either they couldn't read, or the sword left them no time for reading.

I once had an encounter with a representative from Neustadt, and was not very impressed by him. It was during a discussion about the cleaning of the cemetery. As I recall, in my time—in my youth—every Jewish congregation managed itself. Some congregations had a rabbi who came to funerals and took certain responsibilities. In Rülzheim, it was Rabbi Dr. Einstein of Landau. I can still remember his Swabian dialect; he came from Ulm and was related to the famous Einstein. His son Paul died during World War I, and his daughter, Anne, lived her last years in Israel. . . .

MAY 25, 1998

Dear Emil,

Your wonderful birthday letter and enclosures came right on time. Thank you very much for the beautifully written words as well as for the warm melodies from the olden days. When I listen to the music, I feel as if I am transported back millennia, and in my thoughts I can picture the epochs when the composer lived and worked. And it took hundreds of years before people were capable of writing down his work. During the course of this period, his name was forgotten, like the names of so many who were productive long ago. Even though many of our ancestors could read and write, their work was only written down and kept if it had something to do with religion. Religions were often the impetus for art, perhaps because they [the religious groups] were the only ones who could support it financially. That is—to be ironic—a good reason for the existence of religions. Yet I am going too far, and so I will end with that and thank you again for your wishes on my birthday.

I would very much like to know the dates of your and your wife's birthdays, so that I might return the act of kindness. Please send them to me with your next letter. I hope that you are well rejuvenated.

All the best, from Greta as well,

JUNE 11, 1998

Dear Paul,

Many thanks for both of your letters in May. My answer is delayed, for after our vacation I fell into the hands of the urologist. I am being operated on tomorrow, June 12, 1998.

Best regards to both of you,

Emil

JUNE 14, 1998

Dear Paul,

First of all, I want to thank you for both your letters in May 1998. Since I last wrote, I am somewhat fit again; my systematic training and the spas at Bad Hofgastein improved my joints a great deal, and the "plumbing" is running better again after the operation the day before yesterday. . . .

I want to get in contact with Rülzheim in the next few days. I am happy that the final form of Class 10's idea has found your approval. I will let you know about my conversations with them.

Since I last wrote, I have found out about another project that impressed me greatly. A high school in Eifel has leased a huge area where a KZ had been constructed during the Third Reich. After the war, however, the spot was completely leveled. The students want to investigate the history of this forgotten camp during their free time, excavate the site, and reconstruct it, which will certainly demand a great deal of time. You see that there are not only "skinheads" here. Even if, as always, the peacefulness in the country hardly finds a response from the media, one shouldn't disregard the efficacy of that kind of behavior.

I have no objections to Rovan's theses. However, it would be more accurate if he didn't point his statements toward "the Germans"; his comments are just as valid for the entire "Western world" of the Middle Ages. Even

Karl the Great, whom our French friends happily claimed as "their" kaiser, could neither read nor write. He had his specialists for that. Even his international treaties were not always written down; he employed people who had to learn them by heart. Mainly, things were written only in the monasteries in order to make copies of the Holy Scriptures, and for the studies there. Before the invention of the printing press, no one wanted the public to be able to read either—even reading the Bible was forbidden to non-priests. "Biblical history" should instead be preached to the people from the pulpit. For this purpose, depictions of "biblical stories" were painted on the church walls; with their help the preachers could enlighten the people about the meaning behind the Church. The series of paintings were called "Biblia pauperum" (Bible for the poor people). The later emancipation of the European population from "Church and Throne" began step by step with the Reformation. The "French Revolution" was in 1789. Our Rhineland-Palatinate became French in 1792, which is why the liberation of the Jews had begun here then. With Napoleon in 1808, that liberation was contained somewhat, but we were nevertheless several decades ahead of the other remaining German regions in Rhineland-Palatinate.

Statistic: you know that the number of Nobel Prize winners is not dependent on the size of the population, but on qualities that certainly have nothing to do with "head counts." We were often told in school how many holy or famous men came from especially large families. But they always forgot to mention how many wrongdoers or criminals would not have been born had their parents just limited themselves. An English scientist is supposed to have said once: "I only believe those statistics that I have falsified myself." Nevertheless, it is interesting and useful to work through such examples. In doing so, one might even learn some things. . . .

You ask about my birthday, so that you can possibly "return the act of kindness" for the cassette. I just happened to discover the recording in a library and thought that it might interest you. Naturally you can know my birthday; it is December 3, 1920. But listen, we have made an agreement with all of our acquaintances that in the future we won't give presents on any of these commemorative days. We have everything that we need, and we're tired of racking our brains over presents because of some certain day. When we see something that we think could give pleasure to one or another of our friends, then we give it to them without any particular reason and regardless of the date. . . . On my next birthday, for the first time in my life, we won't be at home, but spending several days in the mountains with a group. I will be very happy if we both leave things as they have been. Just write me some greetings—and remain healthy yourself so that we can continue to exchange our thoughts for a long time. (My wife Elli was born March 31, 1924). . . .

———— ✿ ————

July 5, 1998

Dear Emil,

First of all, many thanks for your letter of June 14th. You didn't wait long to renew the correspondence after your return from the hospital. I am happy that the "plumbing" is functioning again. I didn't know that it was causing you trouble. Usually everyone of increasing age has something to complain about. My doctor explained to me in a nice way that I will just have to get used to my "sore" feet. And yet that is not bad when considering my age, or thinking about my son-in-law.

I haven't received any answer to my letter to Rülzheim. Why not? I would have liked to explain to them that during the period of mourning, the men didn't shave, and the rabbi from Landau always came to the funerals. Perhaps you can tell them that at some point. I was surprised that they had completely overlooked the children's burial grounds. Questions to me would have explained some things.

Even though during my time antisemitism was customary at the universities, it would be interesting to find out what kind of education the skinheads have today. I always thought that a good education would steer the children and youth onto the right track. The conduct of the high school in Eifel emphasizes that idea with the current generation. Perhaps you have an opinion of it.

You write that "biblical history" was preached to the people from the pulpits in the church. Falsities about the Jews were also spread with this "biblical history," and with them antisemitism. Those are memories from my youth in Rülzheim. Was that not the case in Schifferstadt? You, nevertheless—I assume—went to church regularly and heard the priests' sermons. Was Schifferstadt an exception? In any case, you have more or less acknowledged that a part of the "enlightenment" came from the pulpit of the church. What, then, was the "enlightenment"? Religions are difficult to describe and understand. But we know that all religions, such as Buddhism, Jainism, Confucianism, Taoism, Shintoism, Zoroastrianism, Judaism, Christianity, Islam, and the Reformation, were invented by a man, who in so doing, created his own God. We don't know how many men and women there are today who do the same thing. But we see no end to how many gods there will be in the future. Everything would be good and acceptable if religion didn't include a hatred of others. I believe that in some way I am repeating myself. Forgive me. . . .

———❦———

JULY 18, 1998

Dear Paul,

Before I get into your letter of July 5, 1998, I have to tell you something interesting:

Speyer received a visit from a Jewish class of its Israeli sister-city Javne. It was the first time that such a class came to Germany for a true student exchange. There were twenty-two young people, aged fifteen and sixteen, boys and girls. They were distributed between two high school classes of the same age in Speyer. They went to school with their German classmates and lived with their families for two weeks. It was an attempt that de Gaulle and Adenauer had started with great success after the last war between the former "arch-enemies," France and Germany. None of the guests spoke German, not even the teachers who came along.

Erez, the guest who was staying with the family of our daughter Martina, actually spoke English (along with Modern Hebrew) that, according to his boasting, he had learned on the street, but which supposedly he could not write. Initially he had some problems coping with his situation; it was the first time in his life that he was without his parents. He didn't eat or drink anything the first evening, and he hardly spoke a word. He closed himself off completely. I had the impression that he was simply afraid of us—or that he was homesick, or both. The other students must have been in a similar situation. I heard that some said they would be afraid to ride on the train or take a shower here—it reminded them immediately of the German concentration camps (with two generations distancing them from the Third Reich!). This mistrust and caution remain very deeply ingrained, and have been very visible in the majority of people. And it will stick with us for generations more.

But it reminded me of my own experience when I met Fritz Löb, which I've already written you about. He had pneumonia and I had to examine him. No one could tell that I had to overcome some inhibitions within myself to touch his (Jewish) body during the examination! The conditioning by the Nazi propaganda penetrated so deeply into my being, even with the ensuing knowledge of the events in the KZ, and despite my earlier internal rebellions! It took me some time before I could be uninhibited with Fritz—and then a friendship developed between the two of us.

Similar for me were my first few days in Israel, during which time the pictures from Auschwitz constantly thrust themselves between me and my conversation partner even though we had grown close in our letters beforehand. There, too, it took me some time before I was able to overcome my prejudice.

Now I have clearly become more inwardly liberal and no longer have any inhibitions speaking with Jews. On the first evening, I wanted to save Erez from his cocoon and draw him into a conversation with me, so I asked him to explain a Hebraic expression. As I was talking, I consciously touched him lightly on the arm—and I noted how he jumped with surprise. What mechanisms might have been in his mind at that moment? . . .

Rolf, our partner for Erez, told me that the Israeli children were considerably better informed about the political events in the world, and were more interested in them than our children. They also had much more information about the Third Reich.

Yesterday, the principal from Rülzheim, Mr. G., told me on the phone that during history instruction for the lower classes, the Third Reich is mentioned primarily as an addition to the other material, and that its critical appraisal is reserved for the upper classes. . . .

In your letter, you ask about the "education of the skinheads." I don't have documents about it, only newspaper reports. I once asked two Abitur classes whether they believed it was possible that a right radical group could develop in Germany again. The students claimed that this would be impossible after everything we had experienced here. I, myself, was not so certain. When one looks around the world, he recognizes the radicalism that comes from a great need to change an intolerable situation. There is also the ideological, the religious, and the racist radicalism that serves one's own views of the world. Here there was the leftist radicalism when there was still no unemployment and prosperity was bursting at the seams. And there is the radicalism of the young men, who, caught within the onslaught of their masculine hormones, no longer know where they should even begin with their strength. There is the well-ordered, positive enthusiasm of the masses (unbelievable!), as we have just seen in the stadiums of the soccer championships [the World Cup]—and likewise the negative side of it, the butchering of fans outside one's own arena, even in nations that were actually well known for their proverbial, sportsmanlike fairness. The sociological analyses by the police psychologists were supposed to have revealed that the majority of these nasty thugs are not from the underworld of the needy, who are uneducated and unemployed, but from the "better circles." Their desire for revelry and their aversion to being at the mercy of a restrictive, social order lead to such excesses. The political radical right, whom one would have thought of first, are actually underrepresented here. They could be led quickly out of the underground with their campaigns, and "deployed" with determination using the secret modern instrument of power, the "Internet."

After the Russian revolution at the end of World War I (which was characterized by "Free Love" with the disintegration of civil marriage), there were thousands upon thousands of young people in that country without parents, who marched through the country in bands, stealing and murdering. It led to an intolerable situation. In a few months, Lenin removed this problem of "hooligans" in his own quick and relentless way: a large part of them were simply shot on the spot, and the others were exterminated in camps. But how should a civilized country handle a problem presented by these kinds of "outlaws"? The French dealt with it correctly: they immediately used the law to sentence such people, and they locked them up for a long time. Even a country under the rule of law can deal with this problem; yet it must do so quickly and full of determination, which is very difficult for us, since the murderers have access to every public means of legal redress, while hardly anyone cares for the victims afterwards. It is known that the victims have "no press." Do you know any country that is completely free of this problem?

I have gone to church somewhat regularly for my entire life, even today, and I try to separate completely the all-too-human problems that are there, as everywhere, from the spiritual-philosophical meaning. I am alone with my thoughts in church; I take advantage of the time to read the ancient texts and to reflect. It is a compulsory break, so to speak, that I impose upon myself. I remove myself from the problems of everyday life. The location permits thoughtfulness much more effectively than our everyday surroundings. To a certain extent, my practice is a remnant of the old idea of the "Sabbath" for one's soul. In a much different way than before, I have become a fan of the teachings of the historical "Rabbi Jehoshua," which he preached during a time when doing so meant his certain death. Today he still lives on in the churches that bear his name. I, of course, separate him from the denominational "ecclesiasticism" that came into being after him, and which in his human dimension has often become a completely distorted picture of his teaching. My distance from the Jesus preached about in the many Christian churches has grown for some years, and for some years has been the reason for my theological studies. I also find some older people (seniors) there who have become pensive, who have gotten over the storm of their lives; one can ask them questions. And I try, as much as I can, to translate into action, in my life and my surroundings, those things that I recognize as the essentials of Jesus' teachings. All religions are carried on by human beings who incorporate their own personal interests and behaviors into their ways of looking at the world, and in that respect they are hardly distinguishable. Thus, religion is obviously not a protection against the "basic, inhumane tendencies" born into every person. It can be no surprise to one who has carefully read the Torah to find that the same basic problems are in every society, religion, and ideology.

Religions and ideologies were always put into practice by human beings—and for that reason were always basically distorted. One must always work for a fundamental humanistic attitude within and outside of even religious societies, which becomes a lifelong task, as the prophets knew long ago. After everything, even Cain had descendants who, according to the text of the Torah, were saved from destruction by "a sign" from God himself—and their natural tendencies have been distributed somewhat evenly throughout all of humanity, as one can see from the further course of history. It is exhausting to keep oneself free of primitive, human reactions for the long term. It was not the churches and the religions who invented wars and who make me skeptical, but the people within these institutions who make nonsense of their own ideas. One can probably be a good human being in any religion, even despite such religions. . . .

The Israeli guests of our students have arrived again safely at home with their parents. It was very good that they were all together in Struthof, to the KZ in the Vosges mountains. They cried together there—and this connects one more deeply than any holiday happiness. In the enclosed interviews with the teachers, you can read how much this experience overshadowed all their other undertakings! I don't know whether they were also told details about the camp there. Struthof wasn't an extermination camp. As we found out afterwards, two of our Strasburg University teachers carried out their "scientific" experiments on people there, on chemical weapons and the causes of jaundice. I knew the "professors" who were involved to be completely normal, inconspicuous lecturers. We had no idea about their "field of work" and their work methods behind the curtains and away from Strasburg. Accordingly, we were severely shattered to see their names come up in the Nuremberg doctor trials. Professor Haagen, our hygienist, kept the Allied trials (one after the other, Americans, Russians, and French) busy for years. Everyone examined his research very thoroughly and was interested in it (on virology). Then the French sentenced him to lifelong forced labor in 1952—in 1955 set him free again—and again he was able to do his scientific work at well-known universities. Professor Hirt, who should be judged considerably more severely for his chemical weapons experiments, kept himself hidden in the Black Forest after the end of the war, where he shot himself, as was discovered much later, on June 2, 1945. The results of his experiments also became an important basis for additional "benevolent" research elsewhere. . . .

———❀———

AUGUST 12, 1998

Dear Emil,

I got the chance to hear your voice again, and listening to the Palatinate dialect was like hearing once again the sounds of home. Not sounds of home, actually, but sounds from my youth. We have already talked about the word "home," and I think I said that we find our home wherever we put down our bags. At any rate, it was nice to exchange a few words with you. Why don't you have e-mail? That would make it possible to communicate some brief ideas more quickly.

Now to your letter: you described the visit of the Jewish youth with a great deal of warmth and understanding, and I thought that maybe *Der Aufbau* would be interested in publishing it. I sent it to a man there whom we know, and we will see what he has to say about it. It is easy to understand the attitude of the Israeli youth, and only this kind of exchange will show them that perhaps the new generation will conduct itself humanely. It is possible that the youth today will never understand what motivated their fathers and grandfathers.

Rovan says that a historian wrote the following: "I deny the right to speak about Hitler to anyone who doesn't believe in the existence of the devil." Rovan continues: "Hitler marched through Germany and assembled the masses at events that increasingly began to resemble an ecstatic cult." So we come back to the expression "cult." I maintained in an earlier letter that the origin of every religion was a cult. And that the successful cult was one led by an excellent speaker. We also know that Hitler prohibited all religions and wanted to found a new religion based on Nazism.

Rovan writes, "An antisemitism arose in the middle and upper classes of society that was motivated more by racism than by religion, and which stood in the way of the results of a century of Jewish emancipation and assimilation." Then: "Antisemitism presented itself as a useful means to connect the masses of small farmers with the interests of the big landowners." And: "War may be a horror, but it is also loved. Survivors who came back to their ordinary lives went into raptures about the glorious deeds that they had seen as either participants or witnesses." These few excerpts are examples from a well-written book. When Rovan is speaking about Friedrich II, he is speaking only about the history of Germany, even though other countries also attempted to enlarge themselves at the expense of others. And even today, that hasn't been stopped.

You go to church on a more or less regular basis so that you can be alone with your thoughts. Are you not bothered by the sermon? Albert Schweitzer developed his philosophical ideas in a prison, where he didn't have paper or a pen. I can imagine going to some fields or into the forest to be alone with myself, but not to the synagogue. It is almost the opposite there. Several of the prayers disturb me and make me restless. I just can't believe that some individuals were chosen to speak with God and others weren't. . . .

. . . David continues to go downhill. I take a sedative whenever we visit him or he comes here. He has daily aid now; our daughter can no longer manage it all alone. Just as one asks where God was during the Holocaust, the same question can be asked here. Parents should never have to bury their children; it should be the other way around. But these questions and thoughts will be left unanswered. . . .

———❦———

AUGUST 21, 1998

Dear Paul,

. . . *Der Aufbau* sees its task as reprocessing and preserving the past. As you know, that is also an important concern of mine, but in addition, I also want to deal more with the problem of how we can ensure a better future for the coming generations of both our peoples. The future lies in youth employment. Therefore, we cannot overestimate the importance of such student encounters—next year during Pesach/Easter, our young people are going to school in Israel for two weeks. It is the same course that was successfully followed by the former "arch-enemies" France and Germany.

You write about Rovan's quotation, in which he equates Hitler with the devil. That is certainly not meant realistically and in a scientific sense, but rather as a journalistic bon mot. It reminds me of the more striking statement by the French existentialist Jean-Paul Sartre, who said in one of his plays: "Hell, we ourselves are hell!" And unfortunately, one cannot think that the human devil disappeared from the earth with the death of Hitler. Human society has changed only slightly since primeval times. But there has been a step forward in this area. I am thinking of the "higher law" (the Ma'at) that was supposed to protect even the all-powerful Egyptian Pharaohs from becoming purely unjust tyrants. The social ideas of the Middle Eastern peoples are also relevant here; these ideas could once be condensed to the "rules of Moses from Sinai" (but even the Jewish people, as one can read in the Torah, followed these rules very unsatisfactorily). I am also thinking of the tablets of laws of the ancient Romans, Napoleon's Civil Code, the Bill of Rights, the Geneva Convention, the Hague Land Warfare Convention, the noble and well-meant constitutions of the European peoples, and above all the "Human Rights" of the United Nations—but even after the realizations of these insightful bodies of laws, there is not any less harm being done in today's world than there was before, as a glance in the daily paper shows all too quickly. Human beings have known how it *should* be, and they dream about it. Unfortunately, it is extremely difficult for them to translate their progressive intellectual and humanistic insights into action, since to do so, everyone must first begin with overcoming the atavistic, primeval laws that are living inside of him.

Rovan writes, "War may be a horror, but it is also loved. . . ."

I have read about Spielberg's new film *Saving Private Ryan,* which (perhaps, hopefully, finally) will take the place of this series of harebrained war films where, from the beginning, the heroes and villains are distributed nicely on two separate sides, both of which are exaggerated. But that's how the industry likes to depict it for us on the screen, as seen in its eternally unchanging tendency to do so. Need one wonder about the lack of direction of the youth who grew up in this world of media, who are served this kind of stuff on a daily basis right at home? And who then are supposed to orient themselves nevertheless to sophisticated "higher values," which are realized only with a great deal of difficulty? . . .

SEPTEMBER 22, 1998

Dear Emil,

. . . *Der Aufbau* was the crutch for the newcomers to the United States during the time of Hitler. They spoke little or no English, met each other in clubs that they founded, and read *Der Aufbau* to find out what was happening in the world. Another German newspaper that was published in New York sympathized with the swastika. For the refugees, *Der Aufbau* was the last connection to their German language. It included the obituaries and in the earlier years the marriage announcements, and even today it tells who became eighty, ninety, or one hundred years old. The number of readers of *Der Aufbau* has naturally decreased over the years. The new generations have no interest in history and many can't speak or read German. *Der Aufbau* is scrounging financially in order to be able to exist at all. The older generation helps. During the course of time, the news of *Der Aufbau* has changed. It is no longer news that one reads in the newspaper—but instead are stories from the time of Hitler—new and old—that continue to surface. The older people—we, too, are part of that group—are accustomed to *Der Aufbau,* and we are always eager to read it. Our daughter speaks little German. When she was young, the German language was hated in America;

no one dared to speak German in public. In later years, Greta taught her some German and she continued to study German at the university. . . .

Do we live in hell, as Sartre said? When we look back and regard the great wars and see the fanaticism of people, then we can probably agree with him. Today? We look around and see how hatred grows like mushrooms in moist earth. The basis of hatred may be disputed, but it is there and it does its thing very well. Is there always hell on earth? Will it never come to peace? Perhaps with one religion and under one flag, as Hitler dreamed it? But we shake our heads, unable to find the way.

The war was an experience for many. I remember very well, how, fresh out of school for the first time, I got a position near Homburg near my brother in Erbach. I rented a room from two older women and ate my supper in a nearby inn. That was in the year 1926; the First World War should have been long forgotten. But every evening there were buddies sitting at the table, each with a beer in front of him, one after the other, and they bragged about the deeds in the war that they did for the fatherland. Even at that time, this disturbed me, but I didn't attach any particular importance to it. Only now do I think back about these friends. Have they been talking about their war deeds all these years? And with whom? Isn't the world a little bit crazy? . . .

OCTOBER 16, 1998

Dear Paul,

. . . At the moment, I am unable to tackle Rovan's book because I am almost drowning in reading. I've been asked to lecture on the topic of Edith Stein. She was a Judeo-Christian, canonized in Rome on October 11th, who was murdered in Auschwitz-Birkenau in 1942. They want me to make a statement. I have developed some critical questions on the topic; it will go: "Jew?—Philosopher?—Christian?—Saint? Questions, Information, and Trains of Thought on the Topic of Edith Stein." That could actually be the topic for an entire lecture series. My problem is determining what I can leave out so that the essential aspects can still be covered in two hours. Edith Stein is an interesting woman, and I will certainly look more into her ideas and philosophy afterwards as well.

Rovan writes that the Church treated Hitler kindly, which is quite correct, as we had determined earlier, for at times Hitler needed the Church to be an "unloved ally" in order to keep the people calm. In 1942, the Dutch Catholic bishops wrote a pastoral letter to protest the deportation of the Dutch Jews, whereupon all of the Jews in the Netherlands who had become

Catholic were promptly deported to Auschwitz as well (it is said there were fifty-two people). Among them was the German philosopher and nun Edith Stein, who had escaped from Germany to the Netherlands, all this while the so-called half-Jews within the Reich were (still) untouched. That event prevented the German bishops from saying anything because they feared the same reprisal for the over one thousand Judeo-Christians living within the Reich. Edith Stein's last signs of life came from the train station in Schifferstadt; she was able to throw a piece of paper from the stopped train and exchange a few words with passers-by who were supposed to pass on her regards to her friends in Schifferstadt and Speyer. Edith said, "It is going to the East." During the fifties, when there still wasn't the slightest clue that Edith would be advanced in the Church, I made several recordings of people who had witnessed her life. Later these recordings were used to further elucidate her story. We recently erected a bronze plaque for her on the third platform of the Schifferstadt train station. Thus, they now turn to me again for a lecture about her situation.

It is not only the "Germanness" in Europe, but all of humanity that obviously "still awaits us with more surprises, horrors, and (perhaps also) joys" [this is in response to a quotation from Rovan that Friedhoff sent Sold]. When one thinks about the animal experiments in which the animal habitat is reduced step by step, and it is recognized that such a situation leads to an unbelievable drama of aggression within the herd, one receives an intimation of what could be in store for humanity in the future.

Your explanation of *Der Aufbau* made it clear to me that it deals less with problems of the future than with the reappraisal of the past. It is a rearview mirror for the older generation, and it holds that generation together as much as it can. In doing so, it fulfills a good and useful task. Its counterpart, the *Israel-Nachrichten,* does the same thing there. I wrote one time before that there, too, they have to fight to maintain the existence of the paper because subscribers are dying off in Israel as well, and the people who would be capable of producing such a newspaper are also disappearing. Such is the course of the world.—

You are completely right: there will probably never be one uniform "religion and flag" for everyone. The innate egoism of human beings would never permit it. That can be seen with groups that have been formed merely to pursue the mutual interests of their members. It can't be any different in the big picture than in the small one. We simply must live with this, and attempt in the small picture to ensure that at least our own group is doing what it should.

The war was a far-reaching experience for everyone. It interrupted everyone's daily course of life and changed for good each person's way of looking at the world. I am not surprised that the subject comes up when groups of friends meet at the bar. Those who were oppressed, in particular, could gain in war those feelings of achievement that life had previously withheld from them. . . .

———— ✿ ————

NOVEMBER 6, 1998

Dear Emil,

. . . You wrote about Edith Stein, the Judeo-Christian who was canonized. How did you become an expert on this topic, to the point of giving lectures about it? You didn't say what your attitude about this issue was. What influenced the pope to canonize her? Because she was Jewish, and he wanted to make amends for old sins?

What you reported about the Netherlands was very interesting. Something similar must have happened in Germany as well. A distant relative in Dahn married a Catholic and wasn't bothered throughout the entire war. She later converted to Catholicism out of thanks to God. They first lived in Pirmasens and then in Schweinfurt, where we visited them once during one of our European trips. She is a year older than I and my last letter to her was left unanswered.

In the meantime, it has become November 11th. Without a job, one becomes more busy than before. I have recently read a book that will certainly interest you. The title in English is *The Gift of the Jews.* The author is Thomas Cahill (not a Jew). I don't know if it has been translated into German. Cahill became well known after he wrote the book *How the Irish Saved Civilization.* I assume that he comes from Ireland. One can simultaneously love and hate the book about Jews. He explains in a beautiful style the good and the bad in my ancestors, who at the same time are your ancestors.

What I question in general are the conversations individual men (never women) had with God two or three thousand years ago. Were they conversations or dreams or ideas? During these primitive times, people were also primitive and believed in everything that could help them through their daily lives. I am referring to all religions, certainly to yours as well. And still today—in these modern times—the majority of people believe in these "miracles." That in itself should be regarded as a miracle. Why has no one spoken with God in the last two thousand years? Does God have other projects to carry out? Where was he during the Holocaust, when twelve million people prayed to him and were murdered nonetheless? Are there other "earths" that he now prefers? . . .

———❀———

NOVEMBER 17, 1998

Dear Paul,

. . . "Half-Jews" and "Quarter-Jews" had a special status during the Third Reich, which many of them kept all the way to the end of the war. They were registered, observed closely—and were permitted to serve the führer with their labor (under supervision!). Half-Jews who were not circumcised were left almost completely in peace since it was assumed that such people were not "corrupt" ideologically either. Within the SS, there was a strange discussion about this situation: the orthodox Nazis said: "Wherever a Jew has been involved even once, the Germanic genetic makeup has been corrupted once and for all." Their opponents maintained, "It would be ridiculous if our good Germanic genetic makeup could not in the long term overcome a little Jewish smudge!" Thus, it seems obvious that these crossbreeds were only "saved" to be eliminated in later years, so that the government could temporarily take advantage of their labor (there were some notable experts among them!). Yet there were all kinds of arbitrary, despotic acts on the local level. At home I have a record of the Wannsee proceedings in which this question is discussed.

Edith Stein: she taught for eight years (1923–1931) at the girls' high school of the St. Magdalene convent in Speyer, which my wife Elli also later attended. It is not impossible that one day you even walked past her without noticing it when you went to school in Speyer.

During these years, her spiritual guide and advisor was the canon Josef Schwind, a great-uncle of mine—from whose biography I found out about her after the war. No one had any suspicion that this figure would play a role later. For reasons of family history, I made tape recordings of survivors from the Speyer presbytery. The *Fräulein Doktor* was naturally mentioned in many of these recordings, for she was a guest there every Sunday dinner and embroiled my uncle in witty, intelligent conversations. I later allowed the tapes to be evaluated and came into contact with several people from her sphere. That became well known in Schifferstadt. Twenty years later, it also became well known that I was interested in the Jews and their story.

I had nothing to do with the canonization or anything connected to it. Everyone you could imagine has gone to the public with their "knowledge" relating to this matter. I, however, have not gotten involved with the media extravaganza and haven't uttered a word about her canonization. For that reason, I was asked to give a statement. I promised that I would do it when all the noise had died down. It should take place on December 8th. I will have to straighten out a few misconceptions in the process.

Edith Stein was a remarkable woman in many respects. She was the first woman in Germany to obtain her doctorate in philosophy. But two things stood in the way of her continuing academic career: in the twenties, there still wasn't a single woman in all of Europe who held an academic chair. And her efforts to acquire such a chair were shattered conclusively by Hitler's seizure of power in 1933!

It would be best if I were to send you, if you are interested, my text after my talk on December 8th. We could then discuss some points specifically. At the very least you would receive information about why an intelligent Jew renounced the faith of her childhood, declared herself everywhere as a (well-respected) philosopher without a religion (some say she became an atheist)—and in the end became a committed Christian. We could then get into a discussion about the topic of religion from another point of view. Edith Stein's changing views of the world are worth studying more closely. Thus, I want to postpone my response to the "profession of unbelief" that you expressed in your last letter. . . .

DECEMBER 11, 1998

Dear Paul,

Many thanks for your congratulations on my birthday. . . .

Paul, I am sending you the lecture today that I gave on December 8th about the canonized Judeo-Christian Edith Stein. I was very happy with the audience's response. I was asked to allow the text to be published. I arranged it so that I put the text at the disposal of several suitable people, who will then pass out photocopies to people who are interested.

I think that you will find it interesting to study the text a little more closely. It contains a number of topics that we can both discuss in our old age. I tried to put myself in my audience's position and determine the best way to explain the course that Edith Stein chose. I am anxious to see what part of my explanation you will tackle first. Her path was determined in 1918 when she gave her notice to her superior, professor Husserl. Martin Heidegger took her place at the university and for years afterwards she continued to have discussions with him, as he pursued a completely different philosophical direction. Heidegger became the promoter of existentialist philosophy; in France today, after his death, he still plays a large role as a philosopher (even though he was involved for a while during the Third Reich and was able to make a career for himself at the university). I heard Heidegger give some lectures in my time at Freiburg during the war. One of his theories was that we human beings were thrown into existence from somewhere (he called it the "dereliction into the here"), but unfortunately no knowledge is possible about the kind or manner of this existence. That would certainly be more to your taste than to Edith Stein's, who gave herself into the arms of a faith without resignation and with complete satisfaction.

Human communities need a common idea to bring the people within them together, or else the communities will fall apart. It is good luck for everyone if these societies are organized in a humane way, so that they don't make a hell for each other.

I wish you time of contemplation and spiritual peace for the week of the Hannukah celebration. During these days, I will be together with you in spirit, and I will imagine going with you to the synagogue and keeping very quiet there beside you.

All the best to your entire family, and best wishes to you all, especially to David, for the coming year.

JANUARY 2, 1999

Dear Emil,

The last year of the twentieth century has arrived without a great ado, without *Glühwein* [hot wine], and with a little bit of snow. Actually—I believe—the year 2000 is the last year of the twentieth century. However it may be, we have a new year, and we always hope for something better from it, as all people do. May it be for the good of humanity, and may peace dominate the earth.

I regret having to say that my response to your lecture is not the most complimentary. I learned a great deal about Catholicism, but not that much about poor Edith Stein. You have regarded Judaism from an Israeli viewpoint, without considering that the United States alone has more Jews than Israel does. On the whole, your lecture was very educational, and it certainly met the approval of your audience, the majority of which was probably Catholic. Edith Stein was, as I said above, a poor soul who first became satisfied—and that was not a conscious thing—when she entered into the disciplined Catholic Church. She and others found peace in an environment that consciously promised them heaven if they prayed and believed, and threatened them with hell. . . .

Yes, I know, that we must believe. But in what? I asked our rabbi whether she (she is a woman) really believed that Moses had received the Ten Commandments from God, or whether he chiseled them in the stone himself. She answered that we must believe in God, and that he had given us the Ten Commandments. That is just our religion. That is the central point of our religion; we must believe blindly. And it is perhaps the same in your religion. With the small difference that we don't believe in hell, and are not burdened with the fear of it. And for Moses and Jesus: who wrote all of that down, and after how much time? Who has a memory that good, or was it passed on from mouth to mouth? Wise people want to show us the path we should follow. They were prophets who had some kind of a relationship (conversation) with God. They certainly meant well, even though not everyone was satisfied with it. A friend of mine said that the best religion is a good relationship between one human being and another, and another said that God created the world and then turned his back on it. Who is right? . . .

———— ✸ ————

JANUARY 15, 1999

Dear Paul,

. . . As I can see, you read through my lecture very closely and I am happy to have your critical comments. You guess correctly when you assume that the lecture met the approval of the majority of my (Catholic!) listeners. Yet I have, in the example of Edith Stein, also questioned some of the conventional teachings that the official Church still insists upon today. In order to recognize the details of that claim, however, one must have some inside knowledge. The official ministry has indeed praised, surprisingly, the basic information that I presented, but has thus far kept away from a critical discussion of my conclusions. But many more listeners have asked me to make my text available so that they can take their time to study it. I consented, therefore, so that anyone who wishes to do so may duplicate it and pass it on.

In the months before the canonization, the public here became well acquainted with the details of Edith's life. Thus it was to be expected that by means of word selection and depictions, different sides would be painted of her somewhat idealized saint's legend. I didn't need to go into the general facts for my audience and repeat the story of her life. I wanted to tell them some information that was not so generally known, and in the second and especially the third part, show that our completely dogmatic, or as you say "disciplined," Church has begun to change today and can no longer adhere to old dogmas. At the Second Vatican Council (1962–1965), the Fathers of the Church under John XXIII and Paul VI agreed upon a far-reaching opening and humanization of the Church, a reorientation that affected the Church's relationship with Judaism and Islam and made possible the resolution of old hostilities. Unfortunately, one must have the impression now that the current pope has driven back these ideas, and that within the Church there is supposed to be a return to the strict dogmas of before. As I found out in a conversation with an older Jew in the synagogue in Rome, they have the same impression there because "since then, nothing is happening anymore." Thus it seemed to me all the more amazing that at the same time, John Paul II obviously hurried along the beatification and canonization of the converted Jew Edith Stein, which should show that the Second Vatican Council's resolutions are being valued once again.

I myself could indeed be regarded as a rather regular churchgoer, but more as one who goes there to lose himself quietly in private thoughts. I see the necessity in the Christian Church for a completely new beginning, for a true reformation. I wanted to take the opportunity to smooth the way, in public, for the idea of such a reformation. Edith Stein was, as I was unable to express in detail in my lecture, also a supporter of these new, in the broad sense, ecumenical ideas. Whoever canonizes her with clear knowledge of her ideas, which show the way to the future, cannot at the same time be an opponent of her ideas! In my eyes, her canonization officially reconfirmed the resolutions of the Second Vatican Council for the opening of the Church. Most of the people there certainly understood that. . . .

Do we really have to believe?

For centuries now, religious faith has been retreating from a territory that, since we know too little about it, could really have remained "no-man's-land." But since we wanted "to know" absolutely, it was realized that this area could also be occupied by "faith" for the time being. So far, no one has been able to deny this faith with verifiable statements (see the ancient conception of the world). Then for a while it looked as if the progressing sciences could slowly and surely provide all positions of faith with definite scientific solutions. There arose a "faith in science"; we must only have the necessary patience, and in the end, we will be able to resolve all the questions we've ever had. Since then, science has pushed its horizons to the far parts of the universe, but it hasn't gotten any steps closer to answering our basic questions: What is the world? What was it before the Big Bang? Who are we really, why am I in this world, and where am I going? So everyone is stuck with a conception of the world that remains fundamentally botched. And in the end he stops asking questions, or sinks into the arms of some ideology or religion that saves him from additional questions. Along with the creeds of faith, there are a host of people who proclaim their lack of faith—up to the position of the person who says: there is no sense at all in asking questions that we know from the outset can have no answer. It makes more sense simply to abandon all such questions for good.

Over the past few weeks, I have been working through a book of articles on this topic published in the past years, written by Italian thinkers who are still living: *in cosa crede chi non crede*—what does one believe in, who doesn't believe? (or: what does one believe in, who believes he believes in nothing?).

Observation shows that the human being does not want to stop thinking, and in areas such as this one, where he cannot know, he simply fills the gaps in his knowledge with theories he generates himself.

That's fine because it brings about research and progress. However, if, in the process, one forms new ideologies and doctrines of salvation that try to proselytize and dominate those who think differently, then it becomes dangerous. Then the merry-go-round of wars that is kept running by the constant greed for more and more power will be reinforced by the greed for power brought by ideology or religion. . . .

Paul, a Jewish (!) friend of mine obviously had great difficulties accepting the traditional Sinai legend, which indeed symbolizes the beginning of his Judaism. He didn't want to imagine that a divine being of some sort could have been involved at Sinai. And he couldn't imagine that Moses had chiseled the entire Pentateuch in the stone according to God's dictation either. My friend goes a step further: he is completely convinced that the Higher Being, called "GOD" throughout the world, is only used in order to keep a tight rein on the subordinate masses so that the preachers can more easily translate their own ideas into action (!); he is also convinced that this God is probably an invention of fundamentally malicious humans so that they can use Him to strike terror into people's hearts. That is how he has developed his generally anti-religion philosophy.

This friend of mine, out of a feeling of having to defend himself against such abstruse ideas of God, has reduced his own religious commitments to practically nothing. He now attends synagogue on occasion, only because of a remaining sentiment for tradition (and perhaps also for the sake of his wife).

He has recognized that there are weak and dependent people for whom an ideology or a religion can serve as a useful crutch to help them make it through their lives. He himself became aware of that long ago; for him it was unbearable to surrender himself to such weaknesses. He thinks that religion is damaging to everyone.

But!

However it may have happened at Mount Sinai, the "Moses Legend" still has its effect in terms of history, even for Jews who have become disbelievers three thousand years later! Despite the current worldwide diaspora, and even for those Jews who have become disbelievers, the legend continues to make possible an almost incredible national identification. Adonai [the Hebrew word for God], allegedly superfluous now, no longer necessary for daily life and forgotten, keeps His people together even amid the scattering of the diaspora—and had His people overcome the Holocaust.

Yet my friend, who has coped well in his life even without Adonai (and long ago, his own father should have had to say the Kaddish [the Jewish memorial prayer] for him because of his unfaithfulness to the beliefs of his forefathers!!!), saved over three hundred of his fellow Jews from the Holocaust in an untiring and selfless commitment to their cause.

So faith can be unrealistic and unscientific; perhaps it has even become a nuisance or an encumbrance, and is something that one sheds during the course of his life. Nevertheless, faith always reappears. It is one of the most important driving forces in the gears of human development. Faith can "move mountains," can build cathedrals, can bring about well-being—but it can also make a hell and lead to the abyss. Religious movements are what move the society. They are not automatically good on their own; they must be observed with care. "Ye shall know them by their fruits!!!"

And:

Without faith, mankind would sink back into the *tohubohu* [chaos, formlessness; see Genesis 1: 2] of its biblical beginning.

Paul, my ALS patient in Kassel, can no longer leave his bed. He feels no pain. He has to be fed.

Would you be able to outline briefly for me your current beliefs?

For today, to you and your wife we send our best regards from the Rhineland, where the spring sun is starting to shine on occasion.—

FEBRUARY 5, 1999

Dear Emil,

Today your Jewish (!) friend is going to comment on your explanations, which do not entirely appeal to him. The beginning seems to be, as you yourself say, that the body of laws from Sinai is an unfounded legend, and that Moses gave his people a basis of living for three thousand years. Moses or God? If it was Moses, then you should better understand your Jewish friend. Moses was the first statesman who "led." He became the model for future prophets and wise men. And his paths were easy to understand and easy to follow. And that was and remains the Jewish religion, though it is, as other religions, split into groups.

I am a devout Jew for different reasons. I was born a Jew; in my opinion, the Jewish religion is the religion that attempts the least in terms of dictating a person's life; it is the cornerstone of the three big religions; the Jew has no intermediary between him and God if he is convinced that the legend is well founded.

Your Jewish friend has never claimed that God was the invention of fundamentally malicious people so that they can strike terror into people's hearts. These people are often well meaning and have good intentions. Not all of them.

There has always been faith, even when it was called "myth" or when people prayed to idols. Abraham was the first person to unify all the gods into one, and he became the creator of all the big religions today. But that doesn't mean that with knowledge, but without faith, mankind would sink back into the *tohubohu* of its beginning. Faith "moves mountains"; it gives people reassurance as well as hope for a better life and afterlife. That is, of course, understandable, as long as faith doesn't win people with the sword.

This friend of yours has remained Jewish out of tradition. He goes to the synagogue, where the melodies remind him of the old days, to be with his wife, and if possible, to hear good sermons that suit modern times. Since the death of his parents, your friend has never neglected to say the Kaddish "on *Jahrzeit*." [According to Jewish tradition, on the anniversary of a person's death (following the Hebrew calendar), the family says the memorial prayer and lights a candle.] Even his stomach is better accustomed to Jewish food, though you can't get that here in Chambrel [the elderly community where he and his wife live].

Your friend has never claimed that religion is damaging for everyone. He has said that more people have lost their lives in the name of God than for any other reason. And that it continues like that today. Why does God not stop it? You say that Adonai had his people overcome the Holocaust. After six million had to lose their lives? Is that overcoming?

A saying I have heard claims that you should never discuss religion or politics with friends or acquaintances. Is that true?

Our son-in-law David is not in bed during the day like your friend in Kassel. On the other hand, he is not capable of eating alone; his limbs are completely paralyzed. He doesn't have any pain, though, and is looking toward the future with expectation. He is always finding something that he still wants to do or see. It is difficult to talk with him about his situation. I take a sedative whenever we get together. He has a car that picks up his wheelchair electrically, and he has a young man who takes care of him every day. His speech is so bad that it's great trouble for me to understand him. Parents should never see their children die; it should be the other way around. David is a doctor of marine biology and he taught at the university some time ago.

For today, this should be a spontaneous answer to your letter, which somewhat disturbed me. Apparently, religions are much like roses with many thorns, and can often hurt.

All the best and best regards from both of us,

———✿———

FEBRUARY 23, 1999

Dear Paul,

I am very happy to have a "Jewish friend" with whom I can exchange my thoughts, even about topics that, as you write, "should never be discussed with friends or acquaintances." But what kind of friends would they be if you couldn't talk with them about essential questions? At the end of my last letter, I dared to ask a blunt question, the answer to which is generally private to the person and not happily discussed in an open way. But the question had been going through my head for a long time. And you gave me a wonderful response to my question by allowing me to recognize that within your shell, which has been hardened by more than your fair share of painful experiences, there still remains a tender, sensitive core that you are trying to protect. By letting me see that, you've moved another step closer to me.

I myself was raised a strict Catholic, and indeed, was brought up according to the way the Catholic Church portrayed itself during my youth. My experience before, during, and after the war, with the complete collapse of the environment I was used to, raised the first unanswerable questions in my life. My occupation with science, the study of medicine and psychology, did the rest. I learned to see the world and its problems with different eyes, and to continue to observe. I also learned to change my views on occasion, which naturally put into question the views of my childhood.

I have dealt with people for my entire professional life and have gained the corresponding experience. For the past fifteen years now, I have been taking steps toward retiring from my practice. In doing so, I have gained the time to learn more about our world of people, which, as I realized many years ago, does not develop logically at all, but often by leaps and bounds and with a great deal of chaos. We can watch it every day in the media.

I've continued my outward involvement with the Church. Despite my critical distance from many of its teachings (and even despite my horror over the many perversions and inhumanities that line its path), I still value the rich river of cultural possessions that the Church has handed down to us from earlier centuries. It has offered me the opportunity to go back and study the Tanach [the Hebrew bible—Tanach is an acrostic of the Hebrew words Torah (Pentateuch), Nebiim (prophetic writings), and the Ketubhim (other writings).]; I see the Tanach and the Catholic Church in perfect continuity, despite the dire hostility with which the Church has attempted to separate itself from what it calls the "Old Testament." Although the Christian Church has pursued its own development for two thousand years (which in the meantime has led to the production of over three hundred different Christian denominations!), it is nevertheless a continuum of the longings and thoughts of its fathers, Moses and Abraham.

Man realized long ago that one should not destroy one's house, even if he sees its faults, before obtaining a better one. It is also for that reason that I see myself (and feel!) in a continuum with your ancient patriarchs, which is an important clue for understanding why my studies do not focus so much on the Jesus propagated and presented by the churches, but on the real, historical Jesus, as much as he can still be made perceptible today. I find the additional teachings and ideas devised by the men who became his following to be both interesting and worth thinking about; however, I question their reasons and motives for their dogmas. I consider their works the works of men and thus do not consider them to be implicitly binding. My emotional life is more at home with the older part of the scriptures. I would have no problem going with you to the synagogue and also losing myself in my thoughts there.

There are "ecumenical movements" being conducted by individual church administrations, though still in vain and only with words. But I am seeing that within the individual Christian (and Muslim!) denominations there is a recollection of their common roots in Judaism, and a new opening toward the synagogue. In my opinion, the church administrative machineries that have emerged throughout history would be welcome to survive if a new spirit and a willingness to work together would come to the people involved. I attempted with my Edith Stein lecture, as I did earlier in a different way, to evoke these kinds of thoughts in my local community.

For the most part, we didn't choose our environment ourselves. But we all have our entire lives to react to it, and every day it makes its demands on us. Within our environment, we fight for our financial existence and for our position as a human being. How could one remain spiritually balanced throughout that process if he didn't have an internal, guiding principle, from which life received its meaning? Where we find such a principle is almost less important than whether it can be effective for us. Whoever is going hiking and takes a stick to help him overcome his obstacles is not acting irrationally. His aid should not be taken away from him, since he obviously needs it to continue on, even if someone else doesn't feel the necessity for it. People suffer from the conflict between the reality of their everyday lives and their dreams and yearnings, and in the process, they often lose their inner balance. It is true that such emotional crises can be suppressed by taking medicine. A true balance, however, can only be obtained through the restoration of spiritual peace. Therefore, everything that contributes to one's balance and spiritual peace is a great asset, no matter where it comes from or what it is called, so long as it allows one's neighbors to cope with their lives in their own ways. You see, I move within the constraints of my inherited Church, but within those constraints, I completely lead my own type of life.

Paul, we are having some strange weather here at the moment. There were heavy snowfalls with a continuous frost, but now the weather is milder with a warm rain. Many valleys in the Alps are snowed in and have to be supplied with the necessities by helicopter. Avalanches are falling every day in Switzerland and Tyrol and sweeping away houses; they've already cost several lives. It's raining here in the plains—and the lilies of the valley are coming out, which are sounding the bell for spring. . . .

MARCH 9, 1999

Dear Emil,

Many thanks for your interesting letter. Yes, I believe that we've grown a little closer—though I think that we're too far away from each other to let our masks fall off completely. That would be different, of course, if we could look each other in the eye while discussing such delicate topics. I have the feeling that we're not entirely open with one another, so as not to cause any pain. Religion is simply a personal affair, with different concepts in the eyes of different people. Following the teachings of a "wise man" sounds much better to me than believing in the supernatural. We cannot claim that there is or there isn't a God. In any case, He has never shown Himself. We are waiting to hear from Him. Is he masculine or feminine or both, or a being whose form and body we could not imagine? And I always come back to the bloody sword, brandished in the name of God. And then comes the Holocaust, which God allowed to happen, while it had been in His power to prevent it. Does He hear our entreaties and prayers? Naturally, the believer would say yes. At least, the believer constantly waits for an affirming answer from God, which never reaches him. And his faith is reinforced by his fear of the negative (*hell*—a human invention). And there will always be new cults and religions that preach a new interpretation and guarantee a certain entry to heaven.

In my opinion, human culture, which you speak about, has nothing to do with any religion. I think that I wrote you once that a friend of mine in Clearwater claimed that the best religion is a good relationship between one human being and another. He is right, and this relationship is the basis of our culture.

You go to church in order to think while undisturbed. The founders of old Indian religions sat in the shade of a tree to develop their ideas. Apparently it is solitude that gives people the strength to find the reason for their existence. . . . And everyone finds a different reason, and very often a different god. The supernatural can and will always be interpreted differently.

We were all born into a culture and a religion. And after we grew out of our childhood, no one asked us whether we were satisfied with this culture and this religion. They both became habits for us, and we had no desire to ask any questions. In fact, entirely the opposite is true: we defend what we were born into without becoming critical (Edith Stein was an exception).

I am reading something now about the cultural history of the Jews. A few excerpts from it: Collingswood said: if people could remember, we wouldn't need any historians. Voltaire (not a friend of mine) said: all history is stories! [*"Alle Geschichte ist Geschichte!"* *Geschichte* means both "history" and "story" or "tale."]

The Torah contains various contradictions that are difficult to explain. God's speech came in dreams and visions. It reminds me of a book entitled: *The Bible without Theology* (a history book?).

We are kept well informed here about what is happening with the weather in Europe. We see the avalanches on TV and hear how many people have lost their lives. They, too, were certainly praying as they ran out of breath. Exactly like the twelve million who were murdered by the Nazis. I can't help myself; I keep coming back to the same topic. How can it be forgotten?

As you can see, I'm in a pessimistic mood today; perhaps it is not the right day to be writing to you. But I am not convinced that tomorrow will be better. My thoughts are very much occupied by our son-in-law, whom we keep finding in worse and worse condition. His speech is hardly comprehensible anymore and physically he is completely paralyzed. Thus is life.

All the best to both of you, from Greta as well,

—— 🌸 ——

MARCH 19, 1999

Dear Paul,

Many thanks for your recent letter of March 9, 1999, which for me brought us another step closer, and made it possible for us to continue to lift the "masks" that you wrote about.

We live in our environment and are a part of it. We can remove ourselves from it only partially; and whether everything runs smoothly depends on whether every participant contributes to its harmonization. Theoretically, the gears could be in tune with all parties: but if the machine were operated without the friction-reducing "oil" provided by a fundamental agreement within the society, it would "run hot" and do itself harm.

It is true: we were not asked what kind of society we wanted to be born into. But that society gave us security, a house, and a home during our childhood. And it uses its resources to try and hold on to us. We can only free ourselves from it one step at a time and with a great deal of exertion. The individual can secure for himself a certain freedom within the society, but cannot live entirely without his environment, unless one wants to lead a life like "Robinson Crusoe." And if we want the society to continue to operate, we must, at the very least, pay our taxes and make other contributions in some way.

Much the same is true for the sphere of ideology, of religion. For decades, I have been going through the process of a spiritual transfer. However, I didn't "blow up" the home where I used to live out of a youthful show of strength, but because I didn't feel completely safe in it. I have looked around the world, lived in other inadequate homes, made excursions into my spiritual surroundings, and have investigated whether and how one could sensibly replace or amend one's own, inherited view of the world. I could not discover where else my questions about the world and life could be answered once and for all. Your friend in Clearwater is certainly right when he says that the best temporary solution (not religion!) would probably be to make humane relationships possible among all people. That would be the fundamental requirement that would have to be fulfilled for the time being. But then everyone should have the freedom to think about the world in his own way and have his own thoughts, at least so long as a universally compelling solution to the world's problems doesn't become apparent anywhere. The phrase you quoted from Voltaire indeed puts forth the demand that everyone should be allowed to "lead a life after his own fashion." . . .

That makes me think of a sentence from my last letter, which you very rightfully complained about: without faith, mankind would sink back into the *tohubohu* of its biblical beginning. I didn't mean, however, that no spiritual, economic, or industrial development would have been possible. I didn't use the word *faith* entirely correctly here. . . . It should be replaced by "involvement in generally binding guidelines of conduct."

It says in the Torah that man should not make an "image" of God. But human beings have constantly fashioned such images ever since the beginning. Today I imagine that there must be some instigating (and ordering?) higher principle at work behind all of these incomprehensible processes and real cosmic occurrences, such as when entire worlds disappear into "Black Holes" and new ones come into being simultaneously (I read just yesterday about the discovery of a supernova in the far reaches of space whose light has just reached the earth after billions of light-years!). There must be a higher principle that set the whole scene in motion and continues to keep it on its course. Perhaps people could agree to denote such a higher principle with the word "GOD." But: with such an agreement, we would be leaving the sphere of science and would find ourselves in the midst of many other such imaginary constructions. Very probably, however, one could project his own existence into the series of such far-reaching ideas and then regard himself as a small, disappearing part in that chain of thought. But from that kind of overall view, ideas of a "personal God" who knows you and me, who is responsible for our human destiny in this world, who in the end will hold us accountable for our conduct, could hardly be maintained anymore. In this context, the old question about "theodicy" by the biblical silent sufferer Job could hardly be asked anymore either: where were *you*, God, when this or that injustice happened to us?

Again and again your letter touches on the question of God's justice. Especially after Auschwitz, many people would like to think of a God with whom we could discuss things and whom we could hold accountable, for instance for his considerably "screwed-up" creation. But those people obviously don't realize that those kinds of thoughts were forbidden even to the author of the first commandment from Sinai!

We have also taken a good amount of time in our circles in Landau to discuss the question of God's justice in the Bible. Rabbi Dr. Ydit, who was liberated from Auschwitz as a sixteen-year-old boy, has never been able to resolve this problem for himself completely. In my opinion, our concept of God (that we ourselves have produced) is to blame for the dilemma. Despite the explicit prohibitions in the Decalogue, we have simply attached too many human characteristics to our image of the biblical God (El Shaddai, Jehovah, Adonai).

On the topic of God's justice, I have taken out an excerpt for you from a text about Job, and I am enclosing it in this letter. Naturally, it is from a Christian standpoint, but years ago it kept us pretty busy in our discussion circle in Landau.

Perhaps you notice that my thoughts are not based too strictly on the current views of the Roman Catholic Church, even though I still attend it on a fairly regular basis. But I feel more comfortable in that Church than in any of the other ones. Despite all of the mistakes in its development, for me it remains a "guide rail" back to the historical Jesus, to the "Rabbi Jehoshuah," who was thinking about the legends passed down to him from the generations of his forefathers, and who tried to correct certain parts of them ("You have heard that it was said to the ancients . . . but I say to you . . .").

For me, Abraham and the prophets are important witnesses to their time, a time that was rich in attempts to design a world order that would be binding for all human beings. Systems can be devised from completely different starting points and still allow somewhat well-ordered and useful polities to develop out of human societies, if the individual, who obviously continues to possess primeval tendencies, could only be exclusively "good." But thus far, despite very respectable attempts, human shortcomings have caused every religion to continue to fail in producing a piece of heaven on earth. In spite of these inadequate attempts so far, we must continue to lead our daily lives whether we like it or not. We must do that especially because we, too, have been unable to develop any universal solutions to the problems of humanity. All that we can do is talk with our discussion partners, at least to try to devise better social solutions for the earth, and at the very least to strive for partial solutions to the problems. To do that, we must promote a more humane way of thinking and acting within our own small circles, which should not prevent us from simultaneously observing with interest what new things other great minds can find out about the world.

In conclusion today, with another completely different and less personal, ordinary topic: I had read that there was a great amount of information and specialist literature about the Shoah and its problems, but that thus far there were no belles lettres that had approached the topic. Perhaps the booklet that I sent you by Liana Millu was a first such attempt. I just saw an interesting German film that is also going in this direction (Title: *Aimée und Jaguar*). The content, briefly: during the war, 1943, there is a basement printing press operated in the Berlin underground by hidden Jews for the purposes of espionage, forging passports, and other projects relevant to the Jewish resistance. Its members move around in the city with relative freedom (without a star of David!). They even attend concerts and go to the theater. There they form the connections that are so important to them. One of these Jews (her very telling code name is "Jaguar"; she plays the active partner in the developing relationship) and a German woman (code name Aimée) meet each other in the theater. They become inflamed with an extremely passionate love for each other, which becomes especially racy since the German partner is the wife of a prominent German officer. For that reason, there are an enormous amount of difficult and multi-layered complications. The resistance group breaks up, but if need be the members can still clear out to a foreign country. Jaguar, however, cannot tear herself away from her love affair in time and dies in the KZ.

Aimée, who is not sentenced to death because of her children from her Nazi marriage, survives the war. And here is the other amazing thing: it comes from a story that actually happened! Aimée, today eighty-five years old, lives in Berlin. After fifty years, she allowed her story to be published, and, since then, this award-winning film was made of it. At the end of the film she appears as herself. She goes to a bench in the park to have a conversation with another Jew from the former resistance group in Berlin, who has grown just as old as she has. This woman was also in a lesbian relationship with Jaguar at the time, and it was very painful for her when she found out about the "unfaithfulness" of "her Jaguar" with Aimée, the German. . . .

Good cinematography, and an extremely exciting film about interhuman relationships. It gets its special "kick" from the fact that it interweaves and deals with two topics that have always been taboo: homosexuality and political "race laws"—under the most inhumane conditions possible.

The same group is advertising another film in the same genre now; title: *Meschugge* [Nuts (a Yiddish word)]. I am excited. A Jew from the younger generation is the director of both films.

Paul, now a few more words on the topic from before: besides you, I have no one that I can talk to freely in this way without annoying or confusing them. Almost all of my friends have grown weary; they are happy to be able to cope with the small daily problems that come from being a senior citizen. I don't have any easy answers either, not for either the social or the religious sector. Even after these many years, I haven't gotten beyond my "orientation phase." That is why I asked about your beliefs. I comfort myself with the thought that "an existence of constant intellectual searching" remains in our time the only legitimate type of spiritual existence for human beings. Therefore, your critical letters have become very valuable to me, for which I want to thank you here again.

My best regards to you, your family, and your wife Greta, and shalom on Pesach and Easter!

———⚜———

MARCH 28, 1999

Dear Paul and Greta,

We were very happy with your birthday greetings and good wishes for my wife Elli; we would like to thank you very much for your attention.

On the actual birthday, some of our friends are coming to visit and chat with us. We regret very much that you couldn't be here as well. The family itself is not coming to Schifferstadt until Easter time. Then our house will be full of life. We all get together two times a year: on Easter, which is near the time of my wife's birthday—and also my birthday, which comes around Christmas.

You obviously have the capability to make greeting cards on your computer; several times now I have had the opportunity to admire Paul's creative abilities. . . .

I was surprised by the font Paul printed on the greeting card. It's the old German script in which all our books were printed before, and it's not available in my collection of fonts, though that includes sixteen different options (Style Writer II of Apple). Perhaps it's just connected with the fact that my printer is available internationally. It could also—see here—have political reasons: In a secret decree on January 3, 1941, our mutual friend Adolf Hitler prohibited the old "Gothic" and, thus, the German script for the entire area of the Reich! He didn't like it; it was said that in Austria he didn't learn how to write German but Latin. The official reason was, however, that the Gothic characters (also called *Fraktur*) were now officially denoted as "Schwabacher [type of Gothic print] Jewish characters," and for that reason were forbidden for all future printed material. Yet his book *Mein Kampf* had also been printed in "Schwabacher Jewish characters"! Later this led to an interesting éclat, when years after the end of the war, the painting counterfeiter Kuhnau tried to sell the "lost diary of the führer" to the magazines for millions. At that time, even well-known experts fell for the counterfeits. But when these old leather-bound volumes of his diary were presented to the public on television, and you could see the initials of the Führer A.H. embossed on the metal cover, I said right away: something is wrong there. Kuhnau had, probably from ignorance of the script, embossed a gothic 'K' instead of a gothic 'A' (thus K.H.), which the viewers from the older generation recognized immediately, and which, among other things, very quickly led to the unmasking of the counterfeits.

Paul, if everything goes smoothly, we will be in Bad Hofgastein again in May. Yet I think that I will probably write you again before then. Until then, thank you again and best regards from the birthday girl Elli, and naturally from me as well,

APRIL 7, 1999

Dear Emil,

There are two letters lying here from you that need to be answered, and there is much to say. Apparently we don't have any lack of subject matter for our conversation.

You write: "We live in our environment and are a part of it." Actually, it should be said that we became a part of it—willingly or unwillingly. But somewhere or sometime these parts split up. The reason for this seems to be that one said to the other: do what I command, or you are not my friend. That goes back to the earliest time, when man learned to think, and later, when he was able to write down his "history." But he didn't write this history as it happened. What he wrote down came to him much later, passed from mouth to mouth, and in the meantime it had taken an incredible shape, but it certainly wasn't what and how everything actually took place. And the following generations—in the search for an explanation—accepted everything as a matter of course. Even today we see the birth of new thoughts, and we trot behind these new ideas like madmen. Whatever people don't hear or see, they invent. They are afraid to ask if there is a God who has never let himself be seen. The idea of hell frightens them.

Since we have settled into a certain custom, we automatically accept everything that comes with that custom. Thinking and questioning is disturbing, and for most people unpleasant. So we just continue to move along without turning around and looking the past in the eye.

I very well understand your inner search. I didn't simply blow my house up. It took a long time for me to leave my house and replace it with a question mark. That brought me into the middle, without being either positive or negative. My friend in Clearwater is relevant here again when he says that the relationship between human beings is more important than any religion. After all this time, it doesn't seem to be apparent how the world's riddles could be solved. This way of thinking is not suitable for the general public, which follows all rules blindly.

A small correction: it was Friedrich the Great who said that everyone should lead a life after his own fashion. That was not in Voltaire's vocabulary, for he [Voltaire] was also a pronounced antisemite.

I do not object to calling the higher principle "God." But does He hear our entreaties when we are in great need? Prayers make Him a personal God from whom we expect help, who sets the stars on their predestined path, who has the night come after the day and the day after the night, who has the mountains shake and from whom we demand health and prosperity. Are there people who prayed more than those who were murdered in the concentration camps or those who became refugees today in Yugoslavia? What right does this God have to hold us perhaps accountable if He doesn't see us today and is looking in another direction? These are unpleasant questions with vague or no answers at all. We sit back down under a tree and hope for miracles.

How did it happen that God was given human characteristics? Somewhere in the Bible it says that man was created in the image of God. That is no compliment to God. It is therefore understandable when we imagine God as a man with a long beard (not a woman). As long as we attribute to God the characteristics that all religions proclaim he has, we will be asking ourselves where the justice is that is supposed to be the basis of God. But all of that can be turned off if one believes blindly. And that is what our rabbi (a woman) demands of us. And with that, all discussion ends immediately.

I am happy that I can give you some ideas for your "orientation phase." This discussion is also very valuable to me. It is not often that one can discuss this topic; there is the feeling that you are hurting the other person in the process. The people here in Virginia are especially conservative and always have the Bible under their arms, so to speak. It is not a question of faith; it is more a question of detesting those who don't believe. If something is in the Bible, that means that it cannot be wrong. That reminds me of an old friend who said once that everything that is printed must be true. There are no limits to people's naivete.

Thank you for the story of Job. Naturally I knew it—another piece of fiction from ancient times.

In the course about the Jewish culture, I learned that at the time of Abraham, and later as well, the Israelites sacrificed children to their God: in Exodus 22:28–29, God said, give me your firstborn, man or beast. The same thing appears at other places. Supposedly, Abraham was to have sacrificed his son. But he was resurrected and the angels had all kinds of trouble keeping Abraham from offering him as a sacrifice again. Offering children to one's god appears in all ancient religions. That was like a prayer to comply with the customs of these religions. As you can see, much has changed over the course of time. It always comes back to the simple phrase that man created his God and not the other way around. . . .

Tomorrow Pesach ends, and bread will be served again. Greta wants it like that, and I'm not against the symbols. We're giving a seder [a ceremonial Passover meal in which the story of Exodus is told] this evening for the third time—whenever the time is right for the children and grandchildren. These seders, however, are only explanations of the holidays and they do not go into details. Neither the wife of our grandson nor the husband of our granddaughter is Jewish, but they avoid church. No one asks any questions and we maintain a good relationship with the children. Here, too, one sits down in the shade of a tree and thinks . . .

All the best to both of you, from Greta as well,

———❦———

Dear Paul,

Your letter of April 7th got here very quickly, and I thank you very much.

I have the impression that we've come out of this last phase of our correspondence extremely well, which has demanded something like a confession from both of us. We have spoken of things that one hides from his neighbors during the course of daily conversation, and which we wouldn't immediately touch on within circles of friends either, for fear of causing unexpected pain. When I consider the different paths that our lives have followed, I am amazed at how similar our fundamental philosophies have become in the end.

I have no objections to what you write, and, therefore, can limit myself to a few points:

In your letter I read for the first time the variation of the Abraham legend in which Abraham sacrifices his son for the time being, but then gets him back alive, and then must be prevented by angels from repeating the sacrifice of the firstborn. Naturally, that version could also be interpreted religiously; however, as I've just satisfied myself again, it cannot be read from the text of the Torah. Perhaps this version is from a later rabbinical train of thought, a Midrash, a religious addendum to an earlier legend?

I had written about a "higher principle God." I imagine that it would have its effect in secret and far behind everything that we can perceive in the world. This "principle," however, would not at all be identical with what people themselves have imagined as their God during the course of history in the form of religions. Such a "Prime Mover," far removed from humans, who keeps the universe going, could not also be held responsible for what we humans have messed up in His world and continue to mess up. We could think about how we could align our lives with such a higher ordering principle, and perhaps in the process establish our own, private moral code to which we could commit ourselves (= religion) voluntarily, as to a philosophical faith. Then the individual would have to take the responsibility for his actions—and wouldn't need a scapegoat to free himself from the responsibility of his own mistakes. Then people would even be capable of accepting voluntarily a fate that is not their own, and submitting to it, as the Muslims do with *Kismet* (*Inshallah*) [In Islamic religious thought, *Kismet* means "faith" and *Inshallah* means "God willing."]—and as the existentialists are prepared to do for philosophical reasons.

Religious faith demands unquestioning devotion to a "revelation," about which one shouldn't or doesn't want to think anymore. Yet the Jewish philosopher Maimonides says (mentioned in my Stein lecture) that the irrational shouldn't be the object of a religious faith either. It follows that even religious faith should not remain totally "blind" and without the possibility of questioning.

Today we can hardly argue any longer that man as a creature has developed into his current form through a long biological process, and that he is a part of the creations surrounding him. But in the Torah it says that God created man by His own act "according to His own image." For centuries, that thought made human beings stand out from the rest of creation as something unique "with a special relationship to God," with the task of subjugating the rest of the earth. If the human being that we know were really the image of the religious God, then it wouldn't seem the best for God himself either. So there are many questions that, as you say, one "thinks about best sitting under a tree," letting his mind wander. . . .

Paul, along with this letter, I am sending you a small package by surface mail, in the hope that it might reach you on a certain date. Our grandson Rolf, whom you met, has been in Israel several days as a guest of his exchange friend Erez in Javne. The Israelis chose a good time. Now they can experience the day of memory (*yiskor*!) [*Yiskor* means "to remember." He must be referring to Holocaust Memorial Day, which occurs in April.] with our children in the hosting Israeli school, and it will probably have effects similar to those felt by the Israeli students last year when they visited the KZ Schirmeck in the Vosges mountains. I am enclosing a newspaper article for you that also shows that the students aren't participating in this exchange without a certain feeling of apprehension. I am anxious to see what types of impressions Rolf will bring back from Israel.

At the moment in the Balkans, the powers of Milosevic and NATO have pitted themselves against one another. Would it not make more sense to read through the International Covenant on Civil and Political Rights again beforehand—for spiritual guidance!—not only for the people who must withstand this new drama, but also for both parties? One day (over the rubble of this war), and whether they like it or not, they will have to think back to this organization anyway. I sent you some excerpts from the text of the covenant before.

For today, all the best to you, your wife Greta, and to David's family as well,

———— ❧ ————

MAY 18, 1999

Dear Paul,

Again, my best wishes on your ninety-second birthday.

I am also sending you a copy of all our previous correspondence put together, so that you, too, can have it "as a unified whole." That way, it will be easier to review what we wrote. . . .

. . . I've enclosed my original title as the first cover page: *Correspondence with an American Jew,* but then also the title that I now prefer: *Correspondence with a Jewish Friend.* So you can choose according to your wish. . . .

The copying and formatting of our different letters filled many hours of the past year. But in so doing I wanted to leave my children a document that they can read later—to see what kinds of thoughts were going through the head of their Grandpa during his life. It is much more difficult to leave children with life experiences than it is to leave behind money and property, even though one wishes to leave them such experiences, so that they don't always have to start at the beginning with their own. For that reason, our correspondence has become a part of my family chronicle. . . .

Thus, again in conclusion, all the best for the future to you and your wife Greta, and for you and me, the opportunity to continue our exchange of thoughts for a long time.

In old friendship,

Coda

Friedhoff died August 29, 2001, while these letters were being
prepared for publication. Despite his failing health, he
remained lucid and cogent until his final days, and the
correspondence continued until the end.

Sold still lives in Schifferstadt, Germany, remains active
in his community, and continues, in a variety of ways, to tackle
the difficult questions that stimulated this correspondence.

Afterword

Beyond Opposite Lives and Contrary Worlds

JOHN K. ROTH

*. . . We should use the time that we both have left to reflect together
on a world and a period that we did not intend to create, but in
which we must now live.*
—*Dr. Emil Georg Sold*

. . . One question leads to another.
—*Paul Friedhoff*

They were strangers twice over. Unacquainted until a book about German
Jews and the Holocaust brought them together, Emil Sold and Paul Friedhoff learned that they had once "lived completely opposite lives in what are
almost contrary worlds."[1] An odd couple indeed, yet their correspondence
on the Shoah produced a friendship that revealed "how similar our fundamental philosophies have become in the end."[2]

Their friendship was neither easily developed nor effortlessly sustained.
Sold and Friedhoff were aging. Illness periodically stole their time and
sapped their energy. Frequently and warmly, the German invited Friedhoff
to visit him and his native land. Occasional telephone calls made their
voices audible, but no face-to-face meetings enlivened a relationship that
depended almost entirely on the written word. Such difficulties made it
unlikely that their exchange would last for long, but other threats could
have been even more disruptive.

Unless their correspondence was to be superficial, never getting beyond
what the Holocaust survivor Jean Améry aptly called "false conciliatoriness," Sold and Friedhoff had to find their way through minefields of
emotionally charged Holocaust history.[3] That navigation, at times done

unavoidably by trial and error, had the potential to produce pain, misunderstanding, and hostility that were more than sufficient to break off the communication between a former *Wehrmacht* medic and a Jew who fled Nazi Germany in 1934. Nevertheless, as their letters went back and forth across the Atlantic, Sold, the Catholic doctor, and Friedhoff, the Jewish furniture maker who made the United States his home, found constructive ways "to reflect together on a world and a period that we did not intend to create, but in which we must now live."[4]

Their commitment to keep writing to each other validates Friedhoff's judgment that the two of them had "come into a true friendship without ever having seen one another."[5] Written between September 16, 1994, and May 18, 1999, the letters ably translated by Ivan Fehrenbach and published meticulously in *"That Time Cannot Be Forgotten"* indicate that Sold, the younger by more than a decade, wrote at greater length than Friedhoff. Determined to do what he could to atone for Nazi Germany's genocidal campaign against the European Jews, Sold worked long and hard to preserve the memory of Jewish life in the Rhineland-Palatinate region of Germany where Friedhoff and Sold were born in 1907 and 1920, respectively. His research gave him information, if not answers, to offer in response to many of Friedhoff's questions about Germany, past and present.

While Sold spent much of his retirement time teaching about the Holocaust and Christian-Jewish relations, Friedhoff observed Germany from a distance but no less intensely because Nazism had forced him to abandon his German homeland. The Jew's questions about Germany probe deeply. As "one question leads to another," the lack of closure seems to haunt Friedhoff more than Sold, who offers his historical and philosophical interpretations in greater detail while Friedhoff characteristically finds that "it is difficult to find an answer for what happened."[6] Yet their shared passion for inquiry takes them far in following Sold's urging that "there isn't any reason to hold back any questions."[7]

It takes time for Sold and Friedhoff to get beyond formality. Almost five years after their correspondence began, Friedhoff tells Sold that he still has "the feeling that we're not entirely open with one another."[8] Mindful that they might too easily give offense if their views were completely unmasked, they nevertheless work to communicate their different experiences with honesty and their divergent beliefs with respect. Sometimes they must agree to disagree, an outcome illustrated especially by their wrestling with questions concerning how much the German people knew about the destruction of European Jewry. Sold acknowledges that virtually all Germans knew that Jews were persecuted, pressured to emigrate, often sent to concentration camps, and eventually deported from Germany, but he argues that the majority of Germans did not know about the "Final Solution," the mass murder of the Jews, until after the war. Although Friedhoff remains unconvinced, the partners recognize that this unsettling issue may have to remain unsettled.

From time to time, one writer corrects the other on a matter of fact or a misunderstanding, but scarcely an exchange takes place without their letters showing that the Holocaust does raise one question after another: Why were the Jews targeted for destruction? How did that catastrophe happen? How can human beings commit mass murder? Why do they do it? How should religion—Judaism and Christianity in particular—be understood? What ought to be said about God after Auschwitz? What about the future? Do human beings learn anything good from bad experiences? How should the young be educated, particularly when neo-Nazis and Holocaust deniers vie for their attention? At the end of the day, does might make right? If not, what are morality's source and status?

These men lived too long to believe that history unfolds neatly in a linear progression. "History," says Sold, "has often made leaps or taken completely unexpected paths."[9] With their lives epitomizing that point, it is fitting that the correspondence always keeps close contact with the Holocaust but also jumps from one topic to another, the unpredictable order governed more by the writers' current interests than by any prearranged agenda. At the same time, their discussions avoid abstraction and generality. Books the men are reading, films they have seen, news that is breaking—those ingredients mix and mingle with episodes from personal experience to inform their inquiries. Consequently, the Sold-Friedhoff correspondence encompasses events from the late 1990s that made the Holocaust a present-day reality as well as a historic watershed. Their letters discuss, for example, the controversy surrounding Daniel J. Goldhagen's best-selling 1996 book, *Hitler's Willing Executioners: Ordinary Germans and the Holocaust*, which argued, more to Friedhoff's satisfaction than to Sold's, that vast numbers of Germans knew about, welcomed, and participated in the "Final Solution." Sold and Friedhoff also explore revelations about "Nazi gold" in Swiss banks, and they attend to the issues—still newsworthy in the twenty-first century—about restitution of property and compensation for Holocaust survivors. The Vatican's canonization of Edith Stein, a German exhibition about Holocaust-related atrocities committed by Hitler's armies on World War II's hideous eastern front, ethnic cleansing in the Balkans, the difficulties confronting immigrant workers and asylum-seekers in Germany and other European countries, the Israeli-Palestinian conflict—all of these elements in what I call "Holocaust politics" play important parts in *"That Time Cannot Be Forgotten."*[10]

Consequently, the Sold-Friedhoff exchange grows into an ongoing written conversation, an ocean-spanning, if not an abyss-bridging, transcultural deliberation whose far-reaching scope is matched by the judicious intelligence and clear expression that two wisely experienced interpreters bring to bear upon it. Embedded in the conversation's unfolding is the philosophy that these men come to share. No summary can do it justice, because that understanding evolves through disciplined effort, study, and reflection honed by their years of interaction. The following themes, however, are as important as they are unmistakable: The Holocaust compels attention. That attention should produce a healthy skepticism about nationalism, religious dogma, and every other certitude that divides humanity in ways that pit "us" against "them." Despite the differences that remain, forthright inquiry about the Holocaust can make people more sensitive and bring them closer together. That inquiry deepens, as Sold puts it, "by listening to the other one in silence, then by thinking, and then by asking additional questions."[11] The point is not that such inquiry will completely heal old wounds, but it can help to define and defend what is most important, namely, profound respect for the preciousness of individual life.

Much of the Sold-Friedhoff philosophy emerges in their discussion of religion, a topic that threads through the letters with regularity. Their traditions and practices diverge, but each has taken care to become knowledgeable about the other's ways. They respect these particularities keenly just as they mutually deplore the exclusiveness and hostility that religions so often inflame in spite of their best teachings to the contrary. Practicing Catholic that he is, Sold would not disagree with his more skeptical Jewish friend when Friedhoff suggests that "the best religion is a good relationship between one human being and another."[12]

Neither man is without pessimistic moments, but both refuse indifference and resist despair. Emphasizing that they can neither change the past nor control the present, their commitment to the future is to use their remaining time and energy for purposes that urge people to care responsibly for each other. Encouraging care that can combat our all-too-human tendencies to isolate one another in opposite lives and to leave people stranded in contrary worlds, Emil Sold and Paul Friedhoff show how the Holocaust is best remembered. In tribute to them, it is appropriate for the remainder of this Afterword to extend their shared philosophy by reflecting further on that theme.

"If we stop remembering," the Holocaust survivor Elie Wiesel has said, "we stop being."[13] That warning cannot be heeded well unless careful consideration is given to the fact that memory, memories, and remembering are human realities that raise crucial questions. How can we keep memory alive and well? Which memories most deserve attention? What purposes should remembering serve, and how does remembering best serve them? These are some of the issues that swirl through the ethics of memory. Emil Sold and Paul Friedhoff have responded to those issues particularly well.

As the twenty-first century develops and the Holocaust recedes increasingly into the past, what will happen to memory of the Holocaust? Why should that question be of any concern? What difference would it make if nobody remembered the Holocaust any longer? What dangers would await us if Auschwitz and Treblinka become forgotten places? Are there imperatives that enjoin us, whether we are Jewish or not, always to remember the Holocaust's history?

Sold and Friedhoff make one consider several responses. First, memory of the Holocaust is likely to be less strong, less intense overall in 3001 than it was at the time of their writing. Second, questions about the fate of Holocaust memory should concern us—particularly if my initial response is valid—because the quality of human life depends greatly on what we remember, how we remember, and why we remember. Third, to the extent that memory of the Holocaust disappears, indifference to the wasting of human life will become more prominent. In a world with increasing population pressures, the likelihood of repeated genocide will also expand. Fourth, to the extent that Auschwitz and Treblinka become forgotten places, we will lack warnings that are essential to keep us from a complacency that takes good things for granted. Hence, there are indeed imperatives—moral and religious—to remember the Holocaust's history.

Holocaust survivor Primo Levi, one of the most perceptive witnesses to that event, reminds us that "human memory is a marvelous but fallacious instrument."[14] Memories—I consciously use the plural as well as the singular so as to include our remembering of particular things—can blur and decay. They can become selective, stylized, embellished, and influenced by later experiences and information. In addition, memories can be confused, distorted, repressed, or denied. Still further, they can breed, inflame, and intensify hate.

Writing with the extremity of Holocaust memories in mind—the survivor's and the perpetrator's—Levi noted that "a person who has been wounded tends to block out the memory so as not to renew the pain; the person who has inflicted the wound pushes the memory deep down, to be rid of it, to alleviate the feeling of guilt."[15] Nevertheless, memories can also be as accurate as they are painful, as clear as they are irrepressible. They can be sharpened, recorded, intensified, documented, and even corrected so that they bear witness to the truth with penetrating insight.

Memories are not entirely in our control. For one reason or another—

physiological or psychological—we may lose them. Without memories we could scarcely be moral creatures, for history would dissolve and we would be able neither to identify one another as persons nor to make the connections on which moral decisions depend. But given the fact that we do have memories, we are creatures who cannot avoid responsibility and moral responsibility in particular.

If ethics cannot exist without memory, it is also true that ethical judgment comes to bear on memory. How are we taking care of our memories? Are we doing our best to keep them sharp, clear, documented, and honest? What actions do our memories lead us to take? Do our memories serve good purposes or destructive ones? Such questions stand at the heart of the ethics of memory. Just as our memories say much about who we have been, the uses to which our memories are put say much about who we are and who we will become. Old friends, Sold and Friedhoff model how memory and reflection upon it can serve the best purposes.

Exploring how the Holocaust is best remembered requires recalling what the Holocaust was. The Holocaust scholar Raul Hilberg's conservative estimates indicate, for example, that Nazi Germany destroyed 2.7 million Jews in 1942 alone.[16] That recollection, in turn, leads one to consider how this disaster came to be. These encounters with the past involve details and relations between them. No remembrance of the Holocaust can be adequate without giving those particularities their due, another feature that characterizes the correspondence in this book, and giving them their due builds awareness that the Holocaust was morally wrong or that nothing ever could be. That awareness, in turn, can sensitize the conscience of individuals and help to make them more humanely conscientious than they would otherwise be. That outcome will not necessarily produce agreement about what a nation's domestic or foreign policies should be. It should mean, however, that questions otherwise unasked will be raised, that silence otherwise unbroken will be lifted, that indifference otherwise unchallenged will be disputed, that protest, resistance, and compassion otherwise unexpressed will find expression.

No tradition emphasizes memory more than the Jewish tradition from which Paul Friedhoff comes. That fact helps to explain why one of Elie Wiesel's novels, *The Forgotten,* focuses on the struggle of a Holocaust survivor who strives to transmit his story before the devastation of Alzheimer's disease takes its irreversible toll upon his memories. Especially as we age, we can understand Wiesel's point in our personal lives. No doubt Sold and Friedhoff would agree: We dread memory loss; it means an enfeebled life. And at the end of the day, there is definitely a sense in which we stop existing when we can no longer remember. Wiesel fears that the loss of

Holocaust memory threatens the very existence of human society, another point on which Sold and Friedhoff concur. That loss would leave us bereft of much needed warnings about the destructive power of blindness, arrogance, hatred, and dogmatic convictions that we are right and everyone else is wrong.

The existence of memory, however, is not enough. Memory alone is insufficient for our needs. Everything depends on having *good* memory. Good memory depends on vivid recollection and on lucid connection; it requires recalling details with candor, documenting what is recalled, and discerning patterns of action with honesty. But good memory goes beyond those essential qualities, too. It involves questions not only about what we remember but also about how we remember, what we do with what we remember, and whether we turn memory into something that hurts or something that heals. In those dimensions, good memory compels us to be courageously committed to tell and validate the truth in the best ways we know. Emil Sold and Paul Friedhoff show that these things can be done and also how to do them.

Experience teaches us that memory can be potent. It can hurt and harm. It can incite us to revenge. But as the Sold-Friedhoff correspondence underscores, memory, especially good memory, can also lead us to protest against injustice, to document what is true, to reach out to help others, and to link people together in friendship. Wiesel often suggests that one of the things we need to learn is how to use memory against itself, how to turn memory away from bitterness, revenge, hate, despair, and silence and toward testimony that finds ways to affirm life. Sold and Friedhoff encourage good memory of that kind.

To do that work with the awareness that the ethics of memory entails, encounters with the Holocaust, especially when they take place by reading or listening, require what the Holocaust scholar Lawrence Langer calls "an experience in *un*learning."[17] What has to be *unlearned* is our tendency to hope too easily that all brokenness can be mended, that all suffering has meaning, that all evil can be overcome and redeemed, that the fragmentation caused by disaster can always be repaired, that the human spirit always triumphs. When Holocaust survivor and writer Ida Fink speaks about "the ruins of memory," ethical reading and listening call for us to let those words say what they say.[18]

Especially those of us who encounter the Holocaust at second hand have to learn how to listen and read so that we will approach the ruins of memory without shallow optimism or false hope or glib statements about "the triumph of the human spirit," which all would deceive us. And yet it remains true that Emil Sold and Paul Friedhoff—particularly through the publication of their letters—join survivors such as Ida Fink, Elie Wiesel, and Primo Levi in refusing hopelessness. Instead, they bear witness to help others, to warn, to touch and influence people they never met and will not know. Where encounters with the Holocaust are concerned, the ethics of memory urges us to do the same.

Post-Holocaust encounters with the Holocaust, including the conflicts those encounters may entail, should keep stalking our souls. If those encounters do not happen, the failure will mean that important questions remain unasked, that silence in need of breaking will not be broken, that indifference will not be challenged enough, that protest, resistance, and compassion will ignore or miss needs that should be served.

In particular, encounters with the Holocaust should make us remember how deadly it can be for racism and antisemitism to reassert themselves, for hate and violence to continue their destructive work, for the corrosive conviction to exist that wealth or class determines justice and that might makes right. If such inquiry into the Holocaust does not have a high priority in contemporary life, then not only will the Holocaust be forgotten more quickly, but also the quality of human life may be endangered even more in the twenty-first century than it had been in the bloody twentieth century.

Sold and Friedhoff could scarcely have anticipated that Holocaust encounters would bring them together in the ways that their correspondence so eloquently reveals. Likewise, no one knows in advance who might be permanently affected by a post-Holocaust encounter with the Holocaust—one that might take place by reading this book—or how that impact might change a person's life. At least in some cases, those encounters may move people—as nothing else can—to try to mend the world.

People study the Holocaust because it happened, but not only for that reason. We study it, teach about it, and try to learn from it primarily for ethical reasons that are rooted in deep longing for a safer and more humane world. That deep longing has everything to do with remembering, just as the remembering can change lives and encourage us to make the longing good.

Study of the Holocaust, I believe, aims to give us good memories, but that claim still entails a paradox that calls for explanation. Of course, I do not mean that the *content* of those memories is good. With the exception of the cases of rescue that were too few and far between, most of the content of Holocaust-related memories is bereft of goodness. In that sense, Langer rightly reminds us that "there is nothing to be learned from a baby torn in two or a woman buried alive."[19] Nor do I mean that the good memories

Holocaust study aims to create consist only of figures, dates, and facts, important though those details surely are, because it is through such detail, especially when we focus on what happened to particular people in specific places, that we are helped to learn from the Holocaust.

What I do mean is that, as we learn about and from the Holocaust, our memories will become good in the sense that they will not let us forget what is most important. The Holocaust can and should make us see differently. As Sold and Friedhoff testify, so quickly and in such devastating ways the Holocaust swept away good things—basic ones that every person needs, such as a home, safe and secure—that too often are taken utterly for granted. The Holocaust teaches that good judgment must be honed at memory's edge, to borrow the title of James Young's fine book about Holocaust memorialization.[20] That edge is at the border between honest loss of memory and forgetting, on the one hand, and the distortion, falsification, and even denial of memory, on the other. Memory's edge must be kept sharp, clear, keen, and true.

Emil Sold and Paul Friedhoff kept themselves alert and vigilant at memory's edge. By doing so, they move their readers to inquire about the past and much more. They put memory in the service of humanity. By helping us to consider a time that must not be forgotten, they also summon us to reconsider how to live in the time that is ours.

At some point, if only because death intrudes, people stop writing letters, and a correspondence—even one as long-lived as the Sold-Friedhoff exchange—comes to an end. Such an ending, however, is not the same as a conclusion, for a correspondence like theirs does not conclude, at least not in the sense that there is nothing left to say. One closes this book imagining that these two men, so different and yet so much alike in their caring for each other, want to keep the lines of communication open, on and on.

The last letter in *"That Time Cannot Be Forgotten"* was written to Friedhoff by Sold on May 18, 1999. Sold salutes his friend's ninety-second birthday by sending Friedhoff a copy of their complete correspondence. Just above his signature, Sold's closing line—"In old friendship"—conveys a touching affection, as deeply felt as it is simply stated, especially when one recalls Sold's early observation that the two of them had once lived opposite lives in contrary worlds.[21] Intensified by unexpected Holocaust encounters, theirs was a friendship born in old age and then nurtured to wise maturity that resisted those destructive divisions. Through these pages, their friendship lives on, reaching out to impart its insights to any and all who will receive them.

NOTES

1. Sold to Friedhoff, December 16, 1996, [81].

2. Sold to Friedhoff, April 18, 1999, [192].

3. Améry, a Jewish philosopher who survived the Holocaust and Auschwitz in particular, uses the concept of "false conciliatoriness" in the 1977 preface to his important book *At the Mind's Limits: Contemplations by a Survivor on Auschwitz and Its Realities,* trans. Sidney Rosenfeld and Stella P. Rosenfeld (New York: Schocken Books, 1986), ix.

4. Sold to Friedhoff, December 16, 1996, [81].

5. Friedhoff to Sold, April 15, 1997, [99].

6. Friedhoff to Sold, May 22, 1995, [36] and October 3, 1994 [3].

7. Sold to Friedhoff, February 14, 1995, [14].

8. Friedhoff to Sold, March 9, 1999, [183].

9. Sold to Friedhoff, May 1, 1995, [27].

10. I use the term "Holocaust politics" to refer to the ways—often conflicting—in which the Holocaust informs and affects human belief, organization, and strategy, on the one hand, and in which human belief, organization, and strategy inform and affect the status and understanding of the Holocaust, on the other. For more on these points, see John K. Roth, *Holocaust Politics* (Louisville, Ky.: Westminster John Knox Press, 2001).

11. Sold to Friedhoff, November 27, 1994, [8].

12. Friedhoff to Sold, January 2, 1999, [175].

13. Elie Wiesel, "Let Him Remember," in *Against Silence: The Voice and Vision of Elie Wiesel,* 3 vols., ed. Irving Abrahamson (New York: Holocaust Library, 1985), 1: 368.

14. Primo Levi, *The Drowned and the Saved,* trans. Raymond Rosenthal (New York: Summit Books, 1988), 23. In his letter to Friedhoff on March 19, 1995, [22–26], Sold makes an instructive comment about memory, one that Levi would approve, particularly as it pertains to Holocaust perpetrators or bystanders. The men have been discussing Ralph Giordano's book *Wenn Hitler den Krieg gewonnen hätte* [If Hitler Had Won the War]. Friedhoff has called attention to Giordano's concept of *Geständnisunfähigkeit* [the inability to confess]. Their discussion leads Sold to reflect as follows: "There are obviously circumstances in which the phrase is valid—memory says, 'I did that.' But then conscience says, 'I could not have done that.' Finally memory gives in . . . Strangely enough, this behavior is practiced by all of mankind. We see that in the daily trials, during which no one is willing to admit his own transgressions. It was that way at the trial for the burning of our synagogue in 1938. Those who at the time had boasted about their 'heroic deed' (two of them even had to go to the hospital for a short time because they didn't know how to handle the lighter for their fuel) not only didn't remember their action, but also were able to 'prove' that they were only at the place of the fire because they felt obligated to help (which in reality no one did at all!). It is also strange that the so-called political and religious criminals immediately swore off their own beliefs when they were supposed to be imprisoned for their actions. Obviously there are things and beliefs that we are only prepared to defend if they don't cause us any unpleasantness."

15. Levi, *The Drowned and the Saved,* 24.

16. Raul Hilberg, *The Destruction of the European Jews,* 3 vols., rev. and def. ed. (New York: Holmes and Meier, 1985), 3: 1220.

17. Lawrence L. Langer, ed., *Art from the Ashes: A Holocaust Anthology* (New York: Oxford University Press, 1995), 6.

18. See Ida Fink, *A Scrap of Time and Other Stories,* trans. Madeline Levine and Francine Prose (New York: Schocken Books, 1987), 3.

19. Lawrence L. Langer, *Preempting the Holocaust* (New Haven: Yale University Press, 1998), 10.

20. James E. Young, *At Memory's Edge: After-Images of the Holocaust in Contemporary Art and Architecture* (New Haven, Conn.: Yale University Press, 2000).

21. Sold to Friedhoff, May 18, 1999, [194].

Index

IVAN FEHRENBACH grew up in Williamsburg, Virginia, and studied at Brown University, where he earned a degree in Literary Translation. Recently he completed an English translation of an unpublished memoir by an East Prussian farmer taken prisoner by the Soviets in 1945. Fehrenbach lives in Richmond, Virginia, where he is currently writing a novel.

DATE DUE